The God of Modernity
The Development of Nationalism in Western Europe

Josep R. Llobera

BERG
Oxford • Washington, D.C.

First published in 1994 by
Berg
Editorial offices:
150 Cowley Road, Oxford, OX4 1JJ, UK
22883 Quicksilver Drive, Dulles, VA 20166, USA

Reprinted in 1996.

Berg is an imprint of Oxford International Publishers Ltd.

Library of Congress Cataloging-in-Publication Data
A catalogue record for this book is available from the Library of Congress.

British Library Cataloguing-in-Publication Data
A catalogue record for this book is available from the British Library.

ISBN 0 85496 921 7 (Cloth)
0 85496 940 3 (Paper)

Printed in the United Kingdom by WBC Book Manufacturers, Bridgend,
Mid Glamorgan.

Contents

Contents

Acknowledgements

I have been working on this book for many years and both students and colleagues at Goldsmiths' College have helped in many ways the pursuit of an endeavour which appeared at first rather awesome. If I had to single out individuals, two colleagues who have been particularly supportive are David Lazar and Mike Levin.

As a member of the Historical Sociology Society I have enjoyed over the years the privilege of being part of a group of people who have offered me invaluable critical support. In relation to the present project I have learnt much from Salvador Giner, John A. Hall and Michael Mann and I am particularly grateful to Nikos Mouzelis and Anthony D. Smith for their kindness and intellectual stimulation.

I owe the greatest debt to Ann MacLarnon who has read chapter after chapter, offering concrete suggestions to make it more grammatical and readable. Without her encouragement and understanding the book might have never been finished.

The section on Gallia in Chapter Two was published in a slightly different form in the *Journal of Historical Sociology*, volume 7 issue 3, 1994.

Preface

This book is written in the passionate but scholarly conviction that nationalism represents a major theoretical and political challenge for the foreseeable future. As an ideology it has been haunting us for at least two centuries, but somehow we have failed to come to terms with it. Furthermore, there is a sense of urgency in the present political conjuncture, partly generated by unsatisfied nationalist demands that are exploding around us. Some people had hoped, naïvely, that if they kept repeating that nationalism was on the wane, it would eventually really vanish. But surely the crux of the matter is to ascertain which societal conditions make it possible. Likewise, the continued condemnations of nationalism as evil – particularly the nationalism of others – have had limited effects, perhaps because many people have seen the horns of Leviathan behind the high-ground moralizing. In the final instance, we must be able to account for the consciousness of national identity and the subjective feelings of social communion generated by the participation in acts of national celebration.

It is not easy to read the signs of the times. On the one hand, many new states, in Africa and in Asia, as well as some of the old European states are suffering nationalist ravages in the form of claims for autonomy or for outright independence from subjected (ethno)nations within their borders. Out of the collapse of the Soviet Union and Yugoslavia dozens of new states have emerged. On the other hand, attempts are being made at creating new identities, such as the idea of a European 'community'. More disturbingly, we are not certain beyond some superficial similarities that the label 'nationalism', when applied at a world-wide level, covers the same realities. Is Islamic fundamentalism, for example, a kind of nationalism? It is for these reasons that the book is limited to Western Europe, the birthplace and *lieu classique* of nationalism. It is my belief that any theory of nationalism should start by trying to account for the convergence and development of nationalism in this area. Only when we are clear about the meaning of nationalism in Western Europe can we hope to come to terms with its diffusion to other parts of the world.

The nation, as a culturally defined community, is the highest symbolic value of modernity; it has been endowed with a quasi-sacred character equalled only by religion. In fact, this quasi-sacred character derives from religion. In practice, the nation has become either the modern, secular substitute of religion or its most powerful ally. In modern times the communal sentiments generated by the nation are highly regarded and sought after as the basis for group loyalty. As a symbolic value, the nation is the stake of complex ideological struggles in which different groups participate. That the modern state is often the beneficiary should hardly be surprising given its paramount power.

National ideologies are often said to reflect the French cliché *plus ça change, plus ça reste la même chose*. In this book I shall maintain that if we want to understand nationalism we should reverse the cliché to obtain *plus ça reste la même chose, plus ça change*. In this sense national ideologies are a dialectical precipitate of the old and the new. Though they project an image of continuity, they are pierced by discontinuities; though they conjure up the idea of an immutable ideological core and an adaptable periphery, in fact both core and periphery are constantly redefined.

The history of nationalism in Western Europe offers a good number of examples in which the nation is conceived as a quasi-eternal, motionless reality. The idea of *la France éternelle* is not only a metaphor of romantic French historiography; in fact it has been a first class ideological weapon of all Republican regimes in France. The echoes of such an idea reverberate even in Braudel's posthumous work on French identity.

Why this pretence of continuity? A physicist might say that the explanation must reside in some sort of irrational fear that peoples have of the historical void. It is true that in its origins and fundamentals national identity is an attempt to preserve the 'ways of our foreparents', but reality is constantly changing and the effect of nationalist ideologies is that we tend to perceive the same image where there are in fact different realities. Even modernising or future-oriented nationalisms must pay lip service to this idea of continuity. Expressed in positive terms nationalism emphasizes the need for roots, the need for tradition in the life of any community; it evokes 'the possession in common of a rich heritage of memories' (Renan). The organic analogy is here an inevitable point of reference. And yet the organic conception of the nation is hardly an adequate theoretical tool to handle the complexities of the would-be modern nation-state. For after all, to the ideologists of the nation-state the cultural definition of the nation, as first put forward by Herder, is always subordinated to political objectives or implicitly abandoned because of recalcitrant internal national heterogeneity.

The sociological myth of the nation-state, that is the belief that because the nation-state happens to be the paramount ideology of the modern state it must correspond to a sociological reality, is a serious epistemological obstacle for the explanation of nationalism. But how can one account for the survival of (ethno)national identities in harsh political environments, particularly in cases where the modern state engages all its bureaucratic machinery in policies of cultural, if not physical, genocide? It is my contention that if contemporary (ethno)nationalist ideologies have managed to establish themselves on a sound cultural and political basis, they are extremely resilient and can endure, albeit at times in a hibernating form, all sorts of repressive policies.

In the long run the history of Western Europe is the history of the qualified failure of the so-called nation-state. The celebration of the nation-state, however, continues unabated both by social scientists and politicians. The question to ask is to what extent is state-generated nationalism in Western Europe a success story. There is, of course, no easy answer. The fact of the matter is that the *nation*-state is far from being hegemonical; in other words, most Western European states are, to a varying degree of consciousness, multinational. What is the case is that old national identities originating in the Middle Ages die hard, even if in practice they have to survive in a revamped form. Now historical nationalities or (ethno)nations are not self-propelling entities; they may, of course, survive for a long time as cultural and linguistic fossils, but the question is surely under which conditions they can have a new lease of life. In the final reflection one has to try to explain why certain nations persisted while others perished and why certain nations became nation-states while others remained politically dependent.

The God of Modernity operates at different though interrelated levels. It combines a historical and a systematic approach, from which general conclusions about the origins, types and meanings of nationalism, as well as the causes of its development, are put forward. Although academics are all forced to operate within given institutional divisions and within a fragmented conception of knowledge, I have tried to avoid the partial vision of relying exclusively on a single social discipline. Nationalism is a particularly recalcitrant phenomenon when observed from the vantage point of a narrow specialism. The reader will soon discover that although the book is written by an anthropologist, it is firmly anchored in what for the sake of brevity could be called historical sociology or anthropology, and it has no particular allegiance to school or obvious *parti pris*. In the study of society, however, never has it been better said that science has to build upon the shoulders of giants. To me the towering figures of the Enlightenment and those of nineteenth-century social science (Marx, Weber, Durkheim) are not merely revered classics but authors with whom to conduct an ongoing dialogue of a critical kind. But it would be wrong to infer from such a statement that my book is an argumentation exclusively with past theories. In fact the starting point of my endeavour is the present state of the national question in the social scientific literature. I believe that scientific progress is only achieved when our contenders are considered neither as dead dogs nor as perfect gods, but as figures that, when necessary, one should criticize while respecting them.

It is true that modern nationalism only appeared in the aftermath of the French Revolution, but national identity is a phenomenon of the *long durée*. That is why the book starts by considering, in Part I, how Western European nations were formed. It also introduces the idea of ethno-national potential as a foundational concept. Ethno-national potential appears in the modern period as a given: a region either has it or not. But what I am trying to capture here is the process and the constitutive elements of the formation of national awareness in the Middle Ages. It is important to note that by the end of the medieval period the ethno-national die was cast.

Parts II and III consider, both as preconditions and as conditions of continued existence, the structural and ideological factors, respectively, which make possible the appearance of modern nationalism in Western Europe. Strictly speaking the presentation is not chronological but systematic, though the way in which the different sections are arranged, as well as their contents, have a historical orientation.

It is part of my geological, stratigraphical conception of historical time to conceive of the present as a hierarchical and geometrical accumulation of past ideological constructions, hence avoiding an atomistic view of society. The elements considered cannot be taken in isolation and recombined at pleasure as in a structuralist game; only history can combine them, and in fact has already done so in a definite way for Western Europe. At each historical stage a certain course of action was taken which foreclosed certain future possibilities. This is not to say that history is the realm of iron necessity or that there is an unstoppable march of time. In fact, the ways of history are often undecided and tentative, as if Clio proceeded by trial and error. Then at a certain moment in time a particularly significant event occurs (or better still a series of events) that, retrospectively, from the hindsight of the present, we can recognize as having had a decisive effect in shaping the future. The French Revolution is an excellent example of a constellation of events which, from the experience of its effects, we can say triggered-off modern nationalism.

Of course we can always speculate as to how things could have been under different historical circumstances. What would have happened if Scotland and England had not united their parliaments in 1707, or if

Prussia had failed to create the *Reich* in 1871? Undoubtedly the exercise may have an important heuristic value, but the particular constellation that constitutes the Occident, as Max Weber clearly saw it, is a given and cannot be changed, at least not backwards. And it is precisely this uniqueness that makes nationalism in Western Europe a *sui generis* entity which finds no equivalent in other parts of the world in spite of superficial similarities to the contrary.

Part II examines, by reference to classical and modern literature, two of the major forces of modernity in the West: capitalism and the state. Both forces have affected the development of national identity and nationalism from the sixteenth century until the present. Some authors would go as far as to say that both structures emerged in the latter part of the Middle Ages. Civil society is often seen as the society dominated by the bourgeois class, but the concept of civil society is worth unravelling from its capitalist tentacles and its economistic overtones, particularly in those multinational states where the oppressed nation is economically buoyant. I have hinted before at the idea of nationalism as a secularised religion. The final section of Part II contemplates not only the transformation of the idea of religious community into national community, but also the role of institutionalized religion, Catholic and Protestant alike.

Part III considers the eclosion and development of nationalist ideology in the second half of the eighteenth century and the nineteenth century. By the end of the eighteenth century two main types of nationalist ideology were already clearly visible: political nationalism and cultural nationalism. While the former emphasized the preeminence of the state, the latter gave primacy to ethnic features of a country. On the whole, Rousseau and the French Revolution propagated and enhanced political nationalism; Herder and the Romantic movement diffused and heightened cultural nationalism. The idea of national character, although connected with the cultural definition of the nation, has played such a central role in some nationalist conceptions that it deserves separate treatment.

Part IV focuses on a spatio-temporal examination of the varying ideologies, movements and structures of nationalism in modern Western Europe. It starts by looking into the single most important historical event in terms of nationalist effects: the French Revolution (including the Napoleonic invasions). This event is a nationalist watershed and marks a frontier of no return. In the modern sense of the term, national consciousness has only existed since the French Revolution, since the time when in 1789 the Constituent Assembly equated the people of France with the French nation. The crucial thing is, however, to map out the different constraints that have shaped the nationalist discourse in Western Europe into what it finally came to be: the ideology of mass movements. It is my contention that the nationalist discourse is a privileged semantic field which encapsulates, *in nuce*, the structure and dynamics of modern Western Europe in general and of each specific country in particular. The problem is how to interrogate this discourse, how to uncover the rules of its formation and how to assess its effects in society.

After a theoretical recapitulation, Part V presents, in the form of twenty-two theses, the main conclusions that follow from the study.

Josep R. Llobera

Part I

The Nation:
A Medieval Heritage

-1-

Prelude to Nationhood

Basic Concepts

The idea of the nation as a medieval heritage is used here to indicate a variety of historical elements, cultural and political, which combined over the medieval millennium to leave an imprint, albeit at times an unconscious one, on the collective mentality of the different western European peoples. The locution also assumes that this combination of elements crystallised into what we can call a nation, and that if the sentiment of nationhood may in future time have become dormant (because it was absorbed by an alien state), it could always be awakened in modern times by a variety of cultural and political means.

One of the problems of the modernist conception is precisely that it projects an image of the nation as if it were a reality created *ex nihilo*. This is only acceptable if we take the nation to be a political invention of the modern period – The Enlightenment – and coming into being after the watershed of the French Revolution; in other words, if in the definition of the nation the main emphasis is placed on the idea of popular sovereignty. But we know only too well that the moment we try to operate within this perspective we are blotting out the cultural dimension of the nation and its historicity. To say, then, that nation and nationalism as we understand them today, did not exist in the Middle Ages is mere truism. To abandon for this reason any search into the process of national formation and into the forms of national identity in this period is a recipe for sociological disaster. No doubt what contributed to the triumph of the modernist conception of the nation is the fact that in the sixteenth and seventeenth centuries the consolidation of absolute monarchy blurred the powerful national forces that were emerging by the end of the Middle Ages.

If the nation is, as I have insisted in the Preface, a product of the *longue durée,* we must probe the medieval structures for an answer to the question of how nations were formed. Without travelling all the way along the slippery path of the Hegelian-Marxist idea of 'historyless peoples', there is much to be said about the importance of having constituted a more or less independent, clearly differentiated polity in the Middle Ages: not because of the prestige that might be associated with that polity, but because of the better chances that a growing state bureaucracy, and the literati attached to the state, might have preserved, in a written form, the events and practices of a given time. It will be pointed out rightly that in many cases what obtains in such records is a narrow dynastic perspective, but in fact there are enough side references to the formation of the nation to make this information extremely valuable. In the Middle Ages, as well as in modern times, language is often, though not always, one of the key historical markers of nationhood. Of course, in the medieval period *natio* and *lingua*, to use Latin terms uncontaminated by modernity, were frequently coterminous, as St. Thomas Aquinas forcefully remarked. A written literary language obviously had better chances not only of survival, but also of transmitting culture in a more homogeneous manner and, compared with Latin, it was likely to reach a wider circle of people, even if, given the high levels of illiteracy, the numbers affected would still be rather small.

The ways in which societies organize their lives, from the material to the spiritual realms, are distinctive enough to constitute them into different, separate cultures. There are other facets, however, which may be less visible or forceful, but which are still worth mentioning in the process of the shaping of the medieval nation: territorial frontiers, legitimising myths of descent, concepts of biological kinship (race), symbols of collective identity (flags, shields, shrines, etc.), memories of war, names of the country, etc. All these elements point to the existence of a sense of national awareness, although surely this was not a generalized sentiment except in very rare and ephemerous circumstances. In the changing political world of the Middle Ages, where dynasties and territorial principalities rose and fell, where states absorbed other states through war, marriage alliances, manipulation of feudal law and chicanery, incorporation into a wider political unit did not necessarily mean the end of national identities, though, as we shall see, some national identities survived better than others into modern times.

We are so accustomed to seeing the Middle Ages as a long dismal period preceded and followed by eras of high civilizational attainments, that any attempt to suggest continuities rather than radical ruptures is bound to upset our well-established principles of historical periodization. And yet I intend to show in Part I not only that the roots of modern national identity can be traced back to the Middle Ages, but that in turn medieval political developments cannot be understood properly if we fail to notice their dependency on the real or imaginary institutions of the Roman Empire. The Christianized Roman Empire exerted a mythical appeal on the medieval mind, acting as a sort of ideal to which reality should aspire. In particular, the Middle Ages preserved two powerful and interrelated, universalistic conceptions from the Roman period: the idea of *imperium* and the idea of *ecclesia*. On the other hand, at the level of the political praxis, the administrative divisions of the Roman period, both political and religious, had a particularistic effect which in the long run would gain the upper hand. This is not to suggest, however, that the seeds of medieval political life derived from the Roman period *tout court*. After all this would be to ignore the radically dislocating effects of the so-called barbarian *Völkerwanderung*.

The process by which the different Germanic peoples who settled in Western Europe from the third to the sixth centuries, converted to Christianity and identified to a certain extent with the Roman Empire, whilst progressively developing into unstable kingdoms and territorial principalities, is complex, often contradictory and indeterminate. At this stage the main thing to bear in mind is that there is no historical necessity that explains the form that finally became triumphant in the modern period – the so-called medium sized 'national' state – nor is there a way of predicting which political entities would survive in the end as independent states. As to national identities, once they were formed and had an opportunity to consolidate themselves, their chances of survival were good even if they lost their political autonomy through incorporation into a different state.

The Germanic Invasions

Archaeological records indicate that around 2000 BC a group of Indo-European-speaking tribes settled in north-western Europe. After a long period of isolation, around 1000 BC they began to move in search of better land. They already spoke a form of primitive Germanic language. The Germanic peoples dispersed in all directions, particularly towards the south. These migrations often involved whole tribes and even confederations of tribes. By the beginning of our era, they had reached as far as the Caspian Sea, and from the Rhine and Danube to the Black Sea they were surrounding the Roman Empire. At this time there were five major confederations of Germanic tribes: the North Germani (Scandinavians), the East Germani (Alans, Goths, Vandals, Burgundians, etc.), the North Sea Germani (Frisians, Angles, Saxons, etc.), the Weser Rhine Germani (Franks, Hessians, etc.) and the Elbe Germani (Alemanni, Bavarians, Sueves, Lombards, etc.). The latter three groups are often referred to as the West Germani. This is, in a nutshell, the traditional vision of the Germanic *Völkerwanderung*.

There is, however, much controversy over the economic, social and political organization of the Germanic peoples. For different reasons there has been a long history from Julius Caesar and Tacitus through the nineteenth-century historians and jurists to the present day, of emphasizing a clear cut difference between Roman and Germanic societies. However, recent studies suggest, on the one hand, that the supposed primitivism of the Germanic peoples has been exaggerated and that in many respects they were closer to the Romans than the term 'barbarian' might indicate. On the other hand, it would appear that they lacked unilineal descent groups (either matrilineal or patrilineal) and their basic kin group was the bilateral kindred (Thompson, E.A. 1965; Murray, A. 1983).

In the light of the new historiography it would be erroneous to suggest that the Germanic peoples formed a coherent whole. What we know about them is basically coloured by the lenses of the classical writers. In other words, the Germanic world was a creation of Greek and Roman authors, in the same sense that the Oriental world was an invention of modern European writers. However, this should not be interpreted to mean that there was a homogeneous discourse on the Germanic peoples (or on the Orient for that matter), nor that the texts have no knowledge-value. Another rooted misconception has to do with the nature of the encounter that took place between the Roman Empire and the Germanic peoples. The idea of a continuous confrontation seems to prevail while, in fact, if we take a long historical perspective, a rather different image emerges. In the six centuries that elapsed from the first military victory of the Roman Legions over two Germanic peoples (the Cimbi and the Teutoni) in 102–101 BC to the deposition of Romulus Augustulus by a Germanic mercenary named Odovacar (or Odoacer) in 476 AD, a considerable amount of peaceful contact and accommodation, as well as cultural exchange, took place.

It should be pointed out as well that to define the Germanic peoples as exhibiting an almost 'innate' migratory drive is historically inaccurate, although the East Germani were more 'mobile' than the other groups . This is not to deny their migrations (two of them are well-documented: the incursion of the Marcomanni and allies across the Danube in 167 AD and the crossing of the Rhine by Vandals and Sueves in 406–7 AD), but then most human groups could be characterized as having the same feature. It is much more productive to fix our attention on a peaceful settlement and symbiosis rather than on the disruptive highlights of the invasions. Walter Goffart has put forward a devastating critique of the idea of 'barbarian invasions', and showed how under the label *hospitalitas* the Romans successfully incorporated a variety of barbarian peoples (Goths, Burgundians, Lombards) into the 'fabric of the West' (1980: 230), but in doing that, I would argue, they contributed to their own

downfall. However, as I have made clear before, the reasons for the collapse of the Western Empire must be found elsewhere; in any case, the
barbarian invaders of fourth century AD were few in number (each of
the peoples counted at the most in tens of thousands) and by themselves
they could not not have put an end to the Roman domination. In addition, it is important to remember, as Momigliano rightly suggested, the
image that the Roman Empire actually fell without making a noise. In
fact, the barbarians were not what occupied the imagination of the people living in the fifth and sixth centuries. What mattered at that time was
the 'constant tension with miracles, with the devil, with the pagan's own
past, with Jewish or heretic neighbours and with one's own eternal salvation' (Momigliano, A. 198O: 179).

For later reference it should also be kept in mind that while in the
areas that we shall refer to as Hispania, Gallia and Italia the settlement
of Germanic peoples after the invasions was numerically small, this was
not the case in Germania and Britannia. It is not exaggerated to suggest
that in the former areas the Germanic peoples were linguistically and
culturally swamped by the Romanized local populations, while in the
latter areas there was only a tenuous Roman influence. Things changed
in Germania with Charlemagne, while Britannia had to wait until the
Norman invasion. The presence of the Roman Christian Church in the
whole West, with its strong Roman flavour, no doubt provided an indirect source of 'Romanization'.

The social and political organization of the Germanic peoples was
characterized by the existence of different types of groups. At the basic
level we find the household, which brought together relatives and non-
relatives (dependants and slaves) under the same head or lord. The
household offered protection against a variety of threats. At a higher
level of integration we encounter a group which is alternatively defined
as clan (Fleckenstein, J. 1978) or as a kindred (Murray, A. 1983).
Whether it is envisaged as a clan or as a kindred, the group was a flexi-
ble tool not only for the generation of concrete social relationships, but
also with a specific social function: to keep the peace. In fact it was
within the boundaries of this group that blood-feud and vengeance were
tackled. It would appear that the genealogical memory of the group did
not normally go beyond the third or fourth generation and hence the
members of the clan or kindred would be in the range of hundreds (fifty
families at the most).

The highest level of political integration among the Germanic peoples
was the tribe (*Stamm*), also referred to as people (*populus, civitas*),
nation (*natio*), ethnic unit, etc. It is appropriate to start the discussion by
saying that the level of homogeneity, the character and the size of the
tribes varied tremendously in time and in space. Tribes can be envisaged

as ethnic units based on blood ties and on similar laws and customs, linguistic similarities and common patterns of warfare. Membership was usually acquired at birth, though some of the 'wandering' tribes of the fourth and fifth centuries were aggregates which included individuals recruited from non- Germanic origins (Roman slaves, *colonni*, etc.). Tribes were perceived as different entities by the Romans and were named (Franks, Burgundians, Saxons, Visigoths, etc.). It is a historical fallacy to assume that tribes survived after a long period of time without serious changes in personnel, just because the same name was preserved. However, for the members of the tribe the belief in a common ancestor was essential in order to maintain the sense of identity and unity of the group as a whole. In this respect, as J. Fleckenstein (1978: 9) has remarked, the tribe was seen as the extension of the clan – as a gigantic clan (in any case, as a consanguine community). Consequently, the tribe also performed some of the traditional functions of the clan.

As compared with Roman social and political organization, the Germanic tribe exhibited some fundamental differences. As J. Strayer put it:

> [The Germanic political system] was based on blood ties and personal allegiance to a ruler rather than on loyalty to an impersonal state. It had no territorial basis ... It was directed by unwritten custom and tradition rather than man-made laws and administrative decisions. It demanded more of free men, in expecting all those of military age to serve in the army – less in not requiring taxes and obedience to economic regulations (1982: 28).

With the period of migrations, the Germanic tribes, particularly the East Germani, became larger and more structured, often incorporating other Germanic and non-Germanic tribes and individuals. The idea of a league or confederation of tribes, although not unknown in the earlier period, now becomes more common.

The history of the Germanic peoples shows the appearance and disappearance of tribes which seem to leave no trace behind after a short period of fulgor. It has been suggested by J. Armstrong (1982: 28), following an idea by the German anthropologist Reinhard Wenskus, that the reason for such an occurrence was that tribal names and identities were exclusively maintained by a reduced number of people consisting of the leader, the nobility and its families. They were the ones who had real genealogies. In fact, 'the initial impulse to *Stamm* formation was thirst for adventure, glory, booty, or even subsistence. As he became successful, however, the leader elaborated and inculcated an identity myth. This myth rarely claimed autochthonous status for the emerging identity group; instead, it ascribed a distant, fabulous origin'

(Armstrong, J. 1982: 29). Around this myth the small nucleus would expand to constitute a sizeable *Stamm*. Sustained failure of the tribe to prosper in terms of victories, booty or territories could lead to the disappearance of the group. It is difficult to generalize about how cohesive the *Stämme* were. To start with, the reasons that kept the members of a given *Stamm* together varied tremendously: from territorial contiguity to legal customs, from religious rites to linguistic similarities, from the belief in common ancestors to the attraction of a king. We know that in some cases ethnic identity was preserved over a long period of time despite physical separation, while in other cases some Germanic peoples disappeared completely without trace after a military defeat.

The Germanic peoples exhibited two different types of leadership. In order of antiquity sacred royalty came first: that is, those chieftains who Tacitus referred to as *reges*. Their lineage was believed to be of divine origin, although the role of these kings was not altogether clear: sometimes it was military, sometimes religious. However, some authors, like M. Todd (1972), doubt the divine character of the Germanic kings and suggest that they should be called chiefs. Among the Visigoths the kings had judicial functions. In general their legislative and executive power was limited by the general popular assembly (*mahal*) (Bury, J.B. 1928: 12) and varied according to 'age, birth, military prestige or eloquence' (Wallace-Hadrill, J. M. 1980: 3). Kings could be deposed by the assembly of warriors if they decided that the incumbent king lacked the appropriate qualities. Succession was not based on male primogeniture, rather the assembly chose a male from the royal lineage.

The other type of leader or king was the result of war and enjoyed more power. They presided over a band of warriors who were free men but who swore an oath of loyalty in exchange for protection. This retinue (*comitatus*) was recruited from different households and had a strictly martial role. At first the relationship between the chieftain and the retinue was temporary but by the beginning of the Christian era it had become stable and in the long run the members of the *comitatus* became the tribal nobility, hence curtailing to a certain extent the original democracy of the free warriors. In the early period very few leaders succeeded in establishing a strong personal autocracy. Maroboduus, *rex* of the Sueves, was one of the exceptions; he belonged to a royal lineage which survived the demise of his personal rule. J. M. Wallace-Hadrill (1971) mentions three other *reges* who, in the eyes of the Romans, were spectacularly successful leaders. What mattered for the Romans was not the personal background of the kings or the tribal federation or aggregate that they presided over, but the fact that they had *auctoritas*, and so the Roman Empire could negotiate treaties with the conviction that their kingly power would allow them to convince their followers to go along an agreed path. The difference between the king-warrior (*princeps*) and the military chief (*dux*) was not always clearly delineated, particularly after the third century AD. By the end of the fourth century, we have a leader like Theodoric, who while presiding over a large war band was also the king of the Ostrogoths and of the whole of the peoples of the Italian peninsula.

Under Roman influence some leaders tried to make their power more absolute, but their success was limited and hinged upon their personal military and organizational abilities. Kingship, however, was unknown among some Germanic peoples (Saxons), but with the progressive contact with the Roman world the institution developed quickly. M. Todd (1975: 211) has noted that even in the fourth century most Germanic tribes were commanded by war leaders who had limited and short-term goals to achieve; the Germanic peoples certainly did not intend to conquer Rome, but to settle somewhere in the Empire. It was the pressure of the nomad Huns and of other peoples of the steppe that made the invasions 'inevitable' in the last quarter of the fourth century.

Towards a Synthesis

With their increasing contact with the Romans, their later settlements in the provinces of the Empire, and finally the 'invasions', the Germanic peoples converted progressively to Christianity. At first 'Christianity ... filtered across the northern imperial frontier by way of some of the prisoners taken in barbarian raids on the Roman provinces and by way of Germanic soldiers who returned home after completing their service with the Roman armies; and to a slight extent ... [by way] of traders' (Thompson, E.A. 1963: 62). Conversions by these means were probably very limited; the inability or unwillingness of the Church to send missionaries among the Germanic peoples in the fourth or fifth centuries would explain the paucity of conversions. We know, however, that by the end of the fifth century the majority of the Germanic peoples who had crossed the borders of the Empire and had settled somewhere in Western Europe were Christians, albeit of the Arian denomination. They had learned their Christianity from their encounters with the Goths. The initial conversions to Arianism were due to Bishop Ulfila who had preached for seven years (341–8) among the Visigoths settled in the Western shores of the Black Sea. He invented a Gothic alphabet and translated the Bible into Gothic. He had a certain success; his first converts were probably people of humble origin, but by the time the Goths crossed the Danube in 376 most of them were still pagan.

How was it that by the end of the fourth century the majority of

Visigoths had converted to Arianism? To explain this event we must first look into the Arian doctrine which was a Hellenic heresy of the fourth century and was centred around the teachings of Arius. The Arians believed in a hierarchical trinity in which the divinity corresponded only to the Father, while the Son was a perfect being but created by the Father and the Holy Spirit was the third person and inferior to the Son. There is little doubt that Arianism was an interpretation of the New Testament in the light of the Greek philosophy of the time, and hence represented a less radical break with paganism than the orthodox version. Whether it was this 'pagan' feature that helps to explain its spread among the Visigoths who had settled in Mosia, or whether it was the religious zeal of Ulfila and his missionaries, or the fact that in the idea of a hierarchical trinity the Visigothic king and nobility found a convenient religious model to impose on their society, or because their pagan deities had lost their *potestas* in a different, harsher environment; whatever the reason, mass conversion took place between 382 and 395.

The Visigoths remained Arians until 587, when their king in the Iberian peninsula, Reccared, converted to Catholicism. The Ostrogoths converted to Arianism between 456 and 472 and only abandoned their doctrine after Justinian I defeated them in 552. The Vandals, who converted to Arianism while in Hispania (probably in the second decade of the fifth century) were wiped out by Justinian I in North Africa in 553. Of the peoples who crossed the Rhine in 406, the Burgundians became Arians after entering into contact with the Visigoths in Southern Gallia sometime before the mid 430s and did not accept Catholicism until 517, led by King Segismund. The Sueves in the Iberian peninsula tried first Catholicism in 450, then Arianism a few years later, and they remained in this faith until 570. The Lombards were converted to Arianism at the end of the fifth century and entered the Italian peninsula in 568; their final conversion to Catholicism did not occur until the end of the seventh century. It is true, however, that conversions were often superficial, affecting only the upper crust of the kingdoms. A great amount of missionary work was needed at a later stage to reach downwards into the mass of the population.

Why did Arianism spread among Germanic peoples? L. Musset has attributed the widespread attraction of Arianism not so much to the doctrine itself but to the 'Goths's prestige throughout the German[ic] world after their victory [against the Romans] at Adrianople' (Musset, L. 1975: 184). No doubt once the Germanic peoples had settled within the boundaries of the Western Empire, their Arianism was an additional factor that retarded the unification of the Roman and barbarian peoples. The opposition that the Germanic peoples found was varied, but it affected most visibly the upper layers of society: those who were dispossessed of their landed properties. Was the ensuing conflict, which is often presented as a confrontation between Arianism and Catholicism, just a cloak to hide a conflict between the old and the new landowners? But this would be a rather simplistic explanation, not warranted by the evidence that we have on the period.

Was there also an ethnic conflict which manifested itself in religious terms? This possibility is seriously contemplated by L. Musset who has remarked that Germanic peoples saw in Arianism a way of confronting Empire and Church, thus keeping 'their independence and a sense of identity' (Musset, L. 1975: 184), as well as finding a way to slow down assimilation. E. L. Woodward (1916) concurred with the idea that, in the West, Arianism acted as a buffer between barbarians and Romans. For the former, Arianism meant accepting certain tenets of Roman civilization they admired, while at the same time rejecting the power structure of the Empire (both at the politico-economic and religious levels). From a political point of view, the Arian Church was completely subordinated to the temporal power of the Germanic, particularly Gothic, kings. The Roman Church, though, was hardly defeated; in the long run, with the conversions of the Franks to Catholicism, the invitation of Justinian to invade Western Europe to tackle the Arian Goths and Reccared's recanting towards Rome, meant the beginning of the end of Arianism. With it, most of the Germanic kingdoms carved up out of the fall of the Western Empire collapsed like sandcastles. In the Iberian peninsula the Visigothic kingdom resisted until the Arab invasion, but disappeared afterwards without trace. Only the Frankish kingdom survived and would manage to consolidate and expand its power.

A wider problem concerns the development of ethnic consciousness in the different provinces of the Empire at the time of the Germanic 'invasions'. Much has been made of the success of the Romans in creating an empire based on state patriotism rather than ethnic identity. Even in the third century AD when some parts of the Western Empire like Gaul showed centrifugal tendencies, ethnic consciousness was too weak to overcome the sense of loyalty to the empire. Things were different in the East, where ethnic separatism, often disguised in religious terms, made its appearance in Syria, Egypt and Judea (Walek-Czernecki, M. T. 1929).

In its heyday the Roman Empire was a Mediterranean empire, that is, it embraced all the lands surrounding the Mediterranean sea, plus some fringe areas (i.e. Britannia). Effectively it covered areas belonging to three continents: Europe, Asia and Africa. By the fourth century the eastern and the western parts of the Empire were drifting apart from each other and were heading for an inevitable split. For the Romans the division of the world into continents was not particularly meaningful; in a sense what mattered was whether one was civilized or barbarian. With the advent of Christianity these three continents acquired a much more important ideological meaning. The basis for this was the two chapters of Genesis dealing with the dispersion of Noah's children, which from St. Augustine to Isidore of Seville were interpreted to mean the following: the progeny of Japhet inhabited Europe, that of Shem, Asia and that of Ham, Africa. The peoples inhabiting each of these continents were envisaged in different religious terms: Europe was the continent of Christianity (although it also contained Arian or pagan barbarians), Asia was the continent of the old, inferior religion (Judaism) and Africa, in the aftermath of Ham's curse, was destined to serve the descendants of Japhet and Shem.

The changing fortunes of the barbarian kingdoms of the west, under pressure from nomadic populations (Mongols from the east and Arabs from the south-west) produced a special configuration of Western Europe in which the Church had a predominant presence and role. It was during the fifth century that the idea of the primacy of the Roman Church crystallized. It was justified on the basis that St. Peter was the founder of Western Christianity, having been delegated by Christ to defend the faith and to represent Him on earth (with all the powers involved in that). By the end of the century, Gelasius I had formulated his theory of the two powers: the Pope has *auctoritas*, the Emperor has *potestas*. Both powers emanate from God, but they belong in different spheres; the implication was that civil power was subordinated to religious power. Gelasius I was the first to be recognized as the Vicar of Christ; with him we can see the beginning of the medieval hierocratic model. It also explains why in the Middle Ages both the emerging states and the Holy Roman Empire had to contend with a strong Papacy and operate in a political framework – Christendom – which in the final instant was religiously defined. The appearance of the idea of Europe towards the end of the Middle Ages coincided with the loss of temporal power of the Church, but in effect the meaning of the concept overlapped with that of Christendom. But by that time Europe was becoming a complex civilization, with close economic links and common political features. Reformation did not mean the end of Europe: just the triumph of state particularisms over the ecumenical designs of the Roman Church (Hay, D. 1966).

The fourth and fifth centuries, and to a certain extent the sixth century as well, were a period of great political instability in Western Europe. A historical cartographer would have difficulty in fixing the different Germanic peoples in a map. Take for example the Vandals, who at the beginning of the fifth century moved westwards from their settlement in the origins of the Oder, ravaging the Rhine area and then crossing the whole of Gaul from north to south and entering the Iberian peninsula, North Africa and (re)settling finally around Carthage. From there they conducted raids in the Western Mediterranean. The Vandal kingdom was of short duration: it disappeared, and with it the people, after the Byzantine reconquest of North Africa by Justinian. All in all the African kingdom of the Vandals had lasted about 100 years; as a whole, the Vandals left no trace in history except for giving a bad name to the Germanic peoples. The Visigoths, on the other hand, were probably more numerous and, as we have seen, influenced the other Germanic peoples in a variety of ways (Arianism in particular). Before they managed to create a stable kingdom in the Iberian peninsula and Southern Gaul, which lasted for about 150 years (from mid-sixth century to the Arab invasion of 711), the Visigoths had been roaming the West trying to find accommodation in the Empire, from Moesia to Illiricum and to the Italian peninsula. They served the Empire against other Germanic peoples (Vandals, Sueves) settled in the Iberian peninsula and as a reward they received, as *foederati*, the territory between the Loire and the Garonne (Aquitaine), only to be finally chased out by the Frankish Merovingians in the early sixth century.

The Ostrogoths, after leaving their habitat north of the Black Sea, divided: the larger group became subordinated to the Huns in Pannonia, the other served as an ally of the Eastern Empire and was cantoned in the Balkans. By the time of Theodoric both groups had united and moved westwards towards Rome after the collapse of the Western Empire in the late fifth century. The Ostrogoth kingdom was a first synthesis of Germanic and Roman cultures at a high level. During his reign (463–526), Theodoric was in a sense the moral leader of the Germanic West, but his successful kingdom was the result of extraordinary personal qualities which his successors lacked. Ten years after his death, the kingdom was destroyed by Justinian's troops and the Ostrogoths, as a people, left very little trace in history. Again, the attempt to recreate a unified Roman Empire would be short lived: the Longobards and Arabs put an end to it (Burns 1980).

There is a danger in describing these barbarian kingdoms of seeing in them the precursors of modern states. This illusion should be immediately dispelled, firstly because a look at a map will show that the territories carved up in Western Europe by the barbarian kings of the fifth and sixth centuries in no way correspond to our present day geographical boundaries. Furthermore, they did not survive very long as kingdoms and hence they had limited opportunities to consolidate ethnically. The Visigothic kingdom was not Spain, but rather a territory comprising the Iberian peninsula and southern Gaul, while the so-called Ostrogothic kingdom of Italy spread over south-eastern Gaul and the Balkan peninsula. The Frankish kingdom expanded from a site in northern Gaul, while the Jutes, Angles and Saxons were hardly 'England'. What are we to make of statements such as those by R. Folz (1972: 86) and L. Musset (1975: 45) who would explain modern English, French and Spanish 'nationalities' as the results of the early synthesis originating in these kingdoms? To suggest, as Musset has done, that 'the Visigoths enthusiastically set about forming a united Spain' (ibid.: 43) and created the Spanish national spirit is totally ludicrous.

Before spreading into northern Gaul in the fifth century, the Franks had lived in the areas around the lower and middle Rhine; their contact with the Roman Empire had been so steady for decades that by the late third century they were allies of Rome. They were originally ruled by different kings, but by the late fourth and fifth centuries there appeared a widely-based Frankish confederation led by the Salian kings. However, it would be incorrect to assume that either then or later the Frankish confederation constituted a unified ethnic polity.

With the emergence of the Merovingian dynasty founded by Clovis, the Frankish kingdom was consolidated, and expanded into other areas of Gaul and elsewhere, defeating in turn Visigoths (507), Burgundians and Thuringians (530); they established protectorates over the Alammans (536) and Bavarians (555). A number of factors helped in the persistence of the Frankish kingdom. The Franks had converted to Catholicism at the time of Clovis – prior to that they were not Arian, but pagan. No doubt this helped with the Church hierarchy and with the Gallo-Roman population. Furthermore, if Southern Gaul remained strongly Romanized and in theory as part of the Empire in the period following the different Germanic occupations, northern Gaul, though conquered and controlled by Franks quite early, preserved nonetheless the linguistic inheritance of Rome. But there were clearly differentiated areas within the Frankish kingdom, and while Neustria (the western part of northern Gaul) became fairly Romanized, the eastern part (Austrasia) remained largely Germanic. Succession in the Frankish monarchy followed the principle of equality of all male heirs; in other words, the kingdom was conceived as a patrimony to be preserved and augmented, and to which all male heirs of the royal lineage had the right to a part. Consequently, the expression Frankish kingdoms might be more appropriate when referring to the situation described above in which the system of succession produced constant political fragmentation, only avoided when there was a single male heir or the others died young. Civil wars among the Franks were rife, as an astute contemporary witness like Gregory of Tours observed. In any case, as J. M. Wallace-Hadrill (1985: 76) has pointed out, it would be absurd to impute to the Frankish kings the political objective of unifying the Gaul.

The pattern of barbarian contact with the British Isles was slow and it took place in different stages. Prior to the fifth century there were short-lived incursions which had no lasting populational effects, but a number of barbarians (Saxons as well as Franks and Alammani) also came to the island as allies of the Roman Empire to defend the fortifications against native attacks. With the collapse of the Empire in the Rhine at the beginning of the fifth century, the Roman presence in Britannia thinned out, to the extent that by the mid-fifth century the Saxons raided and later fully invaded the island. Along with Jutes, Angles and Frisians, they conquered Roman Britain without much difficulty. By the sixth century the language, religion and civilization of the Romans had practically disappeared; in its place, a small number of kingdoms (Northumberland, Mercia, Wessex, Essex, Sussex, Kent, etc.) appeared, roughly corresponding to the tribal divisions of the original habitat of the Germanic tribes. Whether by the seventh century all these tribes considered themselves as belonging to an early 'nation of the English', as some presentist historians would like us to believe, is rather quaint, even if we accept that there was a king of kings overseeing the Anglo-Saxon territory (which Bede referred to as *imperium*). Neither Wales nor Cornwall, nor Scotland nor Ireland were part of Anglo-Saxon England; the Picts and Scots were an effective barrier against an expansion towards the north. Many Britons, in the areas of Wales and Cornwall, threatened both by Saxons and Scots (from northern Ireland), had abandoned their territories by the mid-sixth century and had settled in the Armorican peninsula (Britanny), generating a linguistic revival of Celtic, as well as a vigorous development of Christianity through monasticism. However, a number of kingdoms (Gwynedd, Powys, Dyfed, etc.) survived in Wales, while Somerset, Devon and Cornwall constituted the kingdom of Dumnonia. By the sixth century Irish settlers (later called Scots) had established the kingdom of Dalriada in western Scotland.

The Carolingian Empire

The Carolingian Empire, particularly under Charlemagne, was the first serious attempt to unite all the Christian peoples of Western Europe in a single kingdom. The aim was to recreate the Roman Empire as a Christian community. In fact, it was the Papacy which was instrumental in sanctifying the new Carolingian dynasty. It was not only that Carolingian kings were ritually anointed, but also an explicit use was made of kingly biblical language to consolidate their position. The ritual procedures culminated in the crowning of Charlemagne as Emperor of Rome in the year 800. To be emperor was a religious dignity bestowed upon Charlemagne and this undoubtedly brought him prestige, but in no way altered the fact that he was the king of a variety of separate peoples (Franks, Longobards, Saxons, Bavarians, etc.) and not the ruler of a unified empire. The Carolingian Empire never created a citizenship similar to the Roman one, and even less a consciousness of belonging to a political unit.

The unity of the empire was extremely precarious and fragile, and if it was maintained this was due to the exceptional military and administrative qualities of Charlemagne. It was, however, a personal empire. The system created by Charlemagne to govern these vast territories involved delegating his powers to counts (*Grafen*) who carried out the military and judicial duties of the king in administrative districts (there were about between 200 and 250 counties), many of which survived long after the disappearance of Charlemagne. These counts were also vassals (that is, had sworn fidelity to the king) who had been given a benefice (a land tenure); in turn they would sub-contract and generate a new vassalic relationship. It was precisely this combination of vassalage and benefice that characterized Carolingian feudalism, while among the Merovingians these institutions had been kept separate (Werner 1979).

Power, however, rested with the king who could depose his subordinates. To oversee the activities of the counts, who often took undue prerogatives or tried to impose their own law, the emperor appointed special envoys (*missi dominici*), who regularly visited his dominions and had the power to enforce royal authority. Counties were grouped creating larger administrative units, usually governed by a duke or margrave who could be of the royal lineage or belong to the core of the Frankish nobility (Austrasia). These territories controlled by dukes often coincided with the old Frankish tribal dukedoms in that they exhibited the same laws and customs which were a synthesis of Germanic and more or less Romanized local elements. The difference was that under Charlemagne the dukes were merely appointed royal officers. Again, these territories often survived the collapse of the Carolingians and became the nucleus of the territorial principalities of the Middle Ages.

Carolingian kingship exhibited a variety of features which corresponded to its complex origins. On the one hand, it owed a great deal to the Germanic idea that office should be in principle popular: granted that the choice was usually within a narrow royal lineage, but certainly not on the principle of primogeniture. As the Carolingian usurpation of Pippin III in 751 clearly showed, a king without real power could justifiably be dispossessed even without papal approval. A leader who was not good at war was not to be entrusted with the throne. Furthermore, the king and his officials were meant to respect and enforce the law of the land, so individuals who felt aggrieved against them were entitled to resist their encroachments. On this conception of kingship, Christianity superimposed a vision of kingship which assumed that monarchic power was of divine origin, hence undermining its popular accountability. The king could only be challenged if he was seen to betray the will of God. This uneasy combination of kingship conceptions led to a type of society – the feudal order – in which the power of the king was far from being absolute (at least in theory), but was rather countervailed by a variety of duties towards his vassals (Fichtenau, H. 1982; Ganshof, F.L. 1970; Wallace-Hadrill, J. M. 1971 & 1975; McKitterick, R. 1983).

It is debatable how successful Charlemagne was in creating a permanent body of faithful followers at different administrative levels. In fact, the public oath of fealty was not sufficiently binding because the empire lacked a clearly defined role of what public office was (in terms of accountability and incorruptibility); this was absent from the Germanic tradition. It is a sign of the ideological limitations of the Carolingian dynasty that it could not instrumentalize the conceptions of either the Roman Empire or the Christian Church (Zacour, N. 1976). It is worth emphasizing, then, that Charlemagne's empire lacked stable institutions of government both at the central and at the local level. Compared with the early Roman administration or with the Byzantine one, the institutions of the *Regnum Francorum* were provisional, rudimentary and deficient. It was due to the personal qualities of the king that the empire kept its momentum; after Charlemagne's death it soon disintegrated as a castle of cards (Ganshof, F.L. 1971).

What emerged after the collapse of the Carolingian Empire was not the beginnings of France, Germany and Italy (and even less Spain), but the dawning of an era, from the ninth to the thirteenth century, in which territorial principalities constituted the key to the understanding of the Western European political order. It is true that the Treaty of Verdun consecrated in the long run the existence of a Western Frankish kingdom (later to become France) and an Eastern Frankish kingdom (later to become Germany) plus a disputed area in the middle. We have examined a number of reasons why the Carolingian Empire could not last, but the fact that these emerging territorial principalities often overlapped with ethnic areas raises the question of how important the resistance to Frankish rule might have been, both from non-Frankish Germanic peoples (Bavarians, Saxons, Lombards, Burgundians, Goths, etc.) and non-Germanic peoples (Bretons, Gascons, etc.). There is no doubt that Frankish rule was seen as alien and oppressive by a variety of peoples who had a sense of different identity based on linguistic and cultural features. E. Sestan (1952) has suggested that the need to satisfy the conflicting demands of the royal children often led to a break away of ethnic units at the time of succession. The fact that the Carolingians appointed as counts or dukes people originating in the core of the kingdom (Austrasia) did not prevent in the long run the formation of practically independent principalities because of the fusion of interests between the royal representatives and the local populations (Dhont, J. 1948).

According to E. Sestan the Carolingian Empire affected very differently the future realities of Germany, France and Italy. For Germany what really mattered was not only the idea of empire (Holy Roman Empire), but the creation, particularly after the Treaty of Verdun (843) of an East Frankish state between the Rhine and the Elbe and the Alps, very roughly corresponding to the Roman Germania. At least until the thirteenth century the state created a common framework of institutions, historical experiences, memories and destiny that helped to create the idea of the German or Teutonic (*Deutsche*) nation, even if later the principalities dominated German life until the nineteenth century. For France the effects of the Carolingian Empire were not so clear. The empire did not change the fact that Gaul was an ethnic mosaic; in fact, it is possible to sugest that the identity of Bretons, Gascons and other ethnies was preserved. An important point is that the Carolingians managed to stop the penetration of the Arabs in Septimania and the Marca Hispanica, which were areas of Visigothic influence. As to Italy, the empire succeeded in blocking the unification of the country, with the Lombards in the north, a Papacy with temporal designs in the centre and a variety of principalities in the south. An additional problem was the Carolingian linking of 'Italy' with empire, which opened the door to a Christian universalism, but also left the peninsula at the mercy of foreign invaders (Sestan, E, 1952: 352–4).

Bibliography

Armstrong, J. A., (1982) *Nations before Nationalism*, Chapel Hill: University of North Carolina Press.

Burns, T. S., (1980) *A History of the Ostrogoths*, Bloomington: Indiana University Press.

— —, (1980) *The Ostrogoths. Kinship and Society*, Wiesbaden: F. Steiner Verlag.

Bury, J. B., (1928) *The Invasion of Europe by the Barbarians*, London: Macmillan.

Dhont, J., (1948) *Etudes sur la naissance des principautés territoriales en France*, Bruges: Uitverij de Tempel.

Fichtenau, H., (1957) (1982) *The Carolingian Empire*, Toronto: Toronto University Press.

Fleckenstein, J., (1976) (1978) *Early Medieval Germany*, Amsterdam: North Holland Publishing Co.

Ganshof, F. L., (1947) (1971) *The Carolingians and the Frankish Monarchy*, London: Longman.

— —, (1965) *Frankish Institutions under Charlemagne*, New York: Harper Torchbooks.

Goffart, W., (1980) *Barbarians and Romans A.D. 418–584. The Techniques of Accommodation*, Princeton: Princeton University Press.

Hay, D., (1957) (1966) *Europe: The Emergence of an Idea*, New York: Harper Torchbooks.

Herlihy, D., (1985) *Medieval Households*, Harvard: Harvard University Press.

McKitterick, R., (1983) *The Frankish Kingdom under the Carolingians*, London: Longman.

Momigliano, A., (1980) *Selections. Sesto Contributi alla Storia degli Studi classici*, Rome: Edizioni di storia e letteratura.

Murray, A. C., (1983) *Germanic Kinship Structure*, Toronto: Pontifical Institute of Medieval Studies.

Musset, L., (1965) (1975) *The German Invasions*, London: P. Elek.

Sestan, E., (1952) *Stato e nazione nell'alto medioevo*, Napoli: Ed. Scientifiche Italiane.

Strayer, J. R., (1982) *Western Europe in the Middle Ages*, Glenview, Ill.: Scott, Foresman and Co.

Thompson, E. A., (1972) *Everyday Life of the Barbarians*, London: Batsford.

— —, (1966) *The Visigoths in the Time of Ulfila*, Oxford: Oxford University Press.

— —, (1982) *Romans and Barbarians. The Decline of the Western Empire*, Madison: University of Madison Press.

Todd, M., (1975) *The Northern Barbarians*, London: Hutchinson

Walek-Zcernecki, M. T., (1929) "Le rôle de la nationalité dans l'histoire de l'Antiquité", *Bulletin of the International Committee of Historical Sciences*, Vol II, Part II, pp. 303–20.

Wallace-Hardrill, J.M., (1980) *The Barbarian West*, Oxford: Blackwell.

— —, (1971) *Early Germanic Kinship*, Oxford: Clarendon Press.

Werner, K. F., (1979) *Structures politiques du monde franc (VIe – XIIe siècles)*, London: Variorum Reprints.

Woodward, E. L., (1916) *Christianity and Nationalism in the Later Roman Empire*, London: Longman.

Zacour, N., (1976) *An Introduction to Medieval Institutions*, London: St. James Park.

–2–

Domains of Statehood and Nationhood

Introduction

A word of caution should be uttered before entering the issue of national identity in the medieval period. One of the most pernicious illusions concerning the Middle Ages is the assumption that we can look at this period through the presentist lenses of our contemporary political and cultural realities. We are so infatuated with entities such as France, Spain, Italy, Germany or Great Britain that we tend to believe that they are, if not eternal, at least old enough to be projected into the distant past without committing a dangerous historical fallacy. Benedetto Croce warned us against the thought that there can be a history of Italy prior to its political unification in 1870. But even in cases where there has been a continuous state since the Middle Ages, as in the oft mentioned example of France, the political and cultural realities behind the expression 'France' today and in the medieval period are radically different. This simple enough point seems to escape a great number of both historians and social scientists who constantly commit the fallacy of historical displacement, either unconsciously or for chauvinistic cum Whiggish reasons.

How can we scrutinize the medieval past from the perspective of the present without superimposing on it our current political and cultural realities? Any answer to this question must take into account the subtle interplay of real as well as illusory continuities and discontinuities that make the Western European history of states and nations a complex tapestry on which time has drawn variegated and often confusing patterns.

I have divided Western Europe after the collapse of the Roman Empire into five major areas or domains of statehood and nationhood. To refer to them I use Latin terms – Germania, Gallia, Italia, Britannia and Hispania – but make no assumptions as to what is going to happen within and between each of these areas. Although these domains are, to a certain extent, based on administrative and religious divisions of the

Roman Empire and on actual historical clusters of political and cultural influence, they remain in the final instance somewhat arbitrary. They are more ideal types useful in thinking about and contrasting historical reality than an accurate map describing historical facts.

The five domains can simply be described in the following way. Germania corresponded roughly to the territory delimited by the North Sea, the Rhine, the Alps and the Oder. It included not only modern Germany but also Austria, Switzerland, Bohemia, etc. Gallia was limited by the Atlantic Ocean, the Pyrenees, the Alps and a mobile eastern border. Between Germania and Gallia there was, since the Treaty of Verdun (843), a highly contentious 'fringe' running north to south (including Flanders, Holland, Lorraine, Alsace, Burgundy, Provence, etc.). Italia refers to the peninsula south of the Alps, but also incorporating the neighbouring islands (Corsica, Sardinia, Sicily). Britannia comprises the British Isles, that is, Britain and Ireland. Finally, Hispania refers to the whole of the Iberian peninsula plus the Balearic Islands.

Needless to say these geographical approximations are very precarious, precisely because what characterizes the history of medieval Western Europe is an extreme fluidity both inside and across these domains. In other words, there is no suggestion that either the internal subdivisions of the domains or their external limits are fixed; there was considerable turmoil and change. In fact, the picture that emerges from the Middle Ages is difficult to retain mentally in that it is a succession of constantly changing political maps. Furthermore, what is durable and what is transient is also not always forever. Of course, with hindsight from the present we can easily place ourselves in the Middle Ages and adopt teleological arguments concerning the 'eternity' of say France or Spain as states or nations or both. To insist that there is nothing necessary about the persistence of these historical realities is as much anathema to some as it is to say that their geographic, political and cultural meaning has changed over time. And yet the fact that terms like 'France', 'Spain' or 'Italy' (or the Latin equivalents) have now been used for centuries should also alert us to their ideologico-symbolic meaning. Finally, a word on the different length of the five following sections. If Britannia, Gallia and to a certain extent Hispania receive a fuller treatment, it is simply because their medieval period is essential for the understanding of how nationalism has developed in all these domains during modernity.

Britannia

In using the expression Britannia to refer to the territories of England, Scotland, Wales and Ireland during the medieval period, I am well aware that I am committing a historical solecism since the Roman province only covered part of Britain – the non-Celtic lowlands – and not Ireland at all (which was called Hibernia by the Romans). The dominant role played by the English kingdom in the medieval history of Britannia may not be comparable with the hegemonic role played by England in the modern United Kingdom, but it cannot be overemphasized. In spite of that, it is important to note that both in the medieval world and in the modern period we are dealing with a variety of peoples, and whether we write a single or a plural history this fact must be taken into account. It is true that in the long run the history of the UK is the history of the political and cultural domination of the English nation over Scotland, Wales and Ireland, but the process was not without hurdles and bloody struggles (particularly in the Irish case); in the end even the assimilation of the Scots was far from successful. It would also be fair to note that in the history of Britannia the role of the different components was not the same; in the medieval period what was distinctive was the consolidation of the English and Scottish kingdoms, while Wales was progressively incorporated into the English crown and Ireland, or at least part of it, was successfully penetrated (Pocock, J.G.A. 1975).

The prominent role played by England in the medieval history of Britannia is partly the result of the early appearance, in the latter period of the Anglo-Saxon era, of a state with territorial boundaries, no matter how imperfect: a kingdom, that of Wessex-Mercia, which had managed to annex and control smaller kingdoms under the rule of a single reigning house, and which exhibited a common legal and fiscal framework, as well as a single Church organization. The Viking invasions did not radically change this picture. Joseph Strayer (1970) has suggested that the process of state-building taking place in the eleventh and twelfth centuries rested on a rather flimsy economic basis, while at the same time insisting that the Anglo-Saxon kings lacked the social conditions for a long lasting centralized monarchy. Loyalties were not focused at the state level but rather followed local lines (family, neighbourhood and county). What is interesting in the English case is that with the Norman invasion of 1066 and the subsequent elimination of the indigenous aristocracy, the centrifugal effects typical of feudal medieval Gallia and other parts of Western Europe were supressed.

In post-Norman England not only were there no provincial dynasties that could challenge the central power of the monarchy, but also the local institutions and local officials tended to reflect royal presence rather than the autonomous provincial power of earls and barons. Furthermore, the invasion had wiped out those from the Anglo-Saxon period and William the Conqueror and his successors made sure that except in the marches no aristocrat held compact territory. No doubt the fact that England was territorially small when compared with some of the Western European kingdoms helped its consolidation, allowing frequent royal visits to the different parts of the kingdom and hence the stamping out of regional diversification. That is why England became the first centralized, 'modern' state of Europe in a process that took place between 1100 and 1300. The state established after the conquest was also able to exert its overlordship on the Welsh princedoms as well as the Scottish kingdom; and, because of its Norman origins, it had, of course, a royal claim over large parts of Gallia.

The relationships between England and its neighbours were not of the same type. For one thing, Wales had been conquered by the end of the thirteenth century and subjected to English rule, while in Ireland effective English domination, between 1169 and 1534, only affected a small portion of the island (the Pale). Scotland managed to establish itself as an independent state and fought successfully English attempts at subjugation. As to the English presence in Gallia, it followed the dynastic fortunes of the English monarchy which tried to enforce this claim first in Normandy (until 1204) and when the Angevin connection was established in 1154 to vaster territories (Anjou, Poitu and Aquitaine). What started as a feudal dispute became, with the Hundred Years War, a struggle between two territorial, early modern states. The English presence in Gallia came to an end in 1453, although it was not until the beginning of the nineteenth century that the English monarchs renounced their medieval claim to the kingdom of France.

I have mentioned above that the history of Britannia in the Middle Ages is the history of the formation, development and interaction of four peoples: the English, the Welsh, the Scottish and the Irish. As we shall see, these peoples had different degrees of self-consciousness – a fact which was undoubtedly connected with their political institutions. While on the whole the presence of a more or less unified state – a kingdom – helps the development of a sense of identity, as was the case in England and Scotland, it would be premature to dismiss, because of its absence or because of its presence in a rudimentary and unstable form, the existence of a similar, though maybe more diffuse type of sentiment in Wales and Ireland as a purely nineteenth-century nationalist construction.

If we believe Susan Reynolds (1985), a sense of English identity developed rather early, that is, by the eighth century. According to her, the 'English' (a word already used at that time) had developed a common language, had participated in a number of common military expeditions and had a sense of loyalty to Rome via the English Church. Later, with the unification of the kingdom in the tenth century, the sense of solidarity became much stronger precisely because of the medieval belief that people who had political unity and shared culture, language and law were of common descent (ibid.: 399). The Danish invasions did not substantially change this state of things because the invaders, once they had settled in England, lost their language and culture and ceased to be seen as different ethnic entities. Can the same be said about the Norman invasion?

Romantic historiography has always insisted in the long-felt presence of the Norman invading elite as an alien body in the life of medieval England. That the natives were excluded from high office and denied access to land, and that (Old) English ceased to be the official language of government (though not of the populace) is perfectly true, but does not apply to the whole medieval period. Furthermore, the sense of English identity whch was created in the Anglo-Saxon period survived the invasion.

Before entering into any other matter it may be worth considering to what extent English, Scottish, Welsh and Irish identities existed in the pre-Norman period. In his classic *Medieval England*, Sir Maurice Powicke remarked on an often forgotten fact: that England was one of the first European countries to exhibit a sense of unity and identity, and that this was achieved long before the Conquest. By the ninth century Alfred could be referred to as king of the English. But even before that there was a sense in which people like Bede and Alcuin were already seen as English and not as Northumbrians. Unlike elsewhere in Britannia and in the continent, the different Germanic tribes that settled in the country did not developd separate strong identities, as happened in Gallia or Germania, nor were the aristocrats, as officials of the king, given the opportunity to create provincial identities. English history has a sense of continuity that not even the Viking invasions managed to destroy. How different Germanic invaders (Jutes, Angles and Saxons) with diverse origins and customs, managed to develop a common law and life style is not an easy question to answer, but the role of a unifying monarchy (Wessex-Mercia), assisted by the Church which sacralized kingship, created the appropriate conditions. The establishment of the shires by Edward the Elder in the tenth century undermined local auton-omy by cutting across tribal settlements. Another feature of the English monarchy at that time was the importance of what Powicke called the 'personal tie'. If we 'look at Anglo-Saxon history as a whole we find that the title to land was not based upon any claim to independent own-ership, but was the reward or symbol of service' (Powicke 1958: 163). The earls were accorded privileges by the king and had to share the prof-its accrued to them. The land, whether in the hands of Church people or of the thegns, was always granted, and hence the incumbents were always dependants, in the final instance, no matter how glorified.

The success of the Norman Conquest could not be explained without the existence of a previous unified Anglo-Saxon monarchy, independently of how feeble and inefficient the monarchy might have been. It is in this sense that it can be said that William I just superimposed an alien dynasty and aristocracy on a structured and unified kingdom. What Powicke considered the three major achievements of England in the two centuries after the invasion – 'the rapid growth of an administrative system which covered the whole country, the insistence upon the supremacy of the Crown, and the appearance of definite means of cooperation between the king and his vassals' (ibid.: 169–70) – cannot be attributed solely to the genius of the Normans but rested on the solid foundations of the previous period.

We know that from as early as 731 Bede used the expression 'English people' (*gens Anglorum*) to refer to the inhabitants of the territory that is England today. The term meant basically that no matter what the ethnic origins of the population of England, a certain sense of political unity had developed. This followed basically from the loyalty due to the reigning king. It is true that linguistic changes had also taken place and a common language had emerged for quite a large part of the population of England. This does not mean that the expression Anglo-Saxon was not used, but it was probably a concession by kings of Saxon origin to ingratiate themselves with Angle populations. Onwards from the time of king Edgard, in the second half of the tenth century, the monarchs were referred to as 'kings of the English', with England and English as the names for the territory and the people respectively. In England as elsewhere in the continent, kings were at first leaders of their peoples and only later rulers of the country; in this sense England is a derivative of English. It was not until after the tenth century that the English polity was seen basically as a kingdom. This sequence of things has much to do with the early medieval conceptions of what a 'people' was. Susan Reynolds (1983) has remarked that the expressions used in the Middle Ages to refer to a people, that is *natio*, *gens* and *populus*, had two important underlying features: they assumed common biological descent but also common culture (and often the same laws and language). England, in spite of the Viking invasions, managed to preserve a strong sense of what Reynolds calls 'regnal solidarity', which the Normans were able to profit from after an initial period of native resistance.

One element which contributed to enhance the medieval belief that the world was naturally divided in a variety of peoples, was the growing use, after the sixth and seventh centuries, of the Biblical and Trojan myths of descent all over Western Europe. The belief that a king and its people were descended from the eponymous hero of a prestigious people like the Trojans, contributed to unify peoples, particularly where linguistic, legal, cultural and class differences existed. Reynolds concludes by saying that 'because kings were seen as the type of supreme ruler and kingdoms as the type of polity, the most complete sort of people comprised the inhabitants of a whole kingdom. Indeed, kingdoms were as much defined by their people as by their king' (1983: 377).

Much is still to be explained about how in a few centuries the Germanic invaders and the local Britons fused into the rudiments of a unitary kingdom which survived, no matter how precariously, the Danish invasions. An initial point which should be clarified at once is the question of names. In the past few years the traditional expression used for the people who inhabited the territory known today as England between the mid-fifth century and the mid-eleventh century – the Anglo-Saxons – has come under scrutiny. It would appear that the term originated in the continent in the ninth century and that it had limited use among the natives which, as we have seen before, referred to themselves as 'English'.

Much has been made of the break represented by the Germanic invasions of Britannia in the fifth century, but recent research has shown that there was more continuity than was thought previously, particularly in the sense that some of the Germanic peoples were invited to come by the Roman rulers to fight against the Britons. Furthermore, although it had been assumed that the invading peoples had different identities and cultures, there is not much evidence to support this type of thought. However, it would still be true to say that 'in fact we do not know how consistently the Germanic-speaking invaders of Britain behaved like a group or felt themselves to be a group during the fifth and sixth centuries' (Reynolds 1985: 400).

J.G.A. Pocock (1975: 607) has suggested that Scotland began with the consolidation of a small kingdom in the northern part of the lowlands (Pictland) and later expanded by incorporating the Highlands and the land of the northwest. While during Roman domination Hadrian's Wall separated the northern part of Britain from the south, after its collapse by the end of the fourth century there began a period of populational fluidity. One of the Germanic tribes – the Angles – reached as far as the Forth. With the creation of the English kingdom, the northern territories would have been in danger of being annexed had it not been for the existence of a buffer zone – Northumbria – which became an area of Norse settlement and domination in the period prior to the Norman invasion. The territory which today is Scotland was never under Roman control, remaining fundamentally a pastoral economy at the time when England became a grain exporting area. These developments were maintained during the so-called Anglo-Saxon period. It would, however, be untrue to say that Scotland was untouched by Rome. Hadrian's Wall marked the first clear division of the island, and in their military, and sometimes trading and cultural exchanges the inhabitants of northern Britain learned of warlike techniques and heard of Christianity.

Who were these peoples with whom the Romans established contact, if only military? We know practically nothing about them. Different names have been used at different times, but *Britanni* seems to be the most common, though this was also the term used to refer to those people south of the wall. *Caledonii* was the name given to a number of the people who occupied the central part of the Highlands. After the fourth century the name Picts seems to be the most common one to refer to the peoples of Scotland. However, another people was mentioned by the Romans in the third century: the *Scotti*. Now these were the people from Scotia, that is, the Roman word for one people from Ireland. The Scots (Irish) and Picts had fought together against Britons and Romans. Gilda's *The Ruin of Britain*, written in the 540s, stated that it was precisely to defend themselves against the northern raiders that the Britons called in the Saxons to help them. Two centuries later, Bede's *Ecclesiastic History of the English People* mentioned that four peoples inhabited North Britain: the Picts north of the Firth, the Scots (Irish) in the north-west or Dalriada (Argyll), the Britons in the south-west (valley of Clyde) and the Angles (Lothian). These peoples spoke different languages; except for the Angles – who spoke a Germanic dialect – the rest were Celtic-speakers. While Pictish was lost without a literary trace, modern Gaelic derives from Scots (Irish), and modern Welsh from the language spoken by the Britons. It is from these four peoples that the kingdom of Scotland emerged, although its southern boundaries were fuzzy for centuries. It was not until the tenth century that the country north of the Cheviots was referred to as Scotland. However, the present demarcation line between England and Scotland occurred much later, with the Treaty of York in 1237.

The union between these four peoples was not easy. In so far as they constituted themselves into separate kingdoms, they fought each other relentlessly. No doubt the introduction of Christianity by the likes of Columba and Aidan contributed to create a common cultural background. What is important about the missionary activity of Colomba and his followers in the sixth century and later was not so much its religious dimension, but its politico-cultural one. Christianity would have come sooner or later to Scotland, but the fact that Picts, Scots (Irish) and Britons were not 'civilized' by the Anglo-Saxon Church meant also that they kept their cultural and political autonomy – a Celtic civilization survived as a viable alternative, at least for the time being.

By the beginning of the seventh century the English kingdom of

Northumbria was threatening the Scottish kingdoms; the Northumbrians incorporated Bernicia under their rule, penetrated the territory of the Britons and defeated Aidan, king of the Scots (Irish). For a moment it appeared as if the northern part of Britain would be a part of the Northumberland kingdom, but in 685 Brude mac Bile, king of the Picts, defeated the king of Northumbria, hence putting an end to the expansionist policies of the English. Later, in the ninth century, Kenneth MacAlpin created the new kingdom of Alba which brought together Scots and Picts. No doubt the union of these two peoples was made possible by an external threat: the incursions of the Nordic peoples. A century later, Lothian became part of the kingdom of Alba. But it was not until the mid-eleventh century that Duncan I managed to bring Cumbria and Strathclyde under his rule. By 1066 it would still be premature to talk about Scottish identity because the kingdom was lacking in a common law and the different peoples were still seen as separate entities. It took the consolidation of a centralized state along feudal lines, the unifying role of the Scottish Church, and the constant threat of an Anglo-Norman invasion to generate a Scottish 'national spirit' (Dickinson 1962: 39).

The history of Welsh identity started in the post-Roman era, when what is known as Wales today became the main centre of Britonnic resistance. Because the Anglo-Saxons had pushed the Britons westwards, but never succeeded in expelling them from their Welsh mountainous refuges, the latter not only had the chance to preserve their Christianity and part of their Roman culture (including Roman law), but more importantly they developed a sense of separate identity. In the fifth and sixth centuries hundreds of Christian monks converted Wales to Christianity. They operated from a great number of small monasteries scattered all over the land. By the sixth century, Gilda's *The Ruin of Britain* suggested that the distinctive characteristic of the Britons *vis-à-vis* the Picts and Saxons was their Christianity; for the Christian monk, though, the Britons had brought ruin on themselves when in the fifth and sixth centuries their leaders became wicked and tyrannical: from being God's chosen people they brought upon themselves the wrath of the Almighty and were defeated by the pagan invaders.

At this stage in history Wales only exists in the mind of romantic historians. In their westward settlements the Britons fought continuous battles with the Anglo-Saxons, and particularly with the kingdom of Mercia. It is not correct to say that the Britons were politically unified; in fact they were organized in four major kingdoms: Gwynedd in the north, Powys in the centre, Dyfed in the south-west and Morgannwg in the south-east. From Gildas' book we know the names of the tyrants of these kingdoms: Maelgwyn of Gwynedd and Gwrthefyr of Dyfed. But despite Gildas' tirades against the moral depravity (murders, adulteries, incests) of some of the Britonnic kings, there is little doubt that they often commanded the respect and loyalty of their subjects; they were often determined and forceful rulers whose exploits were praised and preserved by poets. The literature produced in this period, no matter how despised by Gildas, allowed for the preservation of the identity (culture, language and history) of the Britons at a time when they were starting to become Welsh (Williams 1979: 2–3). The sixth century was also the time of the creation of the Arthurian legend, which later on was to play a key role in the perception of Welsh history. Whether a king or a military commander, Arthur came to represent the first hero in the continuous struggle of the Britons cum Welsh against the Anglo-Saxon invaders.

With the triumphal advance of the Anglo-Saxons, the Welsh were cut off from the other Britons and were kept within a limited territory established by Offa, a Mercian king; the frontier ran from Dogfeiling in the north to Ergyng in the south. By the ninth century, the inhabitants spoke a form of old Welsh and may already have referred to their country as Cymru; nonetheless, they still had a wider sense of identity in so far as they identified with the northern Britons. A crucial factor which gave impetus to this belief was a myth of common descent: the Britons were thought to have descended from an eponymous Trojan hero, Brutus. Royal genealogies with a more limited sense of local identity attached to a smaller territory were also in use in Wales at that time. In the words of Glanmor Williams: 'The two concepts of being affiliated to a people of ancient British, ultimately Trojan stock and of belonging more concretely to a *gwlad* (region or locality) and its ruling house would long persist in the minds of the free population. The idea of owing loyalty to a country thought of as Wales would come very slowly and relatively late' (Williams 1979: 5).

The Viking invasions, among other factors, contributed to the collapse of the traditional political structure of Wales. By the ninth century the different kingdoms were coming to an end and a new type of ruler of all Wales was starting to emerge. The best known of these high kings was Hywel Dda in the tenth century; under his leadership Welsh law was codified and unified, literature flourished both in Latin and in Welsh and a number of political institutions emerged. But in the century prior to the Norman invasion, Wales was involved in internecine wars, as well as in fighting the constant incursions by the English, the Danes and the Irish. By the mid-eleventh century Gruffyd ap Llywelyn tried once again to unify the country under his leadership; by then the Welsh, however, had also to contend against all odds with a superior enemy: the English (Williams 1985: 47–61).

The Romans, who referred to Ireland as Hibernia, left very few clues about this island, though the Irish (Gaels) often raided the British coast. A Celtic population, the Irish managed to remain culturally and linguistically homogeneous for a long time because neither the Roman nor the Anglo-Saxon invasions of Britain had any noticeable effect on them. Not even the Viking invasions, which started at the beginning of the ninth century, and touched a number of coastal areas of eastern and southern Ireland upsetting the delicate political order of the country, changed things radically, since the Viking settlers accepted Irish culture in the long run.

One important development, however, took place in the fifth century: the spreading of Christianity by Saint Patrick, a romanized Briton trained in Gallia. By the sixth century the whole country had converted. The Irish Church had the peculiarity of being a monastic Church in which monks and missionaries were at the forefront, eclipsing the traditional episcopal Roman structure. The civilizing effect of Christianity was soon to be seen in Ireland, with a flourishing of the arts and literature; the monks also contributed, as we shall see, to creating a sense of Irish identity.

There has been a lively controversy raging for decades concerning the Irish political system prior to the Norman invasion. Traditionally, English scholars saw Ireland as a society lacking the requisites of a proper state; they depicted an anarchic polity divided into nearly two hundred tribes led by provincial chiefs or kinglets; there were changing groupings of tribes and subordination. The high king (*ard-rí*) mentioned in the classical texts was seen by these scholars as more nominal than real. More recent scholarship, and particularly the work of Donnchadh O'Corrain, has presented a different picture in which the country was far from being as divided as it was originally thought. There seems to be little doubt, according to O'Corrain, that there was a hierarchy of rulers from the territorial, tribal king to a king of overkings (which corresponded to a large province the size of Ulster or Leinster). That the system was unstable can be shown easily by looking at the vicious in-fighting among kings at all levels. With the appearance of high kings in the ninth century, the power and status of the tribal kings started to diminish; by the eleventh century they were not referred to as kings (*rí túaithe*) any longer; instead, the word lord (*toísech*) was used (O'Corrain 1972).

In a more recent paper, D. O'Corrain has maintained that 'the Irish were profoundly conscious of themselves as a larger community or natio, that their learned classes were preoccupied with this very notion and that in the eleventh and twelfth centuries the greater kings attempted to turn that consciousness to political advantage' (1978: 4). The Irish shared with other European peoples the belief in myths of descent in which Christian and Pagan heroes were mixed. By the seventh century there was a theory which connected the Irish with the Biblical Adam via Mil of Spain; the basic idea was that the Irish had a common origin and hence constituted a people, a community. The fact that both the legal and ecclesiastical systems of Ireland were different from other parts of Romanized Europe, were additional factors which contributed to make Irish identity more obvious. By the time of the Norman invasion of England, the literati had constructed the idea of an all-embracing Irish monarchy. There were also attempts to sacralize the monarchy, but apparently with limited results. In conclusion, one should say that in spite of a certain degree of state-building and territorial aggrandizement, the kings of Ireland had limited and precarious powers; more importantly, unification was only an ideal, while the struggles to become high king often degenerated into internecine wars. In spite of that, the Irish had a sense of identity which was used by monarchs by the eleventh century to stake their claims as kings of Ireland.

In his comparative study of state-building in France and England in the Middle Ages, Joseph R. Strayer emphasized a well-known but nonetheless crucial fact which facilitated the consolidation of the English state: it was simply that the king exercised his powers over the whole realm. While France was a combination of 'virtually independent provinces' (1970: 48–9), England was, at least from the Norman Conquest onwards, like a single French province, exhibiting a high degree of institutional homogeneity. William the Conqueror brought to England a new ruling class of about two thousand knights, which was invested with large but not compact fiefs resulting from the expropriation of Anglo-Saxon landowners. Norman notables held fifty per cent of the land, while the king and the Church shared the rest in equal parts, except for about eight per cent which remained the property of the Anglo-Saxon aristocrats. The conquering king introduced also an efficient and centralized system of government, including a powerful military machine, in this way consolidating the monarchy. Most historians would agree that the Norman Conquest was, for the reasons just mentioned, a turning point for the country. However, it was not only its internal structure which was affected. The Norman, and later the Angevin connections partly reoriented English policy towards the continent and in particular towards Gallia. The English medieval monarchy did not only try to irrupt in the Welsh, Irish and Scottish spaces, but would also have a constant presence in large sections of northern and western Gallia.

To assess royal rights over the conquered land as well as to find out about the people who lived in it, William the Conqueror organised in 1086 a full survey of England which was recorded in the Domesday

Book. Prior to the conquest, the land was divided into shires (or counties) and hundreds (a subdivision of the shire with its own court). The royal officers, who conducted the investigation most thoroughly, used the shire as the basis for their work. In fact the division into thirty-two counties, including their eleventh-century boundaries, has largely lasted to the present day. The purpose of the survey was to enquire into the smallest detail, at the level of the hide, that is, the measure of land able to support one free family and its dependents (between 60 and 120 acres); who possessed the land before and after the conquest, what was its size and its quality, what amount of produce it yielded, the size of the labour force and the potential of the land.

As has been pointed out by F. M. Stenton (1943), after the survey there followed a massive transfer of land and power in a reasonably orderly manner; out of thousands of small estates there emerged a couple of hundred large lordships. Domesday Book exemplifies the crystalization of feudal law in England, because 'every form of possession is related to a descending system of dependent tenures: the maxim *nulle terre sans seigneur*, which did not emerge in France until the thirteenth century, applied, in practice, in England, from that time' (Mitteis 1975: 202). The idea that in Norman England every portion of land was a tenement was already emphasized by Marc Bloch in his classical *Feudal Society*, and led him to see medieval England as an oddity in the Western European context: a highly feudalised society, but with a strong centralized monarchy.

What is characteristic of English feudalism is that vassals amd subvassals alike owed allegiance directly to the king. This is what followed from the oath that William the Conqueror forced upon all his tenants in the Plains of Salisbury in 1086. Without changing the hierarchical character of feudalism, that is, without wanting to appropriate the services that according to feudal law the subvassal owed the vassal, the king expected fealty from all of them. In other words, 'the king was lord paramount, *dominus ligius ante omnes*; not only would *ligesse* take priority over every other obligation, it would be built into every kind of feudal bond so that, should any tenant in chief revolt, his subvassals would be entitled to save their fealty to the king' (Mitteis 1975: 203–4). The principle was reaffirmed in the reigns of Henry II (1154–1189) and Henry III (1216–1272).

The replacement of the indigeneous ruling class by an alien one produced comparatively little upheaval, perhaps because William the Conqueror was well aware that the only way in which a few thousand (probably about ten thousand) conquerors could dominate one million natives was by not interfering in their culture and law – although of course he built enough castles to face local revolts. By operating within the existing Anglo-Saxon institutional framework William and his successors were able to graft onto it Norman practices which perfected the system by developing its potential. The Anglo-Norman state was a well organized and well oiled war machine, and the king was in a position to exact military service from the aristocracy, whether in the form of armed knights or payment to mercenaries. It is true also that the Norman aristocracy came second to none in their eagerness to conquer and plunder new territories.

Furthermore, the Normans managed to incorporate the local elites in the tasks of governing the country, It is difficult to see how the invaders could have otherwise succeeded, given their small numbers and their frequent continental escapades. The chief officers of the crown in the counties, that is, the sheriffs (from shire-reeves) were nominated directly by the king, though among people who held land in the area. In theory they were independent from the baronial power and could be sacked by the monarch. By giving the sheriffs extensive judicial, military and fiscal powers, the Anglo-Norman kings managed to check the dangers of parcellisation of power typical of feudalism.

That a small country like England was able not only to dominate the rest of Britannia, but more importantly to hold large chunks of Gallia up to the end of the medieval period, was due to the existence of a centralized, cohesive and efficient state which had no parallel in Western Europe. In the final instance, what made the strength of the English state was the loyalty of the aristocracy towards its king, though friction and tension were not absent from the relationship. At the state level what mattered was the development of a series of institutions (judicial, fiscal and political) which blended Anglo-Saxon traditions with Norman inventiveness, producing long-lasting achievements such as the the Exchequer, the common law system and the Parliament.

The origin of the Exchequer can be traced back to the beginnings of the twelfth century. In an attempt at improving the financial control over his subjects, Henry I appointed Roger d'Avranches to manage his affairs; the latter introduced an advanced reckoning system from the north of France, which allowed the performance of arithmetic operations that were otherwise extremely cumbersome due to the use of Roman numerals. The system involved a long, oval-shaped table covered with a chequered cloth. Around the table sat the various king's dignitaries ready to scrutinize the accounts of the sheriffs who twice a year paid in the income from their shires. The Exchequer is an early clear indication of the degree of centralization and efficiency of the English state, and as such is rightly seen as a milepost in the administrative history of the country. The Exchequer acted also as a court which settled disputes originating in the process of auditing. 'No other country in

Western Europe', wrote Doris May Stenton, 'could boast of a depart-
ment of state comparable to the Exchequer of the English kings' (1965:
41). In the later medieval period, there was an expansion of the
Exchequer, the functions of which were diversified to handle the
appearance of new forms of taxation which accompanied the development of England as a territorial state. Foreign wars, particularly in
Gallia, put a strain on the royal finances, requiring the introduction of
often unpopular poll taxes.

What is most astonishing about the common law system in England is
its continuity; or as Maitland put it, the fact that although the rules might
have been changed, the body of law survived from the medieval period
to the present day. There has been much controversy as to the origins of
the system and its distinctiveness. Rather than to attribute it to the legislative qualities of any ethnie in particular, be it that of the Romans, the
Anglo-Saxons or the Normans, it is probably more accurate to suggest
that it was a synthesis of many different contributions, and 'the system
took the form it did because it developed in the period of the twelfth
century renaissance and it retained that form for centuries thereafter
because bureaucracy perpetuated' (Clanchy 1983: 158). As compared
with the Anglo-Saxon period and in contradistinction to medieval Wales
and Scotland, English common law shifted away from the regulation of
bloodfeud, first to a system of a system of feudal law under William I
and then to the idea of public prosecution of criminal offences by jury
during the reign of Henry II. Although there were local variations, the
jurisdiction of common law was applied to the whole country. It was not
feudal or customary law, but royal law. There is no doubt that the existence of a unified legal system – a unique development in the European
context, where regional legal systems ruled – facilitated the consolidation of England as a political unit.

G.O. Sayles has remarked that the 'English constitution was the
product of three forces, represented by the king, the feudal barons and
the subject people' (1977: 448). In the thirteenth century these forces
amalgamated to give rise to parliament. It should be emphasized,
however, that the role of the centralized monarchy was paramount in
the emergence of parliament; the king saw parliament as an instrument aimed at facilitating the tasks of government. To avoid misleading historical extrapolations from the present to the past, it should be
made absolutely clear that originally the English parliament was
mainly concerned with administrative and judiciary functions, and
that popular representation was circumstantial. In other words, what
became typical of the English parliament towards the end of the
medieval period and later – bicameralism with growing power to the
House of Commons – was absent. The prehistory of the parliament

was connected with the issue of decision-making: the king needed information about the realm and obtained it by the administrative procedure of asking the responsible and knowledgeable people in the local communities (Holt 1985). An important feature of parliament is that 'from the beginning it was a national assembly – it had no regional competitors' (Corrigan and Sayer 1985: 28).

From the early form of representation there developed, between the last quarter of the thirteenth century and the fourteenth century, parliament in all its basic features. With the Magna Carta of 1215 and the Provisions of Oxford of 1258, the idea that the king had to rely on the consent of the community of the realm became apparent. Meetings were called regularly by the king; these became progressively more representative of the 'whole' community and would gather to discuss a variety of affairs. By 1321 the Modus Tenendi Parliament specified that the first objective of the parliament was to attend to the affairs of the monarch in matters of general policy in the pursuit of war and in the collection of taxes. Because the communities of the shires were involved in the financing of foreign wars, their advice had to be heard in parliament; and that's why both lords and commons had to give their consent and cooperation to the royal policies. In addition, parliament attended also to judicial, legislative and other matters (Harris 1975).

By the fourteenth century parliament used to meet once a year in Westminster; the lords, including religious dignitaries *qua* royal officials, were summoned individually by the king and numbered one hundred, while the commoners, elected in the shires and the towns, were two hundred. Because of continuous and increasing war expenditures, taxation was probably the factor that most contributed to consolidate parliament (Given-Wilson 1986). By the fifteenth century parliament had lost many of its judicial functions. Although one should not overestimate the power of the commons, the king came to depend more and more on their support for a variety of policies. However, most initiatives still originated in the aristocracy. One of the essential features of the emerging political constitution of England was that the king was powerful but only in so far as his subjects consented to it. By the end of the medieval period 'parliament was fast becoming in a new sense the community of England gathered together as one body in head and members' (Wilkinson 1969: 383). King, lords and commons, as the three estates of the realm, had reached a *modus vivendi* within the framework of the parliamentary institution. I have insisted that the English parliament was different from its European equivalents. For one thing, there was never a consolidation of the clerical estate. In fact the term 'estate' is inappropriate to both seignorial and popular representation. More importantly, due to the relatively small size of the country and its early unity the parliament had no provincial competitors – unlike the emerging parliament of the Kingdom of France which had to compete with an array of local parliaments (Myers 1961).

I have said at the outset of this section that the consolidation of the English state after the Norman invasion created a threat not only to the Welsh, Scots and Irish, but also to the attempts of the French monarchy to establish itself over the territory of Gallia. This is not to imply that the relationships between England and its neighbours were of the same type. For one thing, Wales had been conquered by the end of the four-teenth century and subjected to English rule, while in Ireland, English domination only affected a portion of the island. Scotland managed to establish itself as an independent state and fought off English attempts at subjugation. As to the English presence in Gallia it followed the dynastic fortunes of the English monarchs who tried to enforce their claims first in Normandy (until 1204) and, when the Angevin connec-tion was established in 1154, to vaster territories (Anjou, Poitou and Aquitaine). In the section on Gallia I mention that what started as a feu-dal dispute became, with the Hundred Years War, a struggle between two territorial, modern states. The English presence in Gallia came to an end in 1453 (except for the enclave of Calais), although it was not until the beginning of the nineteenth century that the English monarchs renounced their medieval claim to the Kingdom of France.

Romantic historiography has always insisted on the long-felt pres-ence of the Norman invading elite as an alien body in the life of medieval England. That the natives were excluded from high office and access to land (and that they resented that) and that (Old) English ceased to be the official language of government (though not of the populace) is perfectly true, but this does not apply to the whole medieval period. Furthermore, the sense of English identity which was created in the Anglo-Saxon period survived the invasion. The fact that monarchs pre-ferred foreign advisors for centuries, mostly from Anjou, Poitou or Savoy, and enriched them munificently, was widely criticized, to the extent that in the mid-thirteenth century the barons petitioned the king against the practice of granting castles to people who were not English-born and against betrothing English maidens to non-nationals.

The language issue is more complicated than it is usually presented. Much has been made of the fact that the Normans introduced Latin as the standard language of government displacing (Old) English which, as a consequence, lost status. The predominance of Latin was not a specif-ically English phenomenon; in fact it was common to most European countries. In the thirteenth century the languages of Gallia (*langue d'oc* and *langue d'oïl*) started to acquire prestige as literary as well as lan-guages of government. At this time English had then to compete with

Latin and French. However, during the thirteenth century (Middle) English had become the native language of practically everybody – the royal family excepted. Latin persisted as the language of the Church, in the same way that the prestige of French culture gave a political and literary role to the two main variety of Gallic dialects (Clanchy 1983).

The loss of Normandy in 1204 and the royal decrees of 1244 forbidding the nobility from holding land both in England and Normandy, sounded the death-knell of French as the language of the ruling class. In the second half of the thirteenth century there was a massive borrowing of French words in (Middle) English – a sign that there was a linguistic shift from French to English among the educated classes. While up to 1250 literature was produced in French, in the following century English became the norm, to the extent that the anonymous author of a romance written around 1325 could note that English had become the universal language of the country, and that French was being relegated to the role of a cultural ornament (Baugh 1976). By mid-fourteenth century the Sheriff's Courts of London instituted English as their official language, the high courts following suit in 1362. A year after the Chancellor used the English language for the opening speech of Parliament. The second half of the fourteenth century produced such figures as Chaucer, Wyclif and Langland. English was not, however, a unified language and different dialects proliferated in different parts of the country. In the long run, the dialect of the east Midlands, which was spoken in London and the circles of government became the basis for modern English (Du Boulay 1970).

One should not expect to find a clear idea of England as a nation in the majority of the population, though no doubt the educated elite had a remarkable awareness of national identity. As Clanchy has noted, nation 'meant a kindred group and hence by extension it was applied to the people of each distinctive country' (1983: 242). This sense of English identity developed mainly as a result of confrontations with, and in opposition to, other emerging nations. The literature of the period shows how the Welsh, the Scots, the Irish and the French were perceived as different peoples. That they were also often presented in terms of disparaging stereotypes, and even depicted as exhibiting non-human characteristics, does not alter the basic distinction. Wars and travelling were the two main factors accounting for the awakening of national identity. It was in the context of these two activities that contacts were made and cultural and linguistic differences noticed and registered, to be elaborated ideologically later on in the form of stereotypes of national character in the literature of the period.

Recognition of the identity of England at the international level, particularly *vis-à-vis* the French monarchy, was essential. At the Council of

Constance, in the early fifteenth century, the English delegation asserted their autonomy in the following manner: 'Whether a nation be understood as a people marked off from others by blood relationship and habit of unity, or by peculiarities of language (the most sure and positive sign and essence of a nation in divine and human law) ... or whether a nation be understood, as it should be, as a territory equal to that of the French nation, England is a real nation' (Du Boulay 1970: 20).

In the context of the Church, and without denying its universality, the archbishops of Canterbury – Chichele and Bourchier in particular – often expressed pride about the Church of England and its distinctiveness. By the late fourteenth century and during the fifteenth century patriotic writings were the rule, Chaucer's work being a noted exception. It is true that many of those who chanted of England as a nation were connected, in one way or another, with the crown and tended to identify *regnum* with *patria*; others were aware of internal differences within England (north and south), but neither this nor local allegiances challenged the basic sense of belonging to England (Thomson 1983).

In the long run, the retreat from France strengthened English identity allowing the country to consolidate its features. By 1533 Henry VIII could boast that his ancestors had built up a true nation, when he asserted: 'that this realm is an empire and so has been accepted in the world' (Du Boulay 1970: 30), and it is well-known that the word 'empire' suggested that the English monarchy did not depend on any other spiritual (Pope) or temporal (Emperor) power. It is true, however, that if we look at 'the outrageous elaboration of the law of treason under Henry VIII and the extravagances of Gloriana-worship under Elisabeth' (Cam 1963: 169) there is in evidence a strong identification of monarch with nation, but this is to be expected from the period. For Kohn, who placed the birth of English nationalism in the seventeenth century, 'the accession of the Tudors to power at the end of the fifteenth century laid the foundations for that national homogeneity which was the necessary condition for the later development of nationalism' (1940: 70).

There seems to be a general consensus that by the end of the medieval period there was a clear sense of national identity in England, even if it was shared perhaps by only five per cent of the population. Can the same be said about Scotland, Ireland and Wales? If we combine the definitions of H. Seton-Watson (1981: 5) and A. D. Smith (1986: 22–30) we could say that ethnies are the nations of the Middle Ages or, more precisely, that the medieval period only knew of ethnies. The criteria that Smith puts forward for an entity to qualify as ethnie (nation in my terminology) are the following: a collective proper name, a specific myth of common ancestry or a common myth of descent, one or more differentiated elements of culture which are shared, an association with a specific homeland or history and a sense of solidarity for significant sections of the population. As we shall see, an argument can be made to suggest that Scotland, Wales and Ireland fulfill the conditions required.

Scottish identity was much slower to develop than English identity. The history of medieval Scotland was that of a constant struggle against the attempts by England to annex its territory. This situation produced the first 'nationalist' statement in western European history in the Declaration of Arbroath (1370). The document said, in no ambiguous words, that the Scots 'shall never consent to bow beneath the yoke of English domination'. With the recognition by Pope John XXII in 1328 of the right of the rulers of Scotland to call themselves kings (and hence to be crowned and anointed), there began a period in which Scotland was internationally recognized as an independent state. However, the distinctiveness of Gaelic culture and language was progressively undermined by the influence of Anglo-Norman presence and practices which were, if not encouraged, at least accepted by Scottish kings (Dickinson 1962: 1–4).

By the fourteenth century, with a clear delineation of lowlanders and highlanders, Scotland was a 'two-nation' state. However, in the context of the wars of independence that ravaged the country in 1329 and 1371, it was the 'anglicized' lowlanders that developed a sense of Scottish national identity (Barrow 1976). The Scots opposed the English myth of descent which stated that the inhabitants of the island were descended from the Trojan Brutus. They proposed an alternative origin for the people of Scotland: they were meant to have descended from the daughter of the Pharoah of Egypt – Scota – who came via Hispania to Ireland and then to Scotland, and expelled the descendants of Brutus south of the border. The existence of a distinctive law, reflecting the fact that Scotland had been more influenced by continental practices than England, was seen also as a prominent element in the character of the Scottish people and was a focus of identity and pride. In the long run, however, the desire of the English state to expand their territory, thus also securing its northern borders, led first to the Union of Crowns of 1603 and later to the Treaty of Union in 1707. How far the Scots consented to the Union is open to controversy, but their sense of nationhood was strong enough to resist the loss of political independence. Furthermore, Scottish identity was preserved in three institutions: the Church, the legal system and the monetary system.

The Anglo-Norman presence in Ireland was a catalyst for the development of Irish national identity during the medieval period. There are enough references, particularly in the literature of the thirteenth and fourteenth centuries to show that there was a growing sense of national awereness. This is particularly obvious in a narrative in prose entitled

Caithre'im Thoirdhealbhaigh (The Triumphs of Turlough) written
probably around 1330. This document, as J. A. Watt has remarked, contains three basic themes of national identity: 'the usurpation and oppression of the foreigner, a myth of the origin of the nation and a political
expression of the unity of the country' (1987: 348).

The parallelisms between the Scottish and Irish cases are striking. At
more or less the same time as the Scottish barons wrote to Pope John
XXII asserting the independence of Scotland, the Irish kings
(Remonstrance of 1317–18) were also asking the Pope to defend their
right to govern themselves alleging to that end that the Irish kings were
not descended from Brutus but from Milesius of Spain, that they had
been ruling in Ireland for 3500 years and that the Irish people had
enjoyed political freedom until the English had subjected them to unjust
rule. Between 1534 and 1691 the island of Ireland was conquered in its
totality and subjected to English domination. Henry VIII changed his
title from Lord to King of Ireland. During this period the Irish were
repeatedly defeated and the autonomy of both Gaelic and Anglo-Irish
overlords came to an end. Protestantism became the official religion of
Ireland, though the Catholic Church managed to maintain a parallel
structure which, though illegal, was still powerful. During the seventeenth century there was a massive expropriation of Catholic landowners; their lands ended up in the hands of newly arrived English people.
By the end of the century, waves of immigrants from Scotland popu-
lated Ulster. The scene was set for an endemic conflict.

It was not until the second half of the thirteenth century that the
Anglo-Norman monarchy, in the person of Edward I, decided to annex
Wales. Because the alien rulers replaced only the top layer of government, the Welsh language and culture were not disturbed. If anything,
the invasion of Wales contributed to unify the Welsh and give them a
sense of national identity. Referring to thirteenth-century Wales, Davies
has argued that 'the growth of a sense of national identity need not be
matched by or conditional upon the development of the institutions of
common state authority' (1984: 51). He also alleges that in the absence
of a state, national identity can be found elsewhere: 'in the awareness of
the common genealogical descent of a people, in a shared belief in a particular version of historical mythology and prophecy, in an emotional
attachment to the geographical boundaries of a country, in a heightened
awareness of the distinctiveness of a common language and of common
customs, in the yearning for the prospect of unitary rule, in the articula-
tion of the "we-them" dichotomy to express the distinction between
natives and aliens' (ibid.: 52). In the case of Wales, one of the prominent
factors which separated it from England was the legal system; its emasculation by Edward I in 1284 was consequently also a challenge to

Welsh identity. The revolt of Owen Glendower between 1400 and 1410 was a national rebellion; he 'was the first, indeed the only, Welsh prince to command popular and spontaneous support from every corner of Wales' (Williams 1985: 88). Whether it can be called a (failed) 'war of national liberation' as Williams maintains, is a moot point. In any case, the unified and independent Wales lasted only for a few years.

Gallia

When the first Capet, Hugues, was elected by his peers as king of the Western Franks in 987, his jurisdiction extended over approximately the territory allocated to Charles the Bold after the partition of Verdun in 843, that is, over the western part of the Carolingian Empire. In practice, however, he only controlled a small duchy – Francia or the Ile de France – which amounted to about five per cent of the territory. The sacred character of Carolingian kingship was also inherited by the Capetians, though somewhat weakened. A Capetian king was bestowed with the titles of *rex* and Church's representative through a number of rituals, but he could not enforce his feudal rights beyond the confines of the core of his own duchy; of course, the same applied to the ruler of the other principalities. Up until the thirteenth century Gallia was basically a mosaic of autonomous duchies or principalities; no geographic, economic or political factors can be posited that account for the development of France as we know it today. In fact, what did happen was rather more improbable than what could have happened. And if, as we shall see, between the thirteenth and the mid-fourteenth centuries the Capetian monarchy succeeded in integrating a good number of the principalities within the royal domain, the attempt was only partially successful in that the so-called Hundred Years War was as much a rebellion by the oppressed principalities against an ever-encroaching king, as it was a war between England and France as well (Finer, S.E., 1974: 99–100).

In Gallia the period between the ninth and the thirteenth centuries can be characterised as one in which the power of the individual principalities often equalled if not exceeded that of the monarchy. It is true that none of the *principes* enjoyed the prestige attached to the holder of the crown of western Francia, and that they all accepted the suzerainty of the king. It is clear, however, that the power of the king did not extend beyond the boundaries of the royal domain (the region around Paris) and that in many other respects the Capetian monarchy was just like the other principalities. In fact, the Capetians were only kings by implicit consent of the *principes*. A major venture such as the conquest of England was the work of the Duke of Normandy and the northern nobility, and not of the *rex Francorum*. By the end of the twelfth century, however, there was a change of fortunes and the royal domain started to expand slowly but steadily over the Gallic territory, mainly by means of enforcing feudal rights, but also by arranging marriages and when necessary by military force. It was a time when the prestige attached to the monarch was decisive in helping to construct the kingdom of France.

In considering the development in Gallia it is important to start by remembering that the dismembration of the Carolingian Empire into sub-kingdoms (*regna*) was the basis for the emergence of the territorial principalities. It is also worth pointing out that the rulers of these principalities had originally been legitimated by the Carolingian themselves. By the tenth century the *princeps* or *dux* was really sovereign in his own territory; in fact they had both *potestas* and *auctoritas* and hence they were comparable to the king. The dukes of Britanny, Gascony and Normandy referred to their territorial principalities as *regna*, indicating herewith that theirs was *de facto* royal power. On the other hand, the fact that other territorial principalities, such as Barcelona, Toulouse and Flanders, were ruled by counts should not hide the reality that they considered their territories as *regna*. How long the principalities were able to maintain their unity is another matter; in fact, some of them suffered the same fate that had afflicted the Empire: they disintegrated rather quickly into smaller units (this was the case of Champagne and Burgundy).

The map of Gallia in the eleventh and twelfth centuries gives the impression of a complicated and changing mosaic or puzzle, but in fact a good number of principalities managed to stabilize their power. The *principes* did not only have the usual rights and duties of a king (from the fiscal to the religious spheres), but some of them made important contributions to state-building, especially in the areas of administration (creation of permanent offices) and military and fiscal organization. Most outstanding was the idea that local officials should enjoy considerable power. Many of these institutional developments were later imitated or taken over by the royal domain. The basis for population growth and for economic expansion were laid down by the principalities. They were also centres in which important cultural and artistic developments took place. (Werner, K. 1968).

The role played by ethnic factors in the consolidation of the territorial principalities is difficult to assess. The fact that they preserved well-established names and laws, no doubt helped them to achieve a sense of identity. The *principes* occasionally used these features in an attempt to maintain their autonomy. In some cases, like Normandy, a descent myth existed for the people of the duchy which was different from that of the early Franks. There was no attempt, however, to build on ethnic lines in those principalities where the majority of the population was not of

Frankish origin (Celtic in Brittany, Basque in Gascony and Scandinavian in Normandy); the reason was partly that the ruling elite was of West Frankish origin.

If in the north of Gallia there were a number of principalities, such as Britanny, Normandy and Flanders, with specific ethnic and political characteristics which differentiated them from the emerging royal dominion, south of the Loire and as far as Catalonia a civilizational area of remarkable homogeneity was visible, in spite of local differences, by the eleventh century, if not before. There was to start with a major linguistic division: the Midi and Catalonia had developed similar dialects of Latin referred to as *langues d'oc*, while north of the Loire the *langues d'oïl* had a unity of their own. The Occitan language was not only important in the legal and administrative spheres until well into the early modern period, but it was the poetical language par excellence of Occitania and in fact of the whole of Latin Europe from the eleventh to the thirteenth centuries. The lyric poetry of the troubadours was based on a conception of love in which women were exalted and idealized and men could reach high moral levels by being faithful to them.

The social structure of this civilizational area had developed in an original way. Two new strata had appeared: warriors around a castle and burghers in the towns. In the countryside some peasants were quasi-independent; others in a servile position (until 1050 the development of feudalism in the Midi had not kept pace with the north). Within the Church there were voices trying to promote a more spiritual type of Christianity, and resenting their subordinate position to the powers that be. The heresies of Occitania in later years, and Catharism in particular, reflected a rebellion against the 'terrestrial' leanings of the established Church (Nelli, R. 1969; Le Roy Ladurie, E. 1978).

There were a number of developments – instincts or indigenous traditions as Archibald Lewis (1965: 403) has called them – which throw some light on why Occitania and Catalonia exhibited a *sui generis* configuration. Firstly, there was the question of the preference for allodial over feudal rights; secondly, there was the belief in the centrality of the family as a source of wealth and power, as well as greater equality among the sexes; thirdly, there was the practice of envisaging feudalism more as an economic than a political contract; and finally, there was the judicial role played by informal and voluntary courts which assembled a variety of free men and women (Lewis, A. 1965: 401–4).

In the period between the eleventh and mid-thirteenth centuries the principalities of southern Gallia started to create strong territorial states where before there was a weak and divided sovereignty. They began to play a wider role in affairs across the Pyrenees and around the wider Mediterranean. The Counts of Barcelona were particularly successful in extending their principality through cunning marriages and military conquests in a variety of geographical directions. An important feature of this period was the sustained economic expansion of the principalities, more obviously visible in the emergence of an affluent merchant class in the major maritime and other towns of the area, which started to compete with that existing in the 'Italian' city-states (Lewis, A. R. 1974). The Capetian kings never visited the area and their suzerainty was purely nominal. In the case of Catalonia it is difficult to say when the seignorial rights were relinquished by the Capetians; certainly by the time the Count of Barcelona became King of Aragon in 1137 he was the *de facto* sovereign in his own realm, though official recognition by the Capetians did not occur until the Treaty of Corbeil in 1258.

K.F. Werner (1968: 263–4) has suggested that the system of territorial principalities in Gallia was basically unstable and hence destined to perish – its decline actually having started already by the late twelfth century. His argument is based on the idea that kingly prestige was a determinant factor in the agglutination of the different principalities around the royal domain, particularly when there was an alien threat. The first instance of such a situation emerged when in 1154 an Angevin, Henry II, had acceded to the English throne and had as well a 'feudal' claim on extensive territories in Gallia. There began a period, according to Werner, in which the power struggle was centered around two kings and, in the long run, the *principes* were forced to take sides with their natural ruler, that is, with the Capetian king. As we shall see, this seems to me a rather simplistic solution to the complex series of events that produced a unified French monarchy by the end of the Middle Ages. However, this is not to deny that the myth of kingship combined with the spirit of feudalism (vassalage) were the key ideological mechanisms used by the Capetian monarchy to ensure their survival (Mitteis, H. 1975: 268).

It is true that by the turn of the thirteenth century the royal demesne had increased its territories substantially. No doubt the Capetians, starting with Philip Augustus (some would suggest that the process was initiated by Louis VI at the instigation of Suger of St. Denis) were able to bank on the prestige and sacred character attached to the person of the king as suzerain of the different principalities of Gallia or even on the prestige of the kingdom itself, but it would certainly be one-sided to give too much weight to these factors at such an early period. In fact, the consolidation and expansion of the Ile de France would not have been possible without a major population growth, a sustained economic development and serious administrative reforms. The royal domain soon took the lead in creating a more integrated, thriving type of economy which was based on technological innovations, progressive clearings of the land, the development of market towns and a more monetised system of exchange. This was accompanied by a more effective, centralized administration and a better organized and more powerful army (Teunis, H. 1978).

The Crusades were also an important influence in giving the Capetians an increasing ascendancy and legitimacy, particularly in the eyes of the Church. There were certainly ups and downs in the relationships between monarchy and the papacy, but on the whole the Capetian kings were seen as paladins of Christianity (St. Louis was a good example). As we shall see, those involved in writing the chronicles of the Capetian kings were clerics whose works reflected this situation. No doubt chance, as the Capetian miracle was called, also played a role in the maintenance of the Capetian dynasty: the continued presence of a male heir over a long historical period preserved its survival. The reign of Philip Augustus (1180–1223) was particularly propitious for the Capetian dynasty. Not only did Philip II take possession of Normandy, Anjou, Poitou and Brittany, but by defeating a powerful coalition of English, Flemish and Holy Roman Empire troops at Bouvines in 1214 he consolidated his monarchy in an unprecedented way, checking the territorial ambitions of the English kings and of the Empire. As Baldwin (1987: 119) has put it, the battle of Bouvines taught three fundamental things: '1.– Because Philip defeated the great barons, like the counts of Flanders and Boulogne, he was the supreme feudal lord over the kingdom; 2.– because he vanquished a Roman emperor, the French remained independent of the Empire in fulfillment of their Trojan origins; 3.– because Philip successfully defended the Church against excommunicated enemies, the Capetians vindicated their title *reges christianissimi*, and Philip personally became a candidate for sainthood'. French historiography has tended to see in Bouvines (somewhat prematurely in my view) the first 'national' event of French history. The fact that after the battle there followed, particularly in Paris, a week of popular celebrations has been used as an indication of the existence of the rudiments of the kind of moral unity behind the monarch which is the stuff of which nations are made. For others, like Renouard (1969), Bouvines, along with other events of the early thirteenth century, marked a certain long-lasting political configuration of Western Europe.

One year before Bouvines, in 1213, Simon de Montfort, leading an army of crusaders from the northern principalities but loyal to Philip, defeated the count of Toulouse and the King of the Catalano-Aragonese confederation at Muret, hence putting an end to the idea of an Occitan-Catalan confederation and preparing the way for the integration of the Midi into the Capetian monarchy. The political kudos derived from these successive victories, particularly Bouvines, greatly enhanced the prestige of the monarchy to the extent that the latter, as G. Duby (1973) has observed, became a key marker in the creation of a royal mythology in the following period. The symbolic use of such events is visible in the literature produced by royal panegyrists for nearly a century.

With Philip Augustus there began a period in the history of the monarchy in which a Carolingian fervour developed. This was probably due to the prestige of epic literature such as the Song of Roland. After a few generations, by selective memory and by emphasizing female descent when necessary, the royal propaganda succeeded in creating an uninterrupted succession of kings belonging to the same royal lineage. Merovingians, Carolingians and Capetians had all been fused into a single genealogy (Guenée, B. 1978: 465).

The period inaugurated by Philip II Augustus allowed for an era of consolidation and reinforcement of royal power at the expense of the principalities and of the Church. This process was not without problems as the developments between 1337 and 1475 clearly showed: for over a century the carefully constructed edifice of the French state started to tumble down and nearly collapsed under the combined pressure of centrifugal forces (particularly in Flanders, Britanny and Guyenne in the fourteenth century and in Burgundy in the fifteenth century) and external intervention (by the English). J.F. Lemarignier (1970: 249) has suggested that four basic problems had to be solved to constitute the French state. Firstly, and as we have seen, the territorial principalities had to be incorporated into the royal domain. Secondly, not only suzerainty had to be reaffirmed but it had to be progressively converted into sovereignty. Thirdly, a mechanism had to be found to transmit the crown and to preserve the royal domain. Finally, the king of France had to assert his sovereignty *vis-à-vis* both the Empire and the Papacy.

French historiography tends, on the whole, to emphasize that the territorial consolidation of the Capetian monarchy was done through legal mechanisms rather than violence. The evidence, however, seems to point out at a combination of both; in other words, violence was used to enforce legal claims when peaceful means failed. The legal way in which Philip Augustus savagely dented the fiefs held by King John of England was originally based on a feudal technicality: that the latter failed to appear in the feudal court of Paris to answer a claim from one of his vassals in Guyenne who had sought redress with his suzerain the Capetian king. With his action, so goes the feudal law, King John had forfeited his fiefs in Gallia. This was not, of course, the way King John saw it. In any case, what decided the fate of the Plantagenet possessions in Gallia was the military victories of Philip Augustus and the fact that part of the nobility of Normandy and other territories defected King John (Hallam, E. 1980: 130–1). The matrimonial policies of the

Capetians and the Valois monarchies were also destined not only to 'reintegrate' territorial principalities to the kingdom but often also to acquire new dominions in the eastern frontier (the Empire). Furthermore, at the death without succession of a fiefholder the territory reverted to the crown.

One of the crucial legal developments of the twelfth century was the relaunching of the idea of suzerainty. This was the work of the Abbey of St. Denis, closely associated with the Capetian monarchy, and particularly of Suger. After two centuries in which the territorial *principes* had eschewed paying homage to the Capetian kings, there was an attempt by the monarchy to enforce the feudal hierarchy by requiring from the *principes* both fealty and service. The feudal hierarchy was conceived as a pyramid in which the king was at the top, and hence owed homage to no one. In itself this principle allowed the king to have authority only over his direct vassals, but not on the subvassals; in practice, this meant that only the *principes* or counts penetrated deep enough into the different social layers and had in fact effective power in their own territories.

Until the Capetian kings managed in different ways to become direct lords in each of the territories, their hold on them was purely nominal. We have seen how this was done in the case of the fiefs of the Plantagenets, but other procedures were also used, namely financial inducements. Where the king could not reach the lower echelons of the society, the legal advisers of the thirteenth century came out first with the idea that in case of conflict between a king and a vassal the subvassal could not fight the king unless it was absolutely obvious that he was acting unjustly; later on it was established that the monarch was no longer at the whim of vassalic relations and that the whole of the feudal hierarchy was subordinated to the king. It has been suggested that this principle was already practised in both England and Normandy, and that the Capetians pushed their luck only at a time when they were in a position to enforce their authority militarily. The well-known expression 'the king of France is emperor in his own kingdom', which was coined in about the mid-thirteenth century, reflected a situation in which, under the influence of Roman law, the royal domain was conceived less in terms of a bundle of rights and more in territorial terms. It was up to the juridical experts to transform the notion of suzerainty into that of sovereignty by extending the authority of the king to all the people of the realm, whether they were part of the feudal hierarchy, free peasants or burghers (Lemarignier, J.F. 1970: 256–61).

It was in this context of the thirteenth-century extension of kingly authority to quite a large portion of Gallia that we see used the expression Kingdom of France (as well as just 'Francia'), and also the idea of loyalty to the king and to the kingdom. Susan Reynolds (1984: 283) has used the expression 'community of the realm' to refer to the feeling of collective solidarity within the Kingdom of France, while Bernard Guenée (1967: 27) suggests that by the beginning of the fourteenth century the people who lived in the Kingdom of France believed that they formed a nation. Needless to say these statements, as we shall see, only make sense if properly contextualized.

The idea of the kingdom as a territorial unit took a long time to develop. To the modern mind what is extremely surprising is the fact that the same king who might have gone to great pains to aggrandize the royal dominion, would be prepared to alienate parts of it to endow his younger sons. There is little doubt that the royal domain was conceived for a long time as the patrimony of the royal family. From the thirteenth to the fifteenth century, although the idea that the kingdom was a unit made great strides, we can still find the practice of the king endowing his younger sons with territorial grants known as apanages. Surely these domains contained a growing number of reversion clauses, but they still created a lot of problems for the unification of the kingdom. It was only in the mid-fifteenth century, when the king's domains ceased to be considered his personal property, that the territorial integrity of the kingdom was preserved.

Along with the principle of territorial integrity came the idea that the crown was inalienable. This change did not happen suddenly. From the eleventh century onwards, and unlike during the Carolingian period, there was a customary rule of succession: the crown was transmitted to the eldest son. Later on, in the fourteenth century, not only were women excluded from the throne, but also their male descendants. This strong agnatic principle of succession was justified by reference to the practices of the Salian Franks and hence called Salic Law (*Lex Salica*). But it was not until the fifteenth century that another principle was imagined: that the Crown was not the property of the king and that hence it could not be alienated. The king was just an incumbent in a long, uninterrupted line of trustees and had no right to dispose of the Crown at his will. What was really happening was a progressive depersonalization of the monarchy, which was becoming a public office subjected first to ad hoc rules which were later properly codified. It is in this sense that has also to be interpreted the idea of royal continuity with independence of age or consecration (Lemarignier, J.F.: 277–83).

In the late Middle Ages, then, the pre-conditions had been established for a new stage in the process of state-building: the progressive centralization of the monarchy. By the fourteenth century the Kingdom of France reached a surface of nearly 150,000 square miles and a population of about twenty million, while England had one third of the surface and one fourth of the population. Potentially, the French king was a powerful monarch if he could only succeed in asserting his authority over the territory of the kingdom, and especially in the newly acquired principalities. To that end both Capetians and Valois developed a series of institutions with specific political, financial and judiciary functions. At the political level the king, from the reign of Louis IX onwards, had the power to legislate and he did so through the royal ordinance which became the basis for the creation of a public law. Although some jurists voiced criticisms against this royal prerogative at different times, the status quo was preserved. Furthermore, the king had also the right to appoint court officials and to decide about peace and war. At the judicial level the king was, in the final instance, the source of all justice, even if he delegated its exercise to specialized people. Finally, at the financial level he had the right to raise both indirect and direct taxes, as well as to coin money (Richet, D. 1973: 53).

In the thirteenth and fourteenth centuries there was a remarkable diversification within the traditional royal court. A number of new offices appeared. There were two institutions of particular importance: the Royal Council and the Estates General (both had consultative character). The Royal Council consisted of a small group of people recruited by the king from the higher nobility, but also increasingly from the juridical profession. The king not only requested the advice of the councillors but normally decided the basic affairs of the kingdom when the council was in session. The Estates General was an attempt to widen the consultative audience; its members were recruited from the three major forces of the late Middle Ages: the aristocracy, the Church and the nascent bourgeoisie. The first meeting of the representatives of the three orders took place in 1302. The Estates General were used by the king as a way of legitimizing his policies. In practice, however, they were not always pliable to the king's desires, and at times of monarchic weakness he often made demands or set conditions before accepting new taxes. On the whole their countervailing power was very meagre compared with other countries. At the local level the king appointed paid representatives – baillies – to administer a small portion of the territory (*bailliage*). As the king's delegate the bailli performed the basic political, judicial and financial functions emanating from the royal prerogatives.

While the function of the English Parliament was basically political, the French *Parlement* was, from the thirteenth century onwards, fundamentally a juridical institution. The organization, specialization and institutionalization of royal justice was a long process that occurred with the development of sovereignty and that had to be constituted in constant struggle against other existing jurisdictions (seignorial, ecclesiastic).

The Hundred Years War put a lot of pressure on the French monarchy in that it was a continuous drain on the traditional resources of the king.

The prolonged conflict required increased financial means. Many of the traditional French taxes (*aides, gabelle, taille*) originated in the military needs of the period, though later were used for the general purpose of state- maintenance. Important changes took also place in the organization of war. With the decline of the heavy cavalry, the infantry came to play a key role. In place of the feudal army a more permanent army of mercenaries appeared under the command of officers nominated by the king. Infantry contingents were available for hire from a variety of European areas, and hence the strength of an army was centred in the financial capability of the king to buy soldiers at home or abroad.

In their centralization process, the monarchy had to tread carefully in enforcing sovereignty. Taxes and other types of encroachments by the centre were resisted by the principalities and there were a number of attempts, in the fourteenth and fifteenth centuries, if not to secede at least to regain or preserve autonomy. The three provincial estates played an important role here, particularly in the newly acquired principalities, defusing animosity against the centre and keeping at least a façade of autonomy, though in practice they had merely consultative functions.

The fourteenth century put in evidence in a clear way for the first time that what we have come to call Europe, the West or Christianity was not a homogeneous political space but rather consisted of a number of sovereign states. Two examples may be used to illustrate this state of things. In the second half of the thirteenth century legal royal advisers all over Europe, but particularly in France, were asserting that *rex in regno suo est imperator*, thus reflecting an openly hostile reaction against the pretentions that the Emperor had *auctoritas* over the European kings. In fact, the death of Frederick II in 1250 signalled the loss of vitality of the Empire. The second example can be found in Marsilius of Padua's *Defensor Pacis*, published originally in 1324. To the question of whether those people who were separated by linguistic, cultural and geographic boundaries should live under different governments, the answer was positive (Marsilius of Padua, 1980: 84–5).

The kings of France, from Philip Augustus onward, were at the forefront of checking the more or less open imperial threats to royal sovereignty. A case in point was Frederick Barbarossa, who in the mid-twelfth century had the stated objective of establishing the hegemony of the Empire over the West. There were, however, many European voices, Dante included, who still believed in the need of a universal government to preserve the peace, and the Empire was the next best thing that existed.

Before sovereignty could be properly said to exist another universalistic power – the Church – had to be curtailed. With the crusader fervour at the end of the eleventh century, the Papacy tried to transform its spiritual power into political power. The popes presented themselves as leaders of a vast community – Christendom. The conflict of the Investitures (from the eleventh to the thirteenth centuries) with the Empire put an end to the first attempt of the Holy See to achieve supremacy. The theocratic assertions of the Papacy that had been developed over the twelfth century had been occasionally used, particularly by Innocent III, to attack the Capetians. The main conflict, however, opposed Philip IV and Boniface VIII on a variety of fronts (taxing the clerics, putting on trial a disloyal bishop, etc.) at the end of the thirteenth century. The pope maintained that he exercised *regimen universale*, hence asserting his superiority over the king. After a long controversy, the king assembled the three orders of the Estates General in 1302 and succeeded in having the royal positions accepted. The loyalty of the three estates to the king was a shock to the pretentions of the temporal power of the pope. A year later, Boniface VIII died after he had been captured and had suffered ignomy at the hands of his enemies. Soon the popes settled in Avignon and lived under the 'protection' of the French crown until 1376 (Ganshof, F.L. 1970: 324–7).

In the long run the papacy retreated from its positions and, as J. F. Lemarignier (1970: 266–77) has remarked, this gave rise both to political Gallicanism and religious Gallicanism. By the first is meant that the king was not a political but only a spiritual subject of the pope, while by religious Gallicanism is meant that the Church of France was subjected spiritually to Rome but temporally to Paris: by the fifteenth century the latter had come to mean as well that the ecumenical council was superior to the pope.

This section has hitherto emphasized the dynastic role in the making of the French state; in so doing, it has implicitly conveyed the idea that the monarchy was the determining factor in creating the idea of France and extending it, from an initial nucleus (L'Île de France) to an ever wider geographical circle. It would appear that, in France at least, the state preceded and created the nation, although once the latter was in existence a kind of feedback would operate. It was during the thirteenth century that the expression *regnum Francie* came into use and that the idea of France as the common country of the French people emerged; by that time, a distinction was clearly made between those born in the country (*naturales*) and those born outside of it (*extraneus*). By the fourteenth century the borders of France acquired a 'political, economic fiscal and especially military reality' (Guenée, B. 1967: 25).

The role of the Capetian monarchy, in progressively charging with symbolic value the idea of France as an 'imagined community' was, as we shall see, extremely successful. It would be inaccurate, however, to assume that national awareness was all state-derived; to put it more bluntly, that the monarchy invented it *ex nihilo*. In fact, it was an early elaboration of earlier traditions, in particular Carolingian themes of Frankish cultural and moral superiority, as well as religious messianism; there was also a genuine love of country and language (Zientara, B. 1982: 19). It could rightly be argued that the awareness of France as a nation was limited to only a few layers of the population; furthermore, it has been remarked that the word *patrie* (or its Latin equivalent *patria*) was normally predicated of a principality, rather than of the whole of the kingdom. And yet, as Dupont-Ferrier (1940) noted, during the medieval period the term *patria* also preserved a sense of nostalgia of the Carolingian unity. It was not until the sixteenth century, however, that the word *patrie* (Fr.) was used in the sense of nation.

Is it too extreme to say, with Joseph Strayer (1971: 314) that 'In France the religion of nationalism grew early and easily out of the religion of monarchy'? By religion of the monarchy Strayer meant that the king was conceived of as a holy person who belonged to an ancient lineage, was heir to Charlemagne, was annointed by heaven (the coronation oil was brought down from heaven) and was a worker of miracles (healing of scrofula). Strayer's thesis is that the 'mosaic' origins of the kingdom (that is, the variety of principalities that made France) was only superceded when loyalty to king and country became the main objective of the ruling dynasties. This loyalty, which had to compete successfully with the loyalty due to the local nobility, was not in the main achieved by instilling fear and self-interest in the population, but by generating feelings of love, respect and admiration for the monarchy and for France.

The image of France in the Middle Ages – how it was created and how it was experienced in the collective mentality of the period – is the object of a detailed study by Colette Beaune (1985). The title of the book – *Naissance de la nation France* – indicates that beyond the vagaries in the medieval use of words such as *natio* and *patria*, there is an '*imaginaire national*' which is worth investigating. Beaune considers three major axes: France and its history, France and its God, France and its signs and symbols. The history of France is considered through the eyes of the medieval chroniclers: how they essentially created the French nation and used the past to justify the present. This past was conceived in a double time, through two myths of origin: one pagan (Trojan or Gaul), one Christian (St. Clovis). The first 'national' histories appeared in the twelfth century; in these histories France appeared as a kingdom which was the result of a history taking place in a Christian time which was unique and oriented towards a glorious future; nations are God- given and follow a prefigured path which shows divine intervention (Beaune, C. 1985: 15). The genre of national histories kept its popularity through the medieval and modern periods, only to be eclipsed in the nineteenth century.

The pagan myth of origin followed the model of the foundation of Rome by Aeneas of Troy and his companions. This myth of descent was created as early as the seventh century and lasted until well into the fifteenth century. The myth referred to a mythical ancestor of the Franks – Francion – who left Troy to settle eventually in Germania and whose descendants later moved into Gallia. Having Trojan ancestors had a number of advantages; it guaranteed the ancient character and prestige of the nation and the ethnic and national solidarity on the basis of common blood. In addition, it justified the top rank of the kingdom in the concert of nations and *vis-à-vis* the Church and Empire, as well as the expansionist policies of the kingdom in Europe and elsewhere (Beaune, C. 1985: 54). All national histories, but in particular the *Grandes Chroniques de France* from the twelfth to the fifteenth centuries, dedicated the first chapter to the tale of the migration of the Trojan princely heroes.

By the end of the fifteenth century, the idea of the Trojan origins of the Franks had been undermined by a variety of critics (mostly Italian humanists) and a Gaul myth of origin was inaugurated in which the Gauls were seen as the direct ancestors and as the founders of Troy. However, neither pagan myth of origin could justify the character of France as the most Christian nation of Europe. If the Trojan/Gaul origins represented the biological birth of France, St. Clovis represented the spiritual birth of the nation. As the first Merovingian king to be converted to Christianity, he was a saint (by popular acclaim, not religious recognition) and the founder of the royal religion; he was the founder of the French monarchy and of the French nation; he had fixed the limits of the French kingdom by his conquests; he combined the features of chivalrous heroism and monastic asceticism; and he became a political model.

The second axis of the idea of France was religion. During the medieval period there was a growing sacralisation of the French monarchy which manifested itself in the attribution to the French kings of a number of prerogatives: the anointing by the Holy Ampulla, the healing of scrofula, the possession of the heraldic lily in the royal arms and of the oriflamme (sacred banner of St Denis) (ibid.: 211). In the literature, France is not only described as the most Christian nation, but its people have been chosen by God to defend the Christian Faith. To have access to God the intercession of saints was essential. France produced a generous crop of local saints who gave prestige to the French nation, but the monarchy was especially attached, particularly up to the fifteenth century, to the cult of St Denis; he was the patron saint of the kings, and later on of the kingdom. A close alliance was established between the Capetians and the Abbey of St Denis; the latter kept various regalia and was used as the royal necropolis. Towards the end of the medieval period, other saints like St Louis and St Michael came to be considered as mediators between the divinity and the French people. It is important to note that by the fourteenth century prayers were not only said for the king and the kingdom, but also for the nation.

The final dimension of the community of the realm refers to the signs and symbols of France. For a culture which was essentially non-literary, signs and symbols were the best, in some cases the only, source of access to the idea of nation. Perhaps the most important representation of France in the medieval period was the heraldic lilies in the French royal arms; the lily (three petals bound together near their bases) is also found on coins, royal stamps, etc. Towards the end of the Middle Ages, the white cross and the winged flying deer began to take the place of the lily. Along with these symbols there was also the royal battle cry ('Montjoie Saint Denis'). 'Montjoie' was the flag indicating the marching army, and the French battle cry was opposed to the English 'St. George and my right'; as the French expression went 'Il vaut mieux que St. George et mon droit, St. Denis et montjoie'. It could be argued that these symbols belonged essentially to the aristocratic world, but other worlds were also becoming important, namely the legal and literary ones. In the former, there was the codification and utilization of the Salic Law (*Lex Salica*) to maintain and consolidate the Valois dynasty in the kingdom of France at a time (the fifteenth century) when English kings were staking a claim on the throne of France. The exclusion of women and their descendants from succession to the crown was presented by fifteenth-century jurists as a distinctive feature of France *vis-à-vis* other European countries.

The idea of national culture appeared in the fifteenth century, closely associated with the growing prestige of the French language. But language and culture were not the decisive elements of national sentiment in France at that time. In the kingdom there were other languages besides French (Occitan, Breton, Basque, Flemish, etc), and Latin was still very prestigious. This is not to say, as we shall see, that the politics of culture and language were unimportant. A particularly acerbic polemic followed the statement of Petrarch in 1368 in which he urged Pope Urban V to abandon Avignon and establish himself in Rome, with the argument that this city was the centre of Christendom and the principle seat of culture. The French were not prepared to accept that their culture was inferior to that of Italy. French *literati* had been adhering to the concept of *translatio studii* which assumed that the centre of culture had moved from Athens to Rome, and from Rome to Paris. The struggle was not only about culture, but also about power, and involved the papacy and the French kings (Simone, F. 1969: 81–4). Whether the French humanists who defended French culture *vis-à-vis* the pretensions of the 'Italian' authors could be labelled 'cultural patriots' as Nicholas Mann (1971) has suggested, is, of course, a disputed matter. He considers that the development of a national sentiment amongst the elite in late medieval France was the result of the cultural dispute with the 'Italians' and the military confrontation with the English in the Hundred Years War; the latter, however, would have given rise to a much more political sentiment, emphasizing French identity and unity.

If there was one author who excelled in his defence of his country, and approached a 'ferocious nationalism' (Mann, N. 1971) *avant la lettre* it was undoubtedly Robert Gaguin (1443–1501). In his *Compendium de Francorum Origine et Gestis*, which is a series of biographies of kings, the legendary and supernatural are avoided and the monarchs tend to appear both as religious and powerful. He stated that what moved him to write was the love, glory and honour of his country. Gaugin's conception of *patria* has different registers – political, moral, emotive. In his *Compendium* Gaguin examined the different European countries, often in terms of stereotypes which reflected the specificity and position of France towards each of them; Gaguin is reasonably neutral towards Castile and the countries of Germania, but his statements concerning the English follow the pattern of the French literature of the fourteenth and fifteenth centuries: that is, they depict them as perfidious, dishonourable and disloyal. Italia, not as a political but as a cultural reality, was also the object of criticism. To refer to France Gaguin uses interchangeably *France* (Fr.) and *Francia* (Lat.) but also *Gallia* (Lat.); and these terms are referred to as *patria*. There is a continuity between Gauls, Franks and French (the Roman period is glossed over). His national sentiment was closely related to his vision of history. France is both a land with concrete things one can praise (beauty, fertility, etc.) and a spiritual community which derives from its Christian history. The French, in a nutshell, are courageous and industrious, obedient and loyal to their kings, and extremely religious (Schmidt-Chazan, M. 1977).

The consciousness of belonging to a human community characterized both in ethnic and territorial terms is what defined France in the Middle Ages. According to Beaune the myth of Trojan/Gaul descent was an essential part of the definition of Frenchness from the very beginning, but the idea of a national territory also took shape, albeit in the later period. France was represented in different ways, but mostly as a sweet and beautiful country. The territory was often equated to a paradisical garden. Love of country and sacrifice go together; when the country is in danger, it is appropriate to apply the words of Horace : 'Dulce et decorum est pro patria mori'. But the *patria* that is referred to in the fourteenth and fifteenth centuries, maintains Beaune, is no longer, or not only, the local *patria*, but the whole of France. This *patria* is conceived of in emotive and passionate terms, as a mother to be defended from external enemies and to whom the highest sacrifice is due, if necessary.

What is surprising in the French case is that the local particularisms did not challenge more often the sovereignty of the state, though in the fifteenth century the duke of Burgundy was still hoping to create a new state. More serious is perhaps the question raised by Lucien Musset (1982), when he asked why did Normandy, which had been a leading political and cultural power in the twelfth century, accept the rule of the Capetians. And the answer is that, unlike the English monarchs, the French kings recognized the juridical personality and cultural identity of the Normans.

As for the Bretons (Kerhervé, J. 1980), there is no doubt that by the fourteenth century they had a clear sense of identity which expressed itself through terms such as *natio* and *pais*, although these terms often meant little else than a reference to a common origin. It is clear that the dukes of Brittany tried to encourage loyalty in their subjects and in the course of this they helped to create a sense of regional nationality. As Michael Jones has put it '[The dukes] turned increasingly to various aids which would help them to foster natural feelings of loyalty. Propaganda for their point of view took legal and and literary, visual and symbolic forms, as they sought to create a ducal mystique which reflected ... that which surrounded the king of France' (Jones, M. 1976: 163).

It is surprising, though, that in their attempt to show their separate identity the Bretons did not make use of their Celtic inheritance, but then most of the Breton nobles were not Celts themselves. In the final resort, though, the French court had wider appeal (both culturally and in terms of military and administrative opportunities) than the local, ducal court. This meant that, as Jones notes, 'the growth of regional identity in Britanny ... was slow and uncertain' (ibid.: 167), although by the end of the fourteenth century 'the duke had come to exercise most prerogatives then normally ascribed to a sovereign prince' (Jones, M. 1983: 101). However, by the end of the fifteenth century, the French king was able to annex the duchy, although not until the partisans of Breton autonomy had been militarily defeated. By the close of the medieval period, that is with the emergence of absolutism, sovereignty became indivisible; hence 'it was no longer possible to be both a "Bon Breton et bon Francoys"'(ibid.: 112). And this applied generally to the other regional ethnies of Gallia.

There is little doubt that by the end of the medieval period the idea of France had found expression in a single state (although not a unitary one) and in a sense of national identity (limited, I hasten to add, to a small group of people). This was a remarkable success if we consider the political, linguistic and cultural variety that was characteristic of Gallia in the early medieval period. That by 1500 the French identity was weaker than the English equivalent is hardly a surprise if we take into account the different starting points of both countries: a large, mosaic state for the former, a medium-size, unitary state for the latter.

Germania

The Germanian domain in the Middle Ages is extremely difficult to pinpoint given the fluidity of borders and the variable extent of control exercised by the Holy Roman Empire. If it were possible to believe in 'natural' frontiers, Germania had none – geographical accidents separating more than uniting. Furthermore, Germania moved in different directions: south (Italia), west (Old Lotharingia) and east (Hungary, Poland, Lithuania, etc) (Reuter 1991; Snyder 1975).

J. Leuschner (1980) has rightly pointed out that it is difficult to visualize medieval Germania because it consisted of three different, but intertwined realities: 'Germany', the 'German' kingdom (*Regnum Teutonicorum*) and the Holy Roman Empire (which only from the fifteenth century onwards had the rider added: 'of the German nation'). In the first sense, Germania was understood as a geographical and cultural entity; this conception was in plain view in the thirteenth century Annals of Colmar, but it had existed for a much longer time. The Treaty of Verdun, in 934, instituting the division of the Carolingian Empire, showed already a linguistic gulf between the eastern and western Frankish peoples which foreshadowed the medieval division between Gallia and Germania along political and cultural lines. The third division of the Carolingian Empire, the Lotharingia, became a disputed territory between Germania and France for a thousand years. Finally, a peculiarity worth mentioning is the fact that in German the word to refer to this complex political and cultural reality, that is, *Deutschland* (or in the Middle Ages *deutsche lande*), did not originate from the name of a tribe or territory, but from the popular language spoken in the area (*diutischiu liute*).

The constitution of a separate kingdom took place in Germania at the beginning of the tenth century under Henry I. Now, the *Regnum Teutonicorum* should not be envisaged as a 'German' kingdom for the simple reason that it incorporated territories which would later became independent (like Holland, Switzerland, and Austria) or part of France (Alsace, Lorraine); in addition to this, the kingdom was politically complex, with strong elector states, both secular and ecclesiastical. In no way could it be said that the *Regnum Teutonicorum* was culturally homogeneous because it contained peoples who spoke non-Germanic languages (dialects of Latin, and Slavonic languages), but excluded the Teutonic Knights in Eastern Europe. And finally, the Holy Roman Empire, which in the words of Detwiler, 'was neither a truly universal monarchy ... nor a purely German state' (1976: 20). The jurisdiction of the *imperium* extended much further afield, geographically speaking, than that of the *regnum*; it incorporated Burgundy and large parts of Italia (Fuhrmann 1986: 19–23).

As for the titles used by the monarchs, we find that during the medieval period there were two common expressions: *rex Germanorum* and *rex Teutonicorum*. However, there was also the expression *rex Alamanniae* (Alamania being an old name for the duchy of Swabia) which was used in the late thirteenth century and which reflected the important role played by South Germania (Du Boulay 1983: 20). It was not until Maximilian I, who ruled between 1493 and 1519, that the term *rex Germaniae* was employed. As to the imperial titles, the form of address 'King of the Romans always Augustus' (*Romanorum rex semper Augustus*) prevailed prior to the coronation by the pope, after which the title 'Emperor of the Romans, always Augustus' (*Romanorum Imperator, semper Augustus*) was adopted.

The crowning by the pope in Rome was an essential part of the process of becoming emperor from the tenth century. This procedure lasted until 1508 when Maximilian I, with the consent of the pope, relieved the emperors of such requisite; from then onwards the expression 'emperor elect' (*Imperator Electus*) became the appropriate title. Another development that came at the end of the medieval period was the fact that the empire was referred to as 'Holy Roman Empire of the German Nation'.

One remarkable feature of Germania is that it lacked the processes of state unification and centralization typical of other western European domains. In fact, after 1250 we can observe a progressive political fragmentation which by the end of the medieval period could be characterized as a complex combination of ecclesiastical and dynastic principalities, as well as a variety of small, more or less political entities. To be more precise, the sixteen million people living in Germania by the beginning of the early modern period were divided into 'seven electoral principalities, around twenty-five major secular principalities and ninety ecclesiastical ones, over a hundred courtships, and a very large number of lesser lordships, as well as the towns' (Fulbrook 1990: 27).

The absence of a proper 'German' kingdom did not contribute, as might have been expected, to the consolidation of the larger principalities as 'national' states. And the reason has to be found in the need of the princes to share their acquired powers with the traditional estates of their polities (the aristocracy, the local Church and the incipient urban bourgeoisie). It was only after the Thirty Years War that powerful, absolutist principalities began to emerge (particularly Brandenburg-Prussia).

The death of Fredrick II in 1250 is a convenient date that separates two clearly delinated periods in the history of medieval Germania. From 911 to 1250 there was an attempt, with ups and downs, to create and consolidate a *regnum* and *imperium*. After that time the Holy Roman Empire was only a shadow of the past. By wanting to become a truly European (universal) emperor, Frederick II (called in his time the 'wonder of the world' and celebrated by historians like E. Kantorowicz as the first truly heroic figure of medieval Germania) overstretched the territorial basis of the Empire to a point of rupture, while weakening at the same time the hold that the emperors had (particularly his two immediate predecessors) within Germania itself (Abulafia 1992).

To say that the starting point of medieval Germania was as a part of the Carolingian Empire is perhaps unproblematic, but to insist that the internal subdivisions of Germania also find their origins in the administrative procedure of the empire is against the established consensus which envisages that the fragmentation of the Germanian territory took place along ethnic lines. In other words, to see the so-called national, tribal or stem duchies (Franconia, Bavaria, Swabia, Saxony and Lotharingia) as the creation of the local 'tribal' leaders is historically incorrect; the 'regionalization' which was typical of Germania, and other European domains, in the tenth century and later followed a pattern which reflected the Carolingian institutions. If the duchies did not become independent political units it was in large part due to the efforts initiated by King Konrad I (Duke of Franconia) aimed at obtaining the loyalty of his fellow dukes.

From 919 to 1125, under the Saxon and Salian dynasties, there was a certain amount of state building (centralization and bureaucratization) which consolidated the *regnum Teutonicorum*. There also began a certain sense of identity on a linguistic and cultural basis. Otto I was the first king to be crowned emperor by the Pope in 962. However, the expression 'Holy Roman Empire' did not come into common use in literature until the twelfth century. The sense of continuity with the Carolingians that the Germanian emperors tried to create was present throughout the medieval period. The memory of Charlemagne as the paladin of the universal, Christian empire was a powerful symbolic tool which justified the continued existence of the Holy Roman Empire (Folz 1950). At its height, in this early period, the Holy Roman emperors were 'the protectors, guardians and leaders of the Church and Christendom' (Herr 1966: 74). During this period the

Holy Roman Empire was the highest civilization of medieval Europe.

It would be a crass error of perception to envisage the medieval empire in the light of the modern conception of empire. The first thing to emphasize is that the medieval empire was a multidimensional reality, politico-religious in character, but with socio-economic implications as well. Perhaps the category that allows the capture of this idea of empire in all its complexity is Marcel Mauss's concept of total social fact. The Holy Roman Empire was an attempt, flawed at the best of times, to subsume the whole of Christendom; the empire is what came closest to the reign of God on earth. It is true that in terms of actual reality the geographic limits of the empire never went beyond Germania and northern Italia, but at the ceremonial and ritual level the emperors had pre-eminence over all the other leaders of Christendom, carrying the title of Head of Christendom and Protector of the Catholic Faith (Detwiler 1976: 23).

This element of prestige cannot be overemphasised when we are referring to a historical period which was extremely hierarchically oriented and in which matters of honour played a key role. Empire and Christendom were two sides of the same coin; pope and emperor were both God's representatives on earth, albeit that they had different functions. In this dual power, however, lay the seeds of conflict that characterized the High Middle Ages. Popes became involved in political affairs in the same way as emperors were involved in ecclesiastical ones. The War of the Investitures between 1076 and 1122 was just such an episode in a continuing contest which endured for a much longer period of time. The key issue at stake was the appointment of ecclesiastic dignitaries (bishops, abbots, etc), a privilege that the emperors had been exercising since 962 and that was challenged by Gregory VII. The pope's manifest objective was the spiritual regeneration of the Church. To that end he needed a hierarchy of dignitaries who were directly appointed by and responsible to him, and who had spiritual rather than temporal commitments. The reluctance of the emperors to give in was simply due to the fact that, if they conceded in this area, their powers would automatically be undermined because the religious dignitaries, in addition to their political clout, often controlled important economic and military resources.

There was another source of weakening of royal authority which began at the same time as the War of the Investitures: the rebellion of the aristocracy and of the free peasants of Saxony against Henry IV's attempts to encroach on their rights. What followed was a cruel civil war in which the aristocracy successfully claimed territorial lordship over their possessions. The princes also increased their power to the extent that by the reign of Henry V, in the first quarter of the twelfth century, the monarch had no alternative but to accept that he was only *primum inter pares* and that he did not rule by hereditary right but by the elective principle. Barraclough (1979: 16–17) sees in the consolidation of the princely powers the basis for the emergence of the territorial principalities which were typical of Germania in the later medieval and early modern periods.

With the Hohenstaufen dynasty it appeared, at least at first, that a Germanian state might be in the process of consolidation. This was particularly the case under Frederick I (who ruled between 1152 and 1190). He tried to redress the loss of power of the monarchy, and although he was not as successful as some of his European counterparts, he none the less created a monarchy more in line with the needs of a more centralized and integrated state. This task was pursued by his son Henry VI. Frederick I, known as Barbarossa, managed to keep a balance between the internal requirements of the state and the expansion abroad. During his rule the prestige of the Holy Roman Empire was at its height. The Italian entanglements, however, generated constant headaches for the Hohenstaufen, and under Frederick II took pre-eminence over any other consideration. As I have indicated before, it was under this monarch that the schism between the internal and imperial pursuits came into sharp conflict; in fact, Frederick II abandoned the commitment to a Germanian state. Between 1220 and 1230, in successive compacts with the ecclesiastical princes and the secular ones, he ceded territorial power. Prior to that, in 1213, he had relinquished a large part of his control over the Church. His decision was a monentous action for the distant future. With the Golden Bull of Rimini in 1226 he granted the Teutonic Knights the right of conquest to convert the pagans of eastern Prussia to Christianity; with it, began the *Drang nach Osten*.

With the death of Frederick II in 1250 there followed a long interregnum. From then onwards not only the hereditary principle lapsed once again, but the empire was only a poorly co-ordinated confederation of small principalities. The emperor became increasingly a figure-head at the mercy of the princes. The Concordat of Worms in 1122 represented increased power to the Church. The Golden Bull of Charles IV in 1356 constitutionalized decentralization by establishing the procedures to elect the emperor by the seven prince electors: the king of Bohemia, the duke of Saxony, the margrave of Brandenburg, the count palatine of the Rhine and the archbishops of Trier, Cologne and Mainz (the king of Bavaria was added in the sixteenth century). This constitutional arrangement stayed in use until the collapse of the Holy Roman Empire of the German Nation in 1808 under Napoleonic pressures.

Many commentators tend to agree with Barraclough (1979: 36) that the medieval legacy of Germania is a contradictory one: on the one hand, there is the principle of unity created by the empire and, on the other, the particularistic principle of the territorial principalities. As to the existence of a 'German' (national) identity in the medieval period the issue is rather complicated. There is little doubt that in their contact with peoples within and outside the Empire, there was an awareness of a distinct language and culture which we can provisionally call Germanian. How far there was an identification with a *terra* (country) and a *patria* (fatherland) called Germania is something that can only be predicated of a small, select minority of strategically placed people (aristocrats, clerics, etc.). The development of a literature and of a legal system did not occur until the thirteenth century.

From the Germanian domain there emerged, in the long run, a number of independent countries (Switzerland, Holland), while other territories (Alsace, Lorraine, Burgundy) were incorporated into other states, namely France. The end of the medieval period meant also a retrenchment of the Empire as a result of the loss of Italia. The Reformation, if anything, strengthened the sense of identity, but had no visible effect on the unification of Germania. In fact, the principalities developed as modern states in the early modern period; but only a few of them – Prussia, Austria and to a certain extent Bavaria – acquired a strong sense of national identity, which was linguistically and culturally Germanian, but not necessarily German (Conze 1979). Dickens (1974), however, believes that Protestant humanism helped in the creation of German nationalism. The key ideas were the development of an imperial myth and the idea of the German *Volk*. On the other hand, Lutz (1982) has convincingly shown that the confessional differences and the absence of a national dynasty were the realities of the post-Reformation period and that this was a legacy for internal dissension, not political unity.

Italia

In the medieval period, and well beyond, Italia, like Germania, was little more than a vague cultural and linguistic entity. Politically, it only existed as a multiplicity of more or less autonomous, and more or less durable, communes, principalities and kingdoms. There is no organic continuity between the medieval and the modern periods that would allow us to speak about the history of a single political unit. From the Longobard invasion of 568 to the unification of Italy in 1860 there elapsed thirteen centuries of political dispersion. As Croce has insisted there is no history of Italy prior to that date, although it is, of course, possible to write the parallel histories of the different political entities that existed in each historical period, as well as of their interrelationships with each other and with foreign powers. Such a history should give a prominent place to the role of Church and Empire in shaping the medieval political reality of Italia. What seems to be clear is that at the end of the Middle Ages there was no process of state unification and centralization in Italia, although by 1500 the myriad of medieval communes had been reduced to a few states; and that, furthermore, the expressions of *italianità* that appeared at different moments in time had no political impact.

Medieval Italia, like the other western European domains, started with the collapse of the Roman Empire, or to be more precise, with the Barbarian invasions of the northern territory. The division of the Italian peninsula into two areas put an end to political unity. There emerged a long-lasting dualism between the Longobardian north and the Byzantine south. The presence of the Church, with a spiritual, but also an important temporal role, was a decisive factor in the history of Italia. There was a struggle of the papacy to defend Romanity against the Longobard invaders. Later, the Empire reappeared with Charlemagne, but it was short-lived; after that the Germanian emperors rebuilt it again between 962 and 1152. Because Italia was the centre of Christianity the break between the classical and the medieval world was smoother than elsewhere and went almost unnoticed. The Church preserved many of the traditions of Roman governance: from economic, legal and administrative institutions, to military practices, as well as intellectual patterns. At the ideological level 'the myth of Rome dominates the medieval period. Italia appears as a unit, not because it constitutes a nation, but because it constitutes the core of the Roman heritage, the spiritual and political centre of the Roman Empire' (Valsecchi 1978: 3).

In 568 the Longobards invaded northern Italia and established a kingdom which lasted for about two centuries. They came in small numbers, mixed with the local population and absorbed the language and culture of the land. They failed, however, to dominate the whole peninsula (the rest of which was still ruled by the Byzantines). The struggle between the Papacy and the Byzantine emperor took a serious turn when in 727 the Emperor Leo III forbade the cult of images of Christ. There followed a revolt in which the people of central Italia sided with the Pope. The Longobard threat, however, led the popes to request Frankish help; both Pepin and Charlemagne intervened and the Longobards were eventually defeated. Charlemagne incorporated central and northern Italia (about two-thirds of the peninsula) to his domains. As we have seen in Chapter One, he took the title of Emperor from the Pope in 800. The death of Charlemagne meant the break up of the Empire; there followed 150 years of disorder in the Italian peninsula, particularly after the death of Louis II in 875. Italia was subjected to foreign invasions: the Magyars in the north and the Arabs in the south (Sicily became an Arab state from the ninth century to the end of the eleventh century). The Byzantine Empire continued to operate in the south, while the Longobard princes recovered part of their power in the north. Only the revival of the imperial power, through the recreation of the Holy Roman Empire initiated by Otto I, united a great part of Italia under a single ruler. With it began a political system in which the destiny of Italia was, for a few centuries, in the hands of Germanian rulers. In turn, the Normans established a feudal state in southern Italia, conquering also Sicily in the eleventh century. Norman Sicily experienced a notable revival from the eleventh century onwards; many southern Italian and Sicilian cities became cultural centres during the twelfth and thirteenth centuries (Hartmann 1949; Wickham 1981; Tabacco 1989).

An original feature of Italia, particularly after the eleventh century, was the existence of largely independent communes. Municipal autonomy was typical of the classical period, but as a result of the Barbarian invasions it faded away between the fifth and eleventh centuries. The development of the communes was typical of central and northern Italia, while in the south, which had continued with a landowning aristocratic class during the Byzantine Empire, there developed at different moments in time, one or more large territorial states under the control of foreign powers (Norman, Hohenstaufen, Aragonese). What we see in the north and centre is a victory of the cities over the state; everything becomes localized. As Wickham has remarked, 'the ideology of the integrated state was replaced by the real force of local society. Italy sprang apart. The localities went their separate ways (though often on parallel lines), fortified by a growing sense of their own separate identities. It would take the ideology of nineteenth-century Romantic nationalism and the socio-economic transformation of the Industrial Revolution to force them back together again' (1981: 193). In due course, the prosperous city-states, which often had achieved their wealth through long-distance trade, obtained their autonomy either through force or financial inducement from the religious or secular authorities who had dominated them. In the twelfth and thirteenth centuries the Lombard League, in alliance with the Papal States, successfully confronted the Hohenstaufen emperors who had to accept the political liberties of the communes, although the former preserved their suzerainty over the cities (Waley 1969).

The War of the Investitures between Papacy and Empire, which lasted betweeen 1056 and 1250, allowed the Lombard and Tuscan towns to cash in on the economic recovery that had started in the eleventh century. A number of powerful city-states made their appearance (Genoa, Milan, Pisa, Venice, Florence, Bologna, Verona, etc.). The city-states of the north were neither a continuation from the Roman municipalities (which had been largely destroyed by the Longobard invaders) nor an outcome of the manorial organization. As Mitteis has remarked: 'The decisive factor, without doubts, was the role of bishops, who for many centuries had been leading figures in their cathedral cities' (1975: 214). In due course, the bishops encouraged economic life, and the cities became market centres as well as military strongholds. Progressively, a municipal organization emerged, and those groups with strong commercial and economic power came to enjoy political power as well. The growth of the communes or city-states was facilitated by the geographical position of Italia, which was in the right place to act as an intermediary between East and West. In the long struggle between Papacy and Empire, the city-states often changed sides according to the perception of their interests at each moment in time. Those city-states which supported the papal band were called Guelphs, and those who supported the emperor's point of view were known as Ghibellines. It was only when all city-states were threatened by Frederick I that they managed to present a united front. The factionalism continued even after the Investiture Controversy came to an end (Hyde 1973; Hearder and Wiley 1963).

The last serious imperial attempt to control Italia was that of Frederick II in the thirteenth century. From his stronghold of Sicily he tried to extend his authority to the whole peninsula. His state was efficiently organized and he was able to build an impressive alliance with a variety of principalities (in Piedmont, Savoy, Monferrato, etc.) and communes (Siena, Pisa, Parma, Cremona, etc.). However, one advantage of the communes of the Guelph party (Venice, Genoa, Florence, etc.) was their wealth of economic resources when compared with the southern towns. After years of struggle, the death of the emperor in 1250 was a great blow to the Ghibelline cause. However, the final victory came in 1260 when Charles d'Anjou defeated the imperial armies led by Manfred, Frederick's son. With it came the end of the Holy Roman Empire in Italia. Shortly afterwards, the Angevin Charles also became unpopular, having failed to unify Italia. In 1282 he was ousted from Sicily, though he kept the Kingdom of Naples. The crown of Sicily was offered to Peter III of Aragon, starting herewith the growing presence of the Crown of Aragon in Italia in the latter medieval period (including Sardinia as of 1323) (Procacci 1970).

With the collapse of the Empire the Italian communes entered a period of remarkable commercial activity. They were free to expand economically and territorially. The Italian fourteenth century was also characterized by a process of accentuated political particularism, albeit Dante could still assert the need to revive the Empire. It was a period in which the traditional aristocratic government gave way to the rise of despotism. Most city-states were ruled by political or military tyrants.

Naples was the only monarchic state left. The savage competition among city-states created a world of internecine wars which characterizes more specifically the period between 1350 and 1450.

City-states moulded the personality and outlook of the citizen; it was not only a matter of residence. In fact, the city-state provided the physical, social and political environment that created local patriotism. Citizens gave an oath of loyalty to the commune which involved a variety of duties (fiscal, military, civic). Patriotism flourished as a result of the enmity and confrontation with other cities. The symbol of the patria was the *carrocio* – a special wagon, always drawn by an oxen, which exhibited the standard of each city-state in battle. The *carrocio* was often named and, when engaging in battle, was protected by a special elite force; its loss was considered a major disaster. The *carrocio* was more than a military symbol, because it was also used as a focus of civic patriotism in religious and other ceremonial occasions (Waley 1969: 81–2).

Waley maintains that the city-states 'were a dead-end, and not a direct antecedent of nation-states' (1969: xvi), though he does apply this statement to some of the larger ones (Venice, Florence, Genoa) which remained states until modern times. Strayer for his part is more nuanced; for him after 1300 the attributes of sovereignty were taken by the city-states (1970: 59). In his classical work, Goetz (1937) insisted that the city-states were *patriae*. Abroad, however, Venetians, Pisans and Genovese were perceived as 'Italians', and this helped to create a certain sense of linguistic and cultural identity. By the end of the twelfth century there were about 300 communes; towards the end of the medieval period the number had been drastically reduced to a handful.

A challenge to the established order came in the mid-fourteenth century from the political visionary Cola di Rienzo. 'For the first time', said Fedele, 'the concept of the national and political unity of Italy, separated from the universality of the Empire, was present in the mind of an Italian' (1915: 451). This was the man who made such an impression on Petrarca that led him to write these famous words: 'Oh! if ever...oh! if it would only happen in my day...oh! if I could only share in so noble, so glorious an enterprise' (1986: 6–7). In fact, the political objectives of Petrarca (to unify Italia, to restore the Papacy from Avignon to Rome and to recreate a Rome-centered Empire) largely coincided with those of Cola di Rienzo (Mann 1984).

In 1347 Cola di Rienzo, a man of modest origins who had managed to rise to a political position by rallying the poor masses though electrifying speeches, claimed that Rome should be *caput orbis* and the foundation of Christendom. He declared all Italian cities free and gave the inhabitants of Italia the rights to Roman citizenship. An Italian emperor should be elected to rule over all the territory which was originally the Roman Empire (the peninsula from the Alps to Sicily, but also including Provence, Sardinia and Corsica). In a way his project was much more 'practical' than Dante's universal Roman Empire. Was Cola di Rienzo the first to tap on the reservoir of Italian national identity?

As Mazzei has indicated, Cola di Rienzo rejected both Guelph and Ghibelline ideologies because they were connected with 'supra-national' interests. Both papal and imperial domination were anathema to his political project. His new ideology was based on the need to liberate Italia from foreign rule (a theme echoed by Machiavelli in the last chapter of *The Prince*). Rome was envisaged as the *communis mater* of all Italians (1980: 120–1). However, when Cola spoke of *sacra Italia* this should not be understood in the modern sense of the term, as the expression was used by Foscolo or Mazzini. 'For Cola, who was a profound and sincere religious spirit, Christianity permeated everything; he wanted to bring the Empire to Rome and also the Papacy; he wanted to see again both swords, the spiritual and the temporal, in Rome' (Chabod 1961: 53). Italia was sacred because it housed the Church but also the Empire. But the rule of Cola di Rienzo was short-lived. Both Emperor and Pope felt threatened by Rienzo, who had bestowed upon himself arbitrary titles (Liberator of Rome, Champion of Italy, etc.). However, it was a popular Roman insurrection that put a violent end to his life in 1354.

By the end of the medieval period Italia was divided into five major states: Milan, Florence, Venice, the Papacy and Naples. Generally speaking, the fifteenth century was a period of economic prosperity and of cultural renaissance. Politically, the Italian states were engaged in enlarging their borders and consolidating their power. However, as separate entities they were defenceless in front of the might of the Habsburgs and the Valois who, by the dawn of the early modern period, had designs on the Italian peninsula. After a long period of intermittent wars, the (Spanish) Habsburg domination of Italia became a reality by the mid-sixteenth century and lasted until the beginning of the eighteenth century, only to be substituted, with the exception of the Napoleonic parenthesis, by the Austrian presence until the nineteenth century.

To conclude this section it is appropriate to consider in some detail the issue of *italianità*. Galasso (1979) has insisted in the fact that the Italian peninsula was never conceived, during the medieval period, as a political or 'national' area. What dominated were the identities of the city-states. The fact that, when referring to Italia and Hispania, the plural was often used indicates that the expression had essentially a geographic meaning. What are we to make, then, of the *pris de conscience* of *italianità* that many attribute to the Renaissance? What gave coherence to Italia, according to Volpe, was a 'common passion and a common acknowledgement of the artistic and philosophical values, a common exaltation of Rome and of its not human but divine heroes' (1978: 474–5). This humanistic culture expressed also a mild and diffuse sense of Italian national identity. Italia was seen as a value in itself (at least for the select few), a reference point Platonically invoked (Tenenti 1986: 267).

It is worth mentioning that there were a number of attempts to unite the Italian state during the sixteenth century, but to no avail because particularist interests prevailed. At the intellectual level there was a 'gradual awareness of belonging to a common historical and cultural group' (Ilardi 1956: 339). This group was characterized by a variety of markers (common language, common culture, common history). This was not incompatible with another sentiment, perhaps stronger: that of belonging to one's city-state. A Florentine was first and foremost politically and emotionally devoted to his *patria*; and only secondarily to Italia as a 'larger geographical and cultural entity' (ibid.: 343). *Italianità* was essentially a phenomenon restricted to well-educated people; the majority of the population were anchored in their *campanilismo*. In addition, not all intellectuals were in favour of a unified Italia along the French model. Machiavelli was perhaps a prophet of Italian unity, but his contemporary Guicciardini, although well conscious of the cultural unity, wanted peace, but not necessarily political union between the Italian states. It has to be emphasized, as Galasso has put it that 'there is nothing in Italian history that predestined the different republics to become a state' (1979: 180), but also that when the national state made its appearance in the nineteenth century it was marked by the complex history of the different states.

The use of the Italian vernacular in the late medieval and early modern periods is a well-established fact. Whether in its various dialectal forms, or in the more prestigious Tuscan variety, language became the key link among the different regions, as well as the fundamental expression of cultural unity. How far this linguistic consciousness can be labelled 'national' is another matter. Though Vasoli has insisted that in Renaissance Italia: 'The linguistic question represented, explicitly or implicitly, the affirmation of a living, spoken language ... by the majority of the inhabitants of the peninsula' (1986: 162), the movement in favour of the vernacular was a matter of 'national' dignity, but had no wider political implications.

The strength of *italianità*, in the absence of a political unit that supported it (unlike, for example, the backing that the Catholic Monarchs of Castile and Aragon gave to Spanish), had much to do with 'the heritage of Rome which survived in the Italian soul as a cultural and literary myth, as consciousness of a spiritual tradition of which Italia was the most immediate heir and custodian' (Valsecchi 1978: 4). In spite of the foreign conquests, the sense of cultural superiority remained. Italia survived for many centuries without political content, a dream in the mind of artists and writers.

Hispania

Within Western Europe, Hispania was the domain which most suffered from foreign domination: the Visigoths from 419 to 711 and the Muslims from 711 to 1492. None the less, the existence of a Visigothic Kingdom, which by the seventh century had unified the Iberian peninsula and had defined the country 'by three internal elements (*rex, gens, patria*)' (Teillet 1984: 638), has led some commentators (Maravall 1954; Sanchez-Albornoz 1973) to refer to the emergence of Spain as the first European nation. Furthermore, they see in Isidore of Seville's *History of the Goths* (624) a celebration of the Spanish national spirit. I have already criticized such anachronistic views, although I do not wish to deny that from the early medieval period there exists a unitary conception of the Iberian peninsula, the idea of Hispania, which will be repeatedly used for the ideological purposes of forging a single state within the Iberian domain. Needless to say, the fact that in modern times only two states (Spain and Portugal) exist in the Iberian peninsula is not because of any inexorable and preordained historical logic, but rather the result of chance. If historical circumstances had been different, Hispania, like certain parts of south-eastern Europe, could have consisted of several Muslim and several Christian states, with significant minorities of the opposite sign, and of Jews, in each of the states. In any case, within the modern Spanish state Catalans, Basques, Galicians and perhaps other peoples have a distinctive national identity and consciousness.

Whatever the merits of the idea of the Visigothic Kingdom as the beginning of the Spanish nation are, the truth is that by the eighth century the kingdom was collapsing along protofeudal lines through internal contradictions; more importantly, the Muslim invasions destroyed and completely wiped out the Visigothic political structures. The early resistance to Muslim domination appeared in those areas of the Iberian peninsula which had been either outside the full Visigothic control, such as Asturias, Leon and Navarra, or, as with the Pyrenean counties, were associated with the Frankish monarchy. The idea of continuity between the Visigothic Kingdom and the small Christian kingdoms which emerged after the Muslim invasion, appeared at a later stage and it is a mythological elaboration. Hence, it is more appropriate to speak of a plurality of kingdoms pursuing different policies, including the Hispanic March which was more oriented towards Gallia than Hispania.

The medieval history of Hispania after the Muslim invasion divides neatly into three periods. Between the eighth and eleventh centuries there is a clear Muslim domination, although an array of small Christian principalities challenged its rule in the northern fringe of the Iberian peninsula. After the collapse of the caliphate of Cordoba, Muslim Hispania (al-Andalus) was divided into twenty-three *taifas* or petty kingdoms. From the eleventh to the thirteenth centuries the dimensions of al-Andalus were progressively reduced, in spite of successful *razzias* by Berber invaders from north Africa. The battle of the Navas de Tolosa in 1212 meant the beginning of the end of Muslim domination in Hispania. Of the vast Muslim domain, by 1264 there only remained the Kingdom of Granada in south-east Hispania. At the same time, four Christian kingdoms, of different sizes and characteristics, emerged: Aragon, Navarra, Castile and Portugal. From the mid-thirteenth century to the end of the fifteenth century there was a period of consolidation, but also of internal strife within the Christian kingdoms. The Crown of Aragon expanded into the Mediterranean, while the Kingdom of Portugal explored the south Atlantic. Castile, larger and more powerful but land-locked, experienced a number of internal crises, but was determined to homogenize the kingdom and grow bigger through marriage alliances with Portugal or Aragon; it was only in the late fifteenth century that Castile decided to conquer the Kingdom of Granada, putting thus an end to eight hundred years of Muslim rule. The dynastic union of Castile and Aragon had preceded this momentous event.

The Muslim invaders who unified Hispania and ruled it from Cordoba, first as an emirate and then as a caliphate, called the territory subjugated al-Andalus. The conquerors belonged to two different ethnies: Arabs and Berbers. The former, small in number, were the dominant group and settled in the most fertile areas of the south and east of the country. The Berbers came from north Africa in different waves over a number of centuries. While the Arabs who came in the eighth century numbered about fifty thousand, the total number of Berbers who colonized al-Andalus was probably ten or more times that number. The relations between Arabs and Berbers was often conflictual and created a serious problem for the governance of the dominated lands. In the long run, the tribal divisions prevailed and led to the collapse of the centralized structures and to the appearance of tribal-based statelets. When we compare these figures with the approximately seven million *Hispanii*, it is possible to get a clear picture of the feat that the conquest represented. The conversions to

Islam were massive, although the presence of Christians and Jews was tolerated.

The mountainous northern territory of Hispania was never subjected, or only tenuously. As early as 722 a Muslim army was defeated by the Christian ruler Don Pelayo at Covadonga. This symbolic victory was extremely significant in the historiographic annals of medieval Hispania. The heroic deeds of Don Pelayo, which helped to restore freedom to the Christian people, were first mentioned in a ninth century chronicle; by the tenth century the myth of the royal Visigothic origin of Don Pelayo was enshrined in the Chronicles of Alphonse II; in this way, a clear continuity was established between the Visigothic Kingdom and the newly emerged Kingdom of Asturias.

At first, al-Andalus was governed by the Umayyad dynasty of Damascus, but by the mid-eighth century, after the Abbasid rebellion of Syria, al-Andalus became an independent, Umayyad-based kingdom. As a polity it was plagued by internal dissension and centrifugal tendencies reflecting not only the geographic separateness of the different regions of Hispania, but also the multifarious ethnic composition of its population, with an endemic proclivity to strife and fission. The emerging emirate encouraged the development of irrigated agriculture. Urban life also flourished in cities like Cordoba, Seville, Toledo and Granada. But it was only with the caliphate of Abd-al-Rahman III in 929, that al-Andalus entered a period of brilliant economic and cultural splendour which culminated in a range of literary and scientific achievements that irradiated to the rest of Europe. Under Abd-al-Rahman III the administration of the state was perfected; a fairly efficient system of central government was introduced, but with delegated authority for each of the provinces. The treasury, legislation and the administration of justice reached levels of competency unsurpassed in other western European lands. The essential problem with this powerful Muslim state was that it failed to develop a mechanism of political legitimation, hence its inherent instability.

When one of the rulers, al-Hakam II, died leaving as heir a ten-year-old son, a dictatorial figure – that of al-Mansur – appeared in the horizon. He was a successful military leader, and so was his son Abdul-Malik. However, having lost the principle of religious legitimation, the only alternative was force and political cunning. After Abdul-Malik's death there followed a bitter internecine struggle, in which dynastic rivals fought violently for power. As a historian of the period has put it: 'The disintegration of al-Andalus, now thrown into wild disorder, proceeded without let up. The succession of Caliphes was bewildering, as few of them reigned for more than a year or two, and none of them could claim universal authority' (O'Callaghan 1975: 132). In 1031 the Umayyad dynasty became extinct and the caliphate was supressed. There followed a period in which al-Andalus broke up into innumerable small kingdoms along ethnic lines.

The first Christian kingdom which came into being was that of Asturias. As Vicens-Vives remarked: 'it is a historic paradox that Asturians and Cantabrians, who have always been the groups most obstinately opposed to joining the Peninsular community, should have constituted themselves as the perpetrators of the Hispania tradition' (1970: 32). After modest origins, by the end of the eighth century the Kingdom of Asturias had progressed both westwards, towards Galicia, and eastwards, towards the Basque area, that is, to culturally different lands, an occurrence which was to be the source of conflict in the centuries to come. An important feature of the Asturian Kingdom was the absence of feudalism. The *Reconquista* favoured the existence of a 'strong monarchy and a large class of freemen ... Military success not only enhanced the king's prestige, but also added to his resources. Claiming ownership of all reconquered territory, the king was able to reserve large estates for himself and to reward his followers for their loyalty to him. Those who repopulated the newly conquered lands were for the most part small, free proprietors, hardy frontiersmen, who gave allegiance to no lord save the king. The nobility, on the other hand, lacking the military and financial power which only the possession of large estates could give, were unable to offer serious challenge to the kings's authority' (O'Callaghan 1975: 167).

From the beginning of the tenth century the monarchs no longer resided in Asturias, but further south – in Leon, hence the change of name to Kingdom of Leon or Asturias-Leon. By this time Castile had started to develop as a region with a strong and independent personality. A frontier area, Castile was more autonomous than any of the other regions of the kingdom. In the second half of the tenth century, under the count Fernán Gonzalez, Castile became practically independent. It is interesting to note that the first human groups who settled in Castile were Basques and Cantabrians. In the Pyrenees a number of counties, later to become kingdoms, made their appearance soon after the Muslim invasion. For a long time their existence was precarious and their size small, but towards the eleventh century three clear political entities had emerged and crystallized: the kingdoms of Navarre and Aragon and the principality of Catalonia. Their proximity to Western Europe meant that these territories were closely connected and influenced by European (Frankish) cultural and institutional developments.

Navarre was the kingdom of a part of the Basques; a *modus vivendi* had been reached with the Muslims, which lasted well into the beginning of the tenth century, when the new dynasty wedded Navarre to the

Reconquest. The high point of the kingdom came at the beginning of the eleventh century when King Sancho III brought under his rule all the Christian realms except for Catalonia. He used the titled '*rex Dei gratia Hispaniarum*, thereby laying claim to that peninsular supremacy previously attributed to the King of Leon' (O'Callaghan 1975: 136). Having conquered Leon in 1034, he assumed the title of *imperator*. His patrimonial conception of the monarchy meant that after his death the three different kingdoms (Aragon, Castile and Navarre) went separate ways. After such a momentous reign, Navarre never recovered its grandeur. After the twelfth century, landlocked between the powerful Catalono-Aragonese confederation and the Kingdom of Castile, Navarre had no Muslim space in which to expand. Successive alliances with the French monarchy brought the kingdom closer to French interests. This situation lasted until 1512 when the kingdom was annexed to the crown of Castile.

Aragon consisted originally of a group of small counties in the central high-mountain valleys of the Pyrenees. By the ninth century their leaders were more interested in reaching an agreement with the Muslim regions to the south, than in prolonging their dependency on the Frankish monarchy. However, by the tenth century, Aragon came under the orbit of the king of Navarre and only recovered its independence after Sancho III's death in 1035. The identity of the Aragonese land was, however, preserved, and so were its political institutions. Further to the eastern Pyrenees, there were a number of counties created by the Carolingians as a buffer zone against Muslim incursions into southern Gallia. This area, as we know from the section on Gallia, was known as the Hispanic March (later Catalonia).

Without wanting to read too much into this early period, there is little doubt that it is a formative era in the making of a number of medieval state formations: Asturias, Leon, Castile, Galicia, Navarre, Aragon and Catalonia. Along these lines will develop early national identities, which (with others like Portugal appearing at a later time) will persist in a modified form well into the modern times. On the other hand, the fact that the kings of Leon used the title of *rex magnus* and the kingdom was sometimes referred to as *regnum imperium* has induced Menendez-Pidal (1950) and others to postulate a Hispanic unity in this early period, and the pre-eminence of Asturias-Leon over other peninsular kingdoms. That some Leonese monarchs saw themselves as emperors is not at stake. The question is how far were these pretensions recognized by the other Christian kings. And the answer is only rarely.

The next period in the medieval history of Hispania spans from the mid-eleventh century to the end of the thirteenth century. This is a crucial era for the Christian kingdoms; it was not until 1212, when a combined Christian army defeated the Almohads in Navas de Tolosa, that it was clear that Muslim power would ebb for good.

The *taifa* kingdoms which characterized the political organization of eleventh-century al-Andalus were of short duration. However, Islamic Hispania was to be revitalized by two successive waves of Berber invasions, which created the Almoravid empire (1090–1147) and the Almohad empire (1147–1212). The expansion of the Christian kingdoms, which by the eleventh century had reached the central plateau and central Portugal, was checked. At that time, al-Andalus still comprised two-thirds of the territory of the Iberian peninsula.

During the twelfth century the Christian conquests were limited to lower Aragon, southern Catalonia and parts of Extremadura. The Almoravids, who were Saharan nomads who had spread into northern Morocco and then the whole of north Africa and south of the Sahara, came to al-Andalus to assist the *taifa* kings under increasing pressure from Castile-Leon. The Almoravid empire was short-lived, having failed to galvanize the mass of the population for a long enough period of time, particularly after their promises of a better life for the underdog went unfulfilled. The puritanical, theocratic state that they created was perceived as alien by the refined Muslims of al-Andalus, and collapsed through internal dissension by the mid-twelfth century. In their place came a new movement which started among the Berbers of the Atlas; the people who were involved in it were called *al-muwahhidun* (those who profess belief in the absolute religious unity) or Almohads. Having defeated the Almoravids and the *taifa* kings, the Almohads managed to control al-Andalus, but failed to recover the territory that had been lost to the Christian kingdoms. However, they often raided the Christian lands and presented an increased challenge to Christendom.

Pope Innocent III called a crusade to rout the Almohad peril. An array of Christian soldiers from all over Western Europe joined the armies of the five Hispanic kingdoms of the time and decisively defeated the expeditionary force led by the Almohad leader Miramolin in 1212. In retrospect, the importance of such a victory is captured by the words of O'Callaghan: 'The Christian victory at Las Navas de Tolosa ended once and for all the Almohad threat to Christian Spain and hastened the decline of the Almohad empire. The equilibrium hitherto existing between Christian and Muslims was upset, and the balance of power was tipped decisively in favour of the Christians. The victory was the greatest ever achieved during the Reconquest, and it made possible the subjugation of the greater part of al-Andalus in the next forty years' (1975: 248–9). From the mid-thirteenth century onwards Granada became a vassal kingdom of Castile.

For the Christian kingdoms the period under consideration was of the utmost importance. It was not only a time of major territorial expansion to the detriment of the Muslim kingdoms, but also of internal consolidation, restructuring and identity formation. By the close of the thirteenth century the distinct personality of each of the Christian kingdoms of the Iberian peninsula that had survived (Aragon, Navarre, Castile, Portugal) was well-established and so was the territorial extension of each of them. If we except the small Kingdom of Granada in the south-east, the task of the Reconquest had been achieved. As we can see, the fact that at that moment in time there were four Christian kingdoms, and neither more nor fewer, was the result of historical chance, that is, the unintended result of a process of fusion and fission through dynastic alliances and wars. It was the consequence of a conception of the state which was based on two contradictory principles: expansionism and patrimonialism. In other words, monarchs were keen to extend their rule to ever-vaster territories, but when it came to succession they often divided them among their children (preferably males). It is awesome to think that the fate of kingdoms rested on the unpredictable fact of how many childen a monarch was able to beget and keep alive.

It is not my intention to discard the notion that during the whole medieval period there was a unitarian conception of the peninsula, which originated first in Leon, and then was perpetuated by Castile. However, this was hardly the driving force of the medieval Hispanic kingdoms. As Payne has remarked 'despite an underlying Hispano-Christian peninsular identity, monarchic-territorial pluralism became accepted as a legal and natural fact in the state systems of greater Christian Hispania' (1976: 153). On the other hand, the four peninsular Christian kingdoms were structurally very different. Both in terms of size and population Castile became the most powerful Hispanic kingdom; furthermore, the dynamics of the militaristic, frontier-society that Castile was, led to the overshadowing of the kingdoms of Asturias, Leon and Galicia. The Kingdom of Castile operated a policy of integrating the conquered territories to its direct rule. A notable exception were the Basque provinces of Guipuzcoa, Vizcaya and Alava which incorporated into the Castilian crown in the thirteenth and fourteenth centuries, but they all preserved their own laws or *fueros*. The union of Aragon and Catalonia respected the legal specificity of the separate contracting entities; the conquered or acquired territories both in the peninsula and later in the Mediterranean area were incorporated as members of a federation. As previously indicated, the Kingdom of Navarre, squeezed between two expanding states languished for the rest of the medieval period.

The region delimited by the rivers Minho and Douro, known as Portugal, had had a cultural and political identity at least since the ninth century. As a geographically isolated frontier territory, it soon developed a distinct personality. With a dialect of Latin that it shared with Galicia, it was none the less a self-centered society, unlike Galicia which was more turned towards Leon and later Castile, and thus open to western European influences. In the long run, the aristocracy of Portugal felt alienated from the rule of Castile-Leon and sought autonomy. During a period of internal and external crisis of Castile-Leon, Afonso I emerged as the ruler of Portugal. During his long period in power (1128–1185) he declared himself King of Portugal, greatly expanded the territory of the kingdom and sought to cement his independence from Castile by becoming a vassal of the pope. By the end of the thirteenth century Portugal had already completed the conquest of Alentejo and of the Algarve from Muslim hands, hence bringing its part of the Reconquest to an end. However, the Castilian monarchy never quite accepted the independence of Portugal and during the rest of the medieval period there were a number of attempts to incorporate Portugal to the Castilian crown. It may be correct to say that Portuguese identity originated as a result of the distinctiveness of a territory and the specific historical experience of a group. However, the fact that Portugal became and remained an independent state is to a great extent the result of historical accident.

Perhaps it is worthwhile to consider in some more detail the distinctive features of Castile and Aragon. MacKay believes that three factors account for Castilian quasi-absolutism. The first point to emphasize about the Castilian monarchy is that it rested on the sacralization of power. In many respects it mirrored the Capetian monarchy, except that Castile boasted a continuity with the Visigothic period. All the panoply of the religious symbolism of royal authority was present: the sacred relics, the anointment ceremony, manifest destiny, etc. The second factor was the crusading tradition of Castile; the kingdom was the most militarized of the Iberian peninsula, and its ethos – one of war and conquest – had no rival. But by far the most important factor was the absence of proper feudalism in Castile; there were certainly vassals, but they enjoyed more freedom than anywhere else in the peninsula (MacKay 1977: 97–8).

The union of Aragon and Catalonia, from which emerged the Crown of Aragon, was the result of a dynastic pact, and not of a conquest or fusion. Unlike Castile, in the Crown of Aragon each new component preserved its own identity. The union of Aragon and Catalonia took place in 1137 and it originally came into existence as a move to thwart Castilian and Navarrese political designs on the Kingdom of Aragon. The union is best described as a confederation in which the monarchs respected the autonomy of each component. The fact that within the territory of Catalonia there coexisted different sovereignties allowed the Count of Barcelona, Ramon Berenguer IV, to imagine a contractual solution to a dynastic union which instead of leading to a total separation or a homogenizing unification (as was the case of Castile) resulted in political pluralism. As Vicens-Vives put it: 'The solution devised at that critical moment, later turned out to be extremely fruitful, when the problem arose of how to govern Valencia and the Balearics, and when the even more extensive and complicated problem arose of how to govern the Mediterranean possessions of the Crown of Aragon in Italy' (1970: 53). The House of Barcelona ruled until 1410, when Martin I died without descendants, and the Crown of Aragon passed on to the Castilian ruling House of Trastamara.

Dynastic unions were common in the medieval period. What is surprising about the Crown of Aragon is the fact that it lasted for such a long time and that it was genuinely advantageous for all its members. Part of the explanation for its success has to do with the so called *pactisme* (pactism) as the key political mechanism that regulated the relationships between the different components. The Crown of Aragon always kept a fine balance between homogeneization and fragmentation. Each unit preserved its identity at the socio-economic, institutional and cultural levels. In this sense it is possible to talk about an incipient national identity not only in Catalonia but also in Aragon and Valencia. Sesma (1988: 220–8) has illustrated these developments specifically for Aragon *strictu sensu*, although they can be generalized to Catalonia and, to a certain extent, to Valencia. He emphasizes that from the fourteenth century onwards a number of measures were taken which account for the emergence of separate identities. First, a much clearer territorial delineation of the boundaries of each of the countries was established (the creation of custom offices is a good example of such developments). Second, the existence of legal, political and fiscal institutions controlled by each of the kingdoms. Third, the consolidation of strong cultural identities; here what was at stake was the centrality of the rights and freedoms of each of the territories against the encroachment by the crown. Fourth, the fostering of a collective sentiment; this affected only a rather limited part of the population, but it was real enough. Here the monarchy played a positive role, and the fact that the different component kingdoms shared emblems, flags and myths of origin was useful against outsiders. On the other hand, collective memories were constructed and preserved to enhance the cohesion of each of the kingdoms.

Unity and diversity are themes that are commonly argued about concerning the Hispania of this period. By 1300 the dice had been, to a great exent, cast. Cultures and languages, economic, and political institutions, in a word, the traditional ingredients of which states and nations are made, had began to crystallize. This is not to say that realities were fixed forever. Much could still happen, and in fact it did: like the unification of Castile and Aragon at the end of the fifteenth century. But when it occurred, the personalities of the two crowns – authoritarian absolutism in Castile and constitutionalism in Aragon – were well-established. On the issue of the unity of Hispania, Hillgarth has shown, with a flurry of references, that, for example, the Catalans had a clear sense of institutional, linguistic, artistic and ecclesiastical identity, different from that of Castile and at times from that of Aragon. Even if occasionally the existence of a wider unity was acknowledged, the overwhelming evidence points to the consciousness of separate development. Although Castilian texts tend to reflect a unitary view of Hispania, they none the less tend to show a sense of superiority of Castile over all other Hispanic kingdoms. Hence, 'it was hardly likely that a royal marriage in 1469 between the heirs of Castile and Aragon could unite peoples which possessed for centuries their own character, their own language and their mission to achieve' (Hillgarth 1976, I: 15).

In the latter part of the Middle Ages the struggle for hegemony in the Iberian peninsula was essentially between Aragon and Castile, with Portugal playing also an increasing part. In describing the Hispanic kingdoms Hillgarth (1976) suggests that between 1250 and 1410 there was a precarious balance of power between Aragon and Castile, but that the fifteenth century is definitely a period of Castilian domination. Castile was not only a unified kingdom, but compared very favourably with the other kingdoms in terms of population. Estimates vary, but by 1500 the population of the Crown of Castile was around five million, while the number of inhabitants in Portugal and the crown of Aragon did not exceed the one million mark for each. Whether the volume of population accounts in itself for the final triumph of Castile is a thesis which has recently been disputed (Abulafia 1992: 13). The crisis, and later decline, of the commercially-oriented maritime economy of Catalonia, the accession of a Castilian dynasty to the Crown of Aragon in 1410 and the civil strife of the fifteenth century (particularly in Catalonia) are all factors that indicate that the dynamic role that Catalonia had played in the Catalano-Aragonese federation had greatly diminished. Following the more recent historiography of Treppo and Carrère, Abulafia insists that Catalan economic decadence did not occur until much later. Be that as it may, he agrees, however, that after their marriage, the Catholic monarchs undertook an impressive work of reconstruction of Castile so that by 1492 this kingdom had achieved primacy (Abulafia 1992: 19).

To conclude, there was no 'Spanish nation' or even 'state' at the end of the medieval period. There was certainly an accidental dynastic union of the crowns of Castile and Aragon. The monarchs had good geopolitical reasons for the alliance, but it was only meant to be a short-term agreement. The Catholic Monarchs may have had a common foreign policy, but at the peninsular level one of the few common institutions that they created was the Holy Inquisition. The lack of descendants (particularly of Ferdinand's second marriage) and the weakness of the Crown of Aragon, maintained the union, although preserving to a great extent the original institutional arrangements that enshrined the autonomy of the realms of the Aragonese crown. Hence, the expression 'Spanish monarchy' makes little sense when applied to the sixteenth or seventeenth centuries; and the meaning of term 'Spain' could be limited to Castile or include the Netherlands or the Italian possessions. In fact, the king represented as many persons as there were kingdoms, principalities, counties and dominions (Clavero 1989: 112–3). What existed in the sixteenth century was a Castilian-based Habsburg monarchy. Portugal came to this union in 1580 through another dynastic alliance. In 1640 both Portugal and Catalonia, incensed at the centralizing attempts of Phillip IV, tried to become independent, but only the former succeeded. When a problem of succession arose at the turn of the eighteenth century, the components of the Crown of Aragon sided with the Habsburg pretender. The victory of the cause of the Bourbons meant the end of the autonomy of the Crown of Aragon within the monarchy. With it, a proper Spanish centralized and unified state and a Spanish nation began to take shape.

Provisional Conclusions

At the end of this brief tour of the medieval world, what can be said about the five original domains of statehood and nationhood? If we take into account the original territories more or less arbitrarily assigned to each area, the Gallic domain is perhaps the one which appears to be the most successful in terms of the convergence between state and nation. The Gallic area becomes essentially the nation-state France. This entity survives to our days, even if the 1789 revolution meant the end of the ancient regime. England would appear, at first sight, as an even better placed candidate for the convergence of state and nation. However, England is only a part of Britannia; the United Kingdom is a much later development, and strictly speaking a failed one due to the separation of Ireland and the strong Scottish and Welsh national identities. At the other end of the spectrum, Italia was the least successful area, followed closely by Germania. In these areas the convergence between nation and state did not materialize until the second half of the nineteenth century. On the other hand, the Germanian domain produced early fiercely independent and patriotic states such as Holland and Switzerland. But the point to emphasize is that there is no historical necessity that required that Germania should have become Germany and Italia should have turned into Italy. The Italian peninsula harboured quite a number of states, with distinctive and differential identities, which could have easily survived into the twentieth century. The same applies to Germania. Hispania lies somewhere in between, with a process of unification led by Castile, in which Portugal was only integrated for a short period of time. Furthermore, already in the early modern period Catalonia tried, unsuccessfully, to exit from the union when her voice was not heard. In modern times, both Catalonia and the Basque Country have represented alternative national projects.

From a comparison of the different domains what seems to emerge is a variety of factors which help to explain the appearance of nations in the Middle Ages. For sure, these factors should not be taken in isolation, but rather seen as a whole. It is also obvious that the sphere of applicability of national consciousness is limited; national sentiments were restricted to a small part of the population. With all these provisos, it is still meaningful to speak of medieval nations. To start with, the medieval use of terms such as *natio* and *patria*, even with different meanings from those of modernity, indicate the presence of developing political and cultural realities. Towards the end of the period their centrality is apparent.

Language is an obvious factor to consider. According to the medieval philosopher Thomas Aquinas it determined the essence of the nation. More recently, Marc Bloch (1965: 431–7) emphasized that language brought about other common elements, particularly mental traditions and the like. The development of a distinctive language was obviously a slow process, fraught with dangers. Some events took place very early: the division of the Holy Roman Empire at Verdun in 843 consecrated the separation of Germania and Gallia along linguistic lines. The appearance of a literature in the vernacular was one of the ways in which languages became fixed; in time, vernacular literature provided prestige to a court and to a country. The decision of monarchs to write or commission chronicles in the vernacular rather than in Latin was a momentous one; it increased the prestige of a language and its chances of survival. A written language was also, of course, the best means to preserve historical memories. Understandably these would be, at first, essentially dynastic, but the perspective would progressively become wider.

An early focus for the nation was the notion of blood ties. This was a Germanic conception that persisted during the medieval period in the form of an emphasis on common descent. Myths of descent, as I have shown in some detail for Gallia, were extremely popular and played a key role in legitimating peoples's identities and their rights to be ruled separately from other peoples. As Guennée has remarked, by the end of the thirteenth century a clear distinction emerged between native and foreigner which corresponded to the fact of being born in the kingdom or outside the kingdom (1985: 64). Physical appearance also started to play a role in the way in which nations were identified. At the psychological level, the idea of national character became popular, no doubt prompted by an increasing number of contacts across Europe. National stereotypes began to spread. Most Europeans saw the people of Germania as violent and proud, while the natives considered themselves noble and courageous.

The importance of early administrative divisions, particularly those of the Roman period has already been referred to. Although difficult to assess, they no doubt had an effect. In Italia the impact was obvious, as it also was in Hispania. Having a proper name for a country was also important; it implied the crystallization of a sense of collective identity; in some cases it signified the existence of a state, in others that of a nation, and in some cases both. As to the idea of natural boundaries (mountains, rivers, etc.), although references to the Pyrenees and the Alps as national borders can be found, the idea was far from being widely accepted.

Culture, understood as the manners, habits, customs, laws, etc. typical of an area, also helped to identify nations, particularly in the late medieval period. Certain institutions were clearly identified with specific nations. Some characteristics were more visible than others; especially noticeable were the ways of dressing, the eating patterns and the commercial practices.

An interesting use of the word 'nation' occurred in medieval universities. Students tended to be grouped under 'nations'. There was no unanimous use of the term; in some cases it referred to the country of birth, in others to the common language and in still others to the principle of residence. What is clear from Kibre's (1948) comparative study is that the principle of geographical distance was a decisive factor in the merger of small nations into a single category; that is, from the perspective of a university in northern Germania, the chances of differentiating between the different Hispanic peoples was small.

Towards the late medieval period the sentiment against foreign domination became more explicit. National self-consciousness was closely related to this sentiment. Petrarca expressed this sentiment of oppression in many ways; his call for liberation was often articulated in a language which appealed to the glorious Roman past in order to denounce the present barbarian (Germanian) domination of Italia. The Hundred Years War was a period that greatly contributed to the generation of a sentiment of French national identity. It is in the context of glorious military deeds that hero-worshipping made its contribution to the consolidation of the nation. Joan of Arc was a symbol of resistance against English domination, and as such stimulated French national sentiments.

The union of religion and national politics was also a phenomenon which became obvious by the fourteenth and fifteenth centuries. But long before that, patriotism and Christianity were already married; it was usually through the close association of a saint and nation that the link between country and divinity was established. Saint Denis and Saint Michael protected Gallia, as Saint James interceded in favour of Hispania. Whether there were attempts at attacking the Pope's privileges (as by Wycliffe in England and Huss in Bohemia) or not, the fact is that by the end of the Middle Ages, and long before Luther and Henry VIII had come on to the scene, gallicanism was triumphant. It is no coincidence that, as Kantorowicz remarked, 'at a certain moment in history the state in the abstract or the state as a corporation appeared as a corpus mysticum and that death for this new mystical body appeared equal in value to the death of a crusader for the cause of God' (1951: 491).

Although the list of factors is by no means exhausted (and I have left aside for the time being the crucial role played by the state in the emergence of national identity), it is perhaps useful to return to the issue of whether there were nations before modern nationalism. Social scientists interested in nationalism enter the Middle Ages at their peril. It is a field fraught with various, at times insuperable obstacles. The array of linguistic and historiographical skills required to delve into this period scares away many social scientists, while others have no difficulty in making dogmatic pronouncements. It is interesting to note that while medievalist historians, who ought to know better, are willing to contemplate the idea of national consciousness and even that of nationalism (no matter how 'incipient') as part of the period, most social scientists are obsessed with the modernity of the phenomenon.

Among the different specialists of modernity there seems to be, if not unanimity, at least a majority opinion that national sentiments could have not developed in the Middle Ages. This position was compellingly presented by Hans Kohn in his major work *The Idea of Nationalism* published in 1944. The argument has always been grounded on the assumption that neither religious nor political universalism could be the breeding grounds for national awareness. Furthermore, most medieval people lived in confined physical and mental spaces which could only generate a sense of local community. Kohn was forced to admit, though, that 'towards the end of the Middle Ages national states began to take shape, and the first foundations for the future growth of nationalism were laid' and that 'a few individuals wrote and acted in a way which would justify claiming them for nationalism' (1944: 79). However, this is no obstacle for Kohn to still maintain that national sentiments were alien to the period.

It is important to emphasize, however, that the Kohnian case rests on the fallacy of starting with a modern definition of nationalism and then finding the Middle Ages wanting, that is, at fault for not conforming to the prescribed expectations. In any case, the point in dispute is not the existence of a fully-fledged nationalism in the Middle Ages – an obviously untenable position – but the question of the genesis and development of an incipient national awareness over a long historical period encompassing the Middle Ages and the early modern period. However, it is obvious that, as Zientara has pointed out, 'the modern nation differs from the medieval one in that the former exhibits an incomparably much wider sphere of consciousness, incorporating practically the whole population' (1982: 6). None the less, it is a sign of the profound impact of the work of Hans Kohn that his thesis of the modernity of nationalism has rarely been challenged by social scientists. In recent times the best known exceptions to this rule are Armstrong (1982) and Smith (1986).

Generally speaking, medievalist historians differ from this generalized consensus that nationalism is an exclusively modern phenomenon (Tipton 1972). As we have seen, Marc Bloch, writing approximately at the same time as Hans Kohn, concluded that a sentiment of national consciousness was extant in the Middle Ages from the twelfth century onwards. It is true that the growth of the national sentiment was not to be found in the educated men, who using Latin and being concerned with Papacy and Empire, were universalistic, but in the knightly classes and the semi-educated clerics who had narrower linguistic (more 'national') horizons. As to the mass of the medieval population we know very little about their thoughts and sentiments concerning the nation. I have already indicated that for Bloch language differences greatly contributed to create different mentalities which in the long run crystallized into different nationalities.

A contemporary of Bloch, the Dutch cultural historian Huizinga, also maintained that the emotional attitude that is represented by the words 'nationalism' or 'patriotism' already existed in the medieval period, albeit in a less manifest way. Huizinga pointed out that the Christian West was based on a dual perception: a religious unity and a reality of state power. It was around the twelfth century that a national consciousness made its apperance in Europe. The uses of terms such as *patria* and *natio* in the medieval period show how the sense of national consciousness was acquired. *Patria* referred to many things: a specific jurisdiction, a native land and a fatherland. As to *natio* (which was a more common medieval term), it originally referred to the place of birth, but with a wider meaning than *gens* or *populus*. Huizinga remarked that *natio* brought together tribe, language and region in a single conception which allowed it to be used both to refer, say, to Bretons as well as to the French. The point made by Huizinga was that the emotions attached to the word *natio* were the same whether the group was small or big; what mattered was 'the primitive in-group that felt passionately united as soon as the others, outsiders in whatever way, seemed to threaten them or to rival them' (1984: 107).

To close this brief review of the literature published more or less at the same time of Kohn's *The Idea of Nationalism* I would like to bring forward the testimony of the linguist Roman Jacobson. Writing in 1945 he referred to the emergence of a conscious patriotism, crystallizing around the monarch, already in the twelfth and thirteenth centuries. The idea of a national culture, as well that of a national language, appeared at that time and culminated in the period around the Reformation.

As we have repeatedly seen in Part I, the consensus of medievalists has been, for quite a long time, that states and nations, if not fully-fledged realities, were at least partly embodied medieval concepts. The sentiments expressed by the words 'nationalism' and 'patriotism' were alive and well in the late medieval period, only much less effective than in modern times. Of course, as I have hinted in Chapter One many of these developments came to a halt with the emergence of absolutism in the early modern period. This is a period in which the expansion of the state took precedence over any other consideration, eclipsing to a varying degree national sentiments; it was also the time when imperial themes came to the forefront.

In considering the relation between state and nation in the medieval period historians often advance the cliché that while in France the state preceded the nation, in England the nation preceded the state. Beyond the arguments that can be mustered to defend this thesis, the key point to emphasize is that state and nation reinforced each other. It would be, however, a faulty deduction to affirm that the disappearance of a state (through absorption by, or fusion with, another) involved necessarily the end of a national sentiment, particularly when the polity under consideration had already managed to generate a strong sense of identity: Catalonia is a good case in point. But even in those cases where a state had not quite evolved, or had only developed in a very incipient form, national identities were not necessarily absent. Wales and Ireland prove this point. In both cases the presence of ethnic markers persisting over time is an essential precondition for the emergence of modern national-ism. The idea that nationalism is invented, so dear to Hobsbawm, Gellner and other contemporary observers, is patently untrue. Modern nationalisms are recreations of medieval realities; in fact, they can only be successful if they are rooted in the medieval past, even if the links with it may often be tortuous and twisted.

Bibliography

Abulafia, D., (1992) *Frederick II. A Medieval Emperor*, London: Pimlico.

—— —., (1992) *Spain and 1492*, Bangor: Headstart History.

Armstrong, J. A., (1982) *Nations before Nationalism*, Chapel Hill: University of North Carolina Press.

Baldwin, J. W., (1987) 'Le sens de Bouvines', *Cahiers de Civilisation Médievale*, XXX (2), pp. 119–30.

Barraclough, G., (1946) (1979) *Factors in German History*, Wesport Co.: Greenwood Press.

Barrow, G. W. S., (1976) *Robert Bruce and the Community of the Realm in Scotland*, Edinburgh: Edinburgh University Press.

Baugh, A., (1976) *A Literary History of England*, London: Routledge.

Beaune, C., (1985) *Naissance de la nation France*, Paris: Gallimard.

Bloch, M., (1965) *Feudal Society*, London: Routledge (orig. 1940).

Bulpitt, J., (1983) *Territory and Power in the United Kingdom*, Manchester: Manchester University Press.

Cam, H., (1963) *England before Elizabeth*, London: Hutchinson.

Chabod, F., (1961) *L'idea di nazione*, Bari: Laterza.

Clanchy, M.T., (1983) *England and Its Rulers*, Oxford: Blackwell.

Clavero, B., (1989) 'Cataluña como persona, una prosopia jurídica', in *Centralismo y autonomismo en los siglos XVI–XVII*, Barcelona: Publicacions de la Universitat de Barcelona.

Conze, W., (1979) *The Shaping of the German Nation*, London: G. Prior.

Corrigan, P. & Sayer, D., (1985) *The Great Arch. English State Formation as Cultural Revolution*, Oxford: Basil Blackwell.

Davies, R. R., (1984) 'Law and National Identity in Thirteenth Century Wales' in R. R. Davies et al., (eds) *Welsh Society and Nationhood*, Cardiff: University of Wales Press, pp. 51–69.

Detwiler, D., (1976) *Germany, A Short History*, Carbondale: Southern Illinois University Press.

Dickens, A. G., (1974) *The German Nation and Martin Luther*, New York: Harper and Row.

Dickinson, W. C., (1962) *Scotland from the Earliest Times to 1603*, Edinburgh: Thomas Nelson.

Du Boulay, F. R. H., (1970) *An Age of Ambition. English Society in the Late Middle Ages*, London: Nelson.

—— —., (1983) *Germany in the Later Middle Ages*, London: The Athlone Press.

Duby, G., (1973) *Le dimanche de Bouvines*, Paris: Gallimard.

Dupont-Ferrier, G., (1940) 'Le sens des mots "patria" et "patrie" en France au Moyen Age et jusqu'au debut du XVIIe siècle', *Revue Historique*, 188, pp. 89–104.

Fedele, P., (1915) 'La coscienza della nazionalità in Italia nell Medio Evo', *Nuova Antologia* (5th. ser.), 179, pp. 449–62.

Finer, S., (1974) 'State-building, State Boundaries and Border Control', *Social Science Information*, 13 (4–5), pp. 79–126.

Folz, R., (1950) *Le souvenir et la légende de Charlemagne dans l'Empire Germanique médiéval*, Paris: Société d'Edition les Belles Lettres.

Franco, S., (1961) (1969) *The French Renaissance*, London: Macmillan.

Fuhrmann, H., (1986) *Germany in the High Middle Ages*, Cambridge: Cambridge University Press.

Fulbrook, M., (1990) *A Concise History of Germany*, Cambridge: Cambridge University Press.

Galasso, G., (1979) *Storia di Italia. Introduzione.* Torino: Utet.

Ganshof, F. L., (1970) *The Middle Ages: A History of International Relations*, New York: Harper and Row.

Given-Wilson, C., (1986) *The Royal Household and the King's Affinity*, New Haven: Yale University Press.

Goetz, W., (1937) *Das Werden des Italienischen Nationalgefüls*, Sitzungberichte der Bayerischen Akademie der Wissenschften, Heft 7.

Guenée, B., (1967) 'État et nation en France au Moyen Age', *Revue Historique*, 237, pp. 17–30.

— —, (1978) 'Les généalogies entre l'histoire et la politique: la fierté d'être Capétien, en France, au Moyen Age', *Annales*, 33, pp. 450–77.

— —, (1985) *States and Rulers in Late Medieval Europe*, Oxford: Blackwell.

Hallam, E., (1980) *Capetian France, 987–1328*, London: Longman.

Harris, G. L., (1975) *King, Parliament and Public Finance in Medieval England*, Oxford: Oxford University Press.

Hartmann, L.M., (1949) *The Early Medieval State. Byzantium, Italy and the West*, London: the Historical Association.

Hearder, H. & Waley, D., (1963) *A Short History of Italy*, Cambridge: Cambridge University Press.

Herr, F., (1966) 'The Empire as a Regency for God on Earth' in R. Herzstein (ed.), *The Holy Roman Empire in the Middle Ages*, Lexington, Mass.: Heath.

Herzstein, R., (1966) (ed.) *The Holy Roman Empire in the Middle Ages*, Lexington, Mass.: Heath.

Hillgarth, J.C., (1976) *The Spanish Kingdoms*, Oxford: Oxford University Press, 2 vols.

Holt, J.C., (1985) *Magna Carta and Medieval Government*, London: Hambledon.

Huizinga, J., (1984) *Men and Ideas*, Cambridge: Cambridge University Press (orig. 1940).

Hyde, J.K., (1973) *Society and Politics in Medieval Italy*, London: Macmillan.

Ilardi, V., (1956) 'Italianità Among Some Italian Intellectuals in the Early Sixteenth Century', *Traditio*, 12, pp. 339–67.

Jacobson, R., (1945) 'The Beginnings of Self-Determination in Europe', *The Review of Politics*, 7 (1), pp. 29–42.

Jones, M., (1983) 'Bons Bretons et bons Francoys: the Language and Meaning of Treason in Later Medieval France', *Transactions of the Royal Society*, 5th series, vol. 32, pp. 91–112.

— —, (1976) 'Mon Pais and ma Nation: Breton Identity in Fourteenth Century', in C. T. Allmand (ed.) *War, Literature and Politics in the Late Middle Ages*, Liverpool: Liverpool University Press.

Kantorowicz, F. H., (1951) *Pro Patria Mori* in Medieval Thought', *American Historical Review*, 56, pp. 472–92.

Kerhervé, J., (1980) 'Aux origines d'un sentiment national. Les chroniqueurs bretons de la fin du Moyen Age', *Bulletin de la Societé Archéologique du Finistère*, 108, pp. 165–206.

Kibre, P., (1948) *The Nations in Medieval Universities*, Camb., Mass: Harvard University Press.

Kohn, H., (1940) 'The Genesis and Character of English Nationalism', *Journal of the History of Ideas*, 1, pp. 69–94.

— —, (1944) *The Idea of Nationalism*, New York: Macmillan.

Le Roy Ladurie, E., (1978) *Montaillou*, Paris: Gallimard.

Lemarignier, J. F., (1970) *La France médievale: institutions et sociétés*, Paris: Armand Colin.

Leuschner, J., (1980) *Germany in the Late Middle Ages*, Amsterdam: North Holland.

Lewis, A., (1965) *The development of Southern France and Catalan Society, 718–1050*, Austin: University of Texas Press.

— —, (1974) 'The Formation of Terrritorial States in Southern France and Catalonia, 1050–1270 A.D.' in *Medieval Society in Southern France and Catalonia*, London: Variorum Reprint.

Lutz, H., (1982) 'Die deutsche Nation zur Beginn der Neuzeit', *Historische Zeitschrift*, 234, pp. 529–59.

MacKay, A., (1977) *Spain in the Middle Ages*, London: Macmillan.

Mann, N., (1971) 'Humanisme et patriotisme en France au XVe siècle', *Cahiers de l'Association Internationale des Études Françaises*, 23, pp. 51–66.

— —, (1984) *Petrarch*, Oxford: Oxford University Press.

Maravall, J.A., (1954) *El concepto de España en la Edad Media*, Madrid: Instituto de Estudios Políticos.

Marsilius of Padua (1980) *Defensor Pacis*, Toronto: University of Toronto Press.

Mazzei, F., (1980) *Cola di Rienzo*, Milano: Rusconi.

Menendez-Pidal, R., (1950) *The Spaniards in their History*, New York: Columbia University Press.

Mitteis, H., (1953) (1975) *The State in the Middle Ages*, Amsterdam: North Holland Publishers.

Musset, L., (1982) 'Quelques problèmes posés par l'annexion de la Normandie au domaine royale français', in R. H. Bautier (ed.) *La France de Philippe Auguste*, Paris: CNRS, pp. 291–307.

Myers, A. R., (1961) *England in the Late Middle Ages*, Hardsmonworth: Penguin.

Nelli, R., (1969) *La vie quotidienne des Cathares du Languedoc au XIIIe siècle*, Paris: Hachette.

O'Callaghan, J. F., (1975) *A History of Medieval Spain*, Ithaca: Cornell University Press.

O'Corrain, D., (1972) *Ireland before the Normans*, Dublin: The Irish Press.

— —, (1978) 'Nationality and Kingship in pre-Norman Ireland', in T. W. Moody, (ed.) *Nationality and the Pursuit of National Independence*, Belfast: Appletree Press, pp. 1–35.

Pasley, M., (1972) (ed.) *Germany*, London: Methuen.

Payne, S., (1976) *A History of Spain and Portugal*, Madison: University of Wisconsin Press.

Petrarca, P., (1986) *The Revolution of Cola di Rienzo*, New York: Italica Press.

Pocock, J. G. A., (1975) 'British History : A Plea for a New Subject', *Journal of Modern History*, 47, pp. 601–21.

Powicke, M., (1958) *Medieval England*, Oxford: Oxford University Press (orig. 1931).

Procacci, G., (1970) *History of the Italian People*, London: Penguin.

Renouard, I., (1969) '1212–1216', *Etudes d'Histoire médievale*, I, pp. 25–41.

Reuter, T., (1991) *Germany in the Early Middle Ages*, London: Longman.

Reynolds, S., (1984) *Kingdoms and Communities in Western Europe, 900–1300*, Oxford: Clarendon Press.

— —, (1983) 'Medieval *Origines Gentium* and the Community of the Realm', *History*, 68, pp. 375–90.

— —, (1985) 'What do mean by ''Anglo-Saxon'' and ''Anglo-Saxons''?', *Journal of British Studies*, 24, pp. 395–414.

Richet, D., (1973) *La France moderne: l'esprit des institutions*, Paris: Flammarion.

Sanchez-Albornoz, C., (1973) *El drama de la formación de España y los españoles*, Barcelona: Edhasa.

Sayles, G. O., (1977) *The Medieval Foundations of England*, London: Methuen.

Schmidt-Chazan, M., (1977) 'Histoire et sentiment national chez Robert Gaguin', in B. Guenée (ed.) *Le metier d'historien au Moyen Age*, Paris: Publications de la Sorbonne, pp. 233–300.

Sesma, J.A., (1988) 'El sentimiento nacionalista en la Corona de Aragon y el nacimiento de la España moderna' in A. Rucquoi, (ed.) *Realidad e imágenes del poder. España a fines de la Edad Media*, Valladolid: Ámbito.

Seton-Watson, H., (1981) 'Language and National Consciousness', *Proceedings of the British Academy*, Vol. LXVII.

Simone, F., (1969) *The French Renaissance*, London: MacMillan.

Smith, A. D., (1986) *The Ethnic Origins of Nations*, Oxford: Blackwell.

Snyder, L., (ed.) (1975) *Documents of German History*, Wesport, Co.: Greenwood Press.

Stenton, D. M., (1965) *English Society in the Early Middle Ages*, London: Penguin.

Stenton, F. M., (1943) *Anglo-Saxon England*, Oxford: Oxford University Press.

Strayer, J., (1969) (1971) 'France, the Holy Land, the Chosen People and the Most Christian King', in *Medieval Statescraft and the Perspectives of History*, Princeton: Princeton University Press.

— —, (1970) *On the Medieval Origins of the Modern State*, Princeton: Princeton University Press.

Tabacco, G., (1989) *The Struggle for Power in Medieval Italy*, Cambridge: Cambridge University press.

Teillet, S., (1984) *Des Goths à la nation Gothique*, Paris: Société d'éditions Les Belles Lettres.

Tenenti, A., (1986) 'Profilo e limiti delle realtà nazionali in Italia fra quattro e seicento' in V. Branca and S. Graciotti (eds) *Cultura e nazione in Italia e Polonia dal rinascimento all'illuminismo*, Firenze: Olschi.

Teunis, H., (1978) 'The Early State in France' in H. J. Claessen and P. Skalnik (eds) *The Early State*, Mouton: the Hague, pp. 235–55.

Thomson, J. A. F., (1983) *The Transformation of Medieval England*, London: Longman.

Tipton, C. L., (ed.) (1972) *Nationalism in the Middle Ages*, New York: Holt.

Valsecchi, F., (1978) *L'Italia del Risorgimento e l'Europa delle nazion-alità*, Roma: Giuffré Editore.

Vasoli, C., (1986) 'Sperone Speroni e la nascita della coscienza, nationale come coscienza linguistica in V. Branca and S. Graciotti (eds).

Vicens-Vives, J., (1970) *Approaches to the History of Spain*, Berkeley: University of California Press.

Volpe, G., (1978) *Il Medio Evo*, Firenze: Sansoni.

Waley, D., (1969) *The Italian City-Republics*, London: Longman.

Watt, J. A., (1987) 'Gaelic Polity and Cultural Identity' in A. Cosgrove (ed.), *A New History of Ireland* , Vol. II, Oxford: Oxford University Press.

Werner, K. F., (1968) 'Kingdom and Principality in Twelfth Century France' in T. Reuter (ed.), *The Medieval Nobility*, Amsterdam: North Holland, pp. 242–90.

Wickham, C., (1981) *Early Medieval Italy*, London: Macmillan.

Wilkinson, B., (1969) *The Later Middle Ages in England*, London: Longman.

Williams, G., (1979) *Religion, Language and Nationality in Wales*, Cardiff: University of Wales Press.

Williams, G. A., (1985) *When was Wales?* Hardmonsworth: Penguin.

Yates, F.A., (1985) *Astrea. The Imperial Theme in the Sixteenth Century*, London: Routledge.

Zientara, B., (1982) 'La conscience nationale en Europe Occidental au Moyen Age', *Acta Poloniae Historica*, 46, pp. 5–30.

Part II

The Development of Nationalism: Structural Factors

-3-

Capitalism and Nationalism

Can there be established a causal connection between the development of capitalism and the development of nationalism? Any answer at such high level of generality is likely to be unsatisfactory, if nothing else because terms such as 'capitalism' and 'nationalism' have, respectively, different historical and definitional referata. We have already encountered diverse definitions of nationalism, as well as different positions concerning its modernity. As to capitalism, some authors (Pirenne, Lopez) plainly place its origins within the manufacturing and commercial centres of Northern Italia and in the 'Low Countries' in the Middle Ages. The classical sociological tradition (Marx, Weber), as well as many contemporary social scientists (Braudel, Wallerstein, MacFarlane, Mann) prefer the long sixteenth century as the crucial period for the transition from feudalism (whichever way this is defined) to capitalism. Still others (Landes), do not consider capitalism fully-fledged until the Industrial Revolution of the mid-eighteenth century took place, or even better with the major technological innovations (iron, coal, railways) which only came to life in the second half of the nineteenth century.

This quick perusal of approaches to the question of the origins of capitalism should be sufficient to illustrate the dangers of any attempt to causally correlate 'capitalism' and 'nationalism'. It would appear that unless we can rephrase the original question in a more historically and conceptually precise way, we can only contribute to the ongoing ceremony of confusion, but not to sociological explanation. Recently, a consensus seems to have been emerging around the formulations of Ernst Gellner (1964; 1983); in a nutshell, he suggests that it was the development of industrial capitalism and particularly its unevenness that triggered off the development of nationalism.

Can capitalism be reasonably considered the cause for the development of nationalism? Traditionally, this question had a resounding answer in Marxist circles. It was not only that in an economistic perspective nationalism as an ideology was superstructural and hence determined by the capitalist mode of production *strictu senso*. More specifically, this conception assumed that nationalism was the ideology used by capitalists to ensure a national market for themselves by keeping out, through protectionism, foreign capitalists. At the same time, nationalist ideology was seen as an instrument of the class domination of the bourgeoisie over the proletariat, as a sort of cultural diversion to hide economic exploitation. These are, indeed, very crude schemes, but subtlety has never been a characteristic of vulgar materialism.

There is another sense in which the equation 'capitalism generated nationalism' is of meagre interest as a historico-sociological proposition, and it is simply that it has a tautological ring that adds nothing to the quest for the causes of the development of nationalism in the modern world. This is, of course, only in the case of conceiving capitalism as a total social system which would, as of necessity, subsume all that is distinctive in the life of modern society. Nationalism would be an obvious empirical part of it, but the causality would be so diffused and circular that it would cease to have scientific interest; rather it would just constitute a descriptive statement of the state of modernity.

There are two main areas in which classical and contemporary social thinkers differ, and both have fairly important implications for nationalism. Firstly, there is a transition from a societal approach to one based on the concept of world-system (or its equivalent). Secondly, in modern authors there is a much clearer tendency to take the state as an independent variable than in past writers (particularly Marx). It may well be that nationalism cannot be accounted for at the societal level, and that only a world perspective, or at least an inter-state one, will provide the answer. And again, we may have to conclude that whatever the connection between capitalism and nationalism might be, the latter can only be properly accounted for through the mediation of the state. These are important issues which will be examined later in this chapter and in the next one.

At this stage I should like to remind the reader of the provisional conclusions arrived at in Part I. There I tried to show how sentiments of national identity developed in the medieval period, and the prominent role played by the Western European monarchies in fostering these feelings. Whether we can or cannot talk about nationalism in the medieval period is, as I have repeatedly said, a definitional matter. What can be said with certainty is that if one of the preconditions of nationalism is the existence of a mass movement, then obviously the Middle Ages lacked nationalism. But that there was a cultural conception of the nation, as well as a political one (with a very restricted franchise) is obvious to everybody except to those blinded by a very extreme modernist conception of the nation.

Elsewhere (Llobera 1987) I have emphasized how little the sociological classics have to offer on the nation. The fact is that they did not consider the nation as the central category of their sociological scaffolding. Marx, obsessed as he was with the advent of communism, failed to notice the resilience of national sentiments, at times believing them to be little more than a passing creation of the bourgeoisie. Weber was more sensitive to national realities, perhaps because he was a German nationalist himself, and conceived the nation, albeit in its form as a nation-state, as a cultural value, as a community rooted in the population as a whole and exhibiting a long history. In the final instance, both Weber and Marx considered nationalism as closely connected with the development of capitalism in its industrial stage. Braudel had little to say on the nation or nationalism, although in his posthumous work in three volumes (Braudel 1986) on French identity, he posited the very *longue durée*, including geographical factors, in trying to account for the appearance of the French nation. However, he believed it to be an all too recent phenomenon brought about by the French army, the railway system and compulsory schooling – and not forgetting TV in recent times.

In the wealth of writings that Wallerstein has dedicated to the world-system, he has occasionally touched upon the national question. However, in so far as a theory of nationalism presupposes a conceptualization of the nation, Wallerstein's theory is, by his own admission, seriously defective. This is the result of his failure to elaborate hitherto the cultural aspect of the modern world-system. But if a theory of the nation assumes a theory of culture, the former is likely to be reductionist if we generalize on the basis of the clues that Wallerstein has offered in his work. In his *The Modern World-System II*, he defines cultures as 'the ways in which people clothe their political interests and drives in order to express them in space and time, and preserve their meaning' (1980: 65). Like many other social scientists, Wallerstein does not make a clear-cut distinction between state and nation, although he is aware of the differences; for him the only possible relation is that of nation equalling nation-state.

An interesting development in Wallerstein's work is his attempt to graft into the world-system theory a modified conception of the Weberian distinction between class and 'status group' (*Stand*) to account for the existence of ethnicity/nationalism. According to Wallerstein, Weber's trinity of class, status group and party should not be seen as different overlapping groups, but as three different existential forms of the same underlying reality. The problem is to determine when a stratum embodies itself as class, status or party. The strong Wallersteinian theory of nationalism maintains that within the capitalist world-system classes can be reduced to material interests, and that status groups and parties are blurred, often incorrect, collective representations of classes. In situations of acute class conflict the status group lines tend to coincide with class lines. The weak Wallersteinian theory of nationalism maintains that ethnic consciousness is an assertion in the political arena to defend cultural and/or economic interests. And here culture is to be understood in terms of language, religion, history, life-style, etc. or a combination of these in so far as they are used to define the boundaries of a group. From these premises it follows that Wallerstein's failure to provide an explanation of nationalism is due, in the first place, to his economistic, or at best politico-economic, reductionism which pervades his conception of the capitalist world-system, and in the second place, to his inadequate conception of the nation.

In a personal communication to the author, Wallerstein has objected to my strictures pointing out that in his more recent work (Wallerstein 1987) he has gone a long way to counter my arguments. I am not convinced that this is actually the case. In his paper he insists, like E. Hobsbawm and T. Ranger (eds) (1983), on the invented or constructed character of the nation. In his own words: 'the nation hinges around one of the basic structural features of the world economy', that is, 'the political superstructure of this historical system, the sovereign states that form and derive from the interstate system' (Wallerstein, I. 1987: 381). A nation for Wallerstein 'derives from the political structuring of the world-system' (ibid.: 383), in other words, 'statehood preceded nationhood' (ibid.: 384). In the end, though, Wallerstein will insist that the nation is 'in no sense a primordial stable social reality, but a complex clay-like historical product of the capitalist world-economy' (ibid.: 387).

While in his *Sources of Social Power* (Vol. I) Michael Mann did not articulate his arguments on the connection between capitalism and nationalism, it would have been incompatible with his theoretical approach to postulate an ultimate primacy of the economic power. Given the way he referred to the nation-state, it is obvious that nationalism would appear as heavily mediated by the role of the state. In his contribution to a *Festschrift* in Gellner's honour he concludes that 'industrialization was not the principal cause' of nationalism; in fact, 'it arrived too late'. And he adds: 'There were two principal causes: on the one hand, the emergence of commercial capitalism and its universal social classes: on the other, the emergence of the modern state and its professional armed forces and administrators. Conjoined by the fiscal-military pressures exerted by geopolitical rivalry, they produced the politics of popular representation and these formed several varieties of modern nationalism' (1992: 162).

Anthony Giddens has tried to tackle the nationalist phenomenon in his two volume *A Contemporary Critique of Historical Materialism*

(1981; 1985). He defines nationalism as 'the existence of symbols and beliefs which are either propagated by elite groups, or held by many of the members of regional, ethnic, or linguistic categories of a population and which imply a community between them' (Giddens 1981: 190–1). Giddens regards nationalism as a basically modern phenomenon stemming from the aftermath of the French Revolution. Its association 'in time and in fact with the convergent rise of capitalism and the nation-state' (ibid.: 191), is not sufficient ground, he says, for assuming that it is an excrescence of the nation-state and that the latter is a subproduct of capitalism. Giddens also insists that European nationalism is a world of its own and that it should not be generalized to other areas without reference to what he calls 'world-time'. Interestingly enough, though, the connection between capitalism and nationalism, which is rejected at the economistic level, is re-introduced at the psychological level. Nationalism is seen, in this context, as a response to certain 'needs and dispositions' which would appear at a time when, as a result of the commodification of time and space, the individual has lost his ontological security (ibid.: 193–4). Now, to be sure, Giddens does not deny that nationalism is connected with class domination, and that the uneven development of capitalism strongly influenced the 'origins of oppositional nationalism' (1985: 220). And since the idea of an uneven development of (industrial) capitalism is behind a number of recent theories of nationalism, it is time to consider the best known and more influential representatives. I am referring, of course, to Ernst Gellner, Michael Hechter, Tom Nairn and Benedict Anderson.

At first sight it may be surprising to include Ernst Gellner among the proponents of a theory of nationalism anchored on the uneven development of (industrial) capitalism. For one thing, Gellner avoids the expression 'capitalism' (he prefers 'industrial society' or industrialism) and more importantly his theory has been labelled culturalist or linguistic (Smith 1983). But I would tend to agree with Gale Stokes (1986: 594) that, while Gellner is in no way a Marxist, he maintains that nationalism is the unavoidable outcome of an industrial society which requires a spacially ductile labour force. In this sense he qualifies for an economistic vision of nationalism, though this statement will have to be nuanced below. Gellner's first major and influential statement on nationalism came in chapter seven of his *Thought and Change* (1964). There he emphasized that nationalism could only be understood in the context of the impact of industrialization, of the competition between classes in the newly created industrial stratification and of the integrating effects of language and education. The processes of industrialization undermined the traditional social structures and gave primacy to cultural elements (essentially communication). The identity of an individual was no longer defined in terms of his social relations but in terms of his culture. And culture and nationality are closely related. Only the state could provide through the educational system and the official language the kind of 'cultured' persons required by the process of industrialization. The fact that modernization and industrialization spread in an uneven fashion created a new system of social stratification – a class system – which was felt to be unacceptable because of its illegitimacy. If this overlaps with cultural differences, an uneasy alliance between a culturally displaced intelligentsia and an overexploited proletariat may lead to national secession.

In 1983 came the long awaited publication of Gellner's definitive statement on nationalism in the form of a slender volume entitled *Nations and Nationalism*. The book does not represent a major theoretical shift, though he has tried to account for the more disruptive aspects of nationalism (separatism, violence) which he had neglected in the past. The major thrust of his theory is still very much that 'it was social chasms (doubled with cultural differences) created by early industrialism, and by the unevenness of its diffusion, which made it [nationalist conflict] acute' (1983: 121). And he has no qualms in stating once again that 'the specific roots of nationalism are found in the distinctive structural requirements of industrial society' (ibid.: 31).

The Gellnerian model of nationalist development strongly emphasizes that nationalism has its roots in the new industrial order, and that nothing before this period – Gellner's agrarian society – can be equated to nationalism because political units were not defined in terms of cultural boundaries. Since for Gellner nations can only be defined in terms of the age of nationalism, he cannot conceive of the nation as an imaginative vision created by intellectuals in order to legitimize the medieval (agrarian) state (monarchy) in Western Europe. Besides industrialization, Gellner's second emphasis is on modernization (population explosion, rapid urbanization, labour migration, penetration of local economies by a global economy). Following Weber, he admits that the Protestant Reformation must have had an impact on nationalism; so did colonialism and imperialism.

It is essential in Gellner's conception that nations should be invented; the idea of ethno-national potential is for him that of a raw material of limited if any importance. I believe that industrial society only served to reinforce an existing phenomena; Gellner's theory fails completely to account for the nationalist developments in Western Europe, which were largely present prior to industrialization and in any case followed a different pattern from his predictions. In the final resort, his approach cannot escape the constraints of its economistic scaffolding, and this is why Gellner cannot understand what motivates nationalists, except maybe socio-economic mobility. If this does not smack of vulgar materialism, what does?.

There is a long intellectual pedigree to the idea that ethnonational identities within states can be explained in terms of a theory of internal colonialism (Orridge 1981). The theory is a variant of older, Marxist-inspired imperialist and dependency theories. Its most immediate antecedents, though, can be traced back to the Latin American literature of the 1960s. In a nutshell, the idea that states exhibit strong internal inequalities based on ethnic lines (Indians in Latin America, blacks in the USA) was transplanted to Europe where it received a regional basis. In his classical study of the United Kingdom – *Internal Colonialism* – Michael Hechter (1975) maintained that industrialization aggravated an already existing situation of economic dependency and inequality of the Celtic fringe (Scotland, Wales and Ireland) *vis-à-vis* England and this manifested itself first in differential political behaviour and later in ethnonational movements. Hechter emphasized as well the unequal development of industrialism within states. He suggested that in each country there is a region which is favoured by capitalist development, while the others are subordinated. Furthermore, he also defended the idea that instead of national culture, what we have is a core culture which dominates over the others by establishing ethnic boundaries. The key feature of Hechter's theory is the idea of a cultural division of labour existing between the core and the periphery; that is, there developed a system of stratification by means of which the dominant group at the core was in a position to monopolize social positions, which had high prestige in the society, while the members of the peripheral cultures were assigned social roles which were considered inferior. The further industrialization advanced in its uneven way, the internal differences became more accentuated; ethnonationalism emerged as a response to a situation of perceived dependence and exploitation.

Hechter's intention was to articulate a model valid not only for the UK, but for Europe as a whole. It is unclear whether he meant to give it a wider application, though some of his followers have used it to account for ethnonationalist movements in the newly formed states. The appeal of Hechter's ideas is hardly surprising given the eagerness with which social scientists and politicians alike embrace economistic explanations. The model was convenient, although one must insist that Hechter's argument in relation to the UK was both scholarly and persuasive. Unfortunately, many of his followers translated the theory into an extremely simplistic equation in which ethnonationalism was seen as a direct response to an objective situation of economic dependence.

Returning now to Hechter's theory it was obvious from the start that even as a regional – European – theory of ethnonationalism (and this was already an important limitation) it was plagued with glaring anomalies. A well-aired criticism against Hechter's approach was that his theory was unable to account adequately for major ethnonationalist movements like the Scottish one, and even less for the Basque and Catalan variants which actually developed in the most industrialized areas of Spain. Hechter and Levi (1979) tried to counter some of these criticisms by putting forward a modified theory of internal colonialism which incorporated within it the notion of a cultural division of labour, the idea of a segmental division. In their own words: 'the members interact wholly within the boundaries of their own group' (1979: 263) and an elite manages to monopolize the key positions in the social structure. It is arguable how far this modified approach, which also gives more prominence to the role of the state, can be seen as a retreat from the original idea that the uneven development of industrialism was the primary factor which accounted for the development of ethnonationalism. While Anthony D. Smith (1983) seems to believe that in spite of the amendments Hechter's theory is still 'flawed by its reductionist assumptions that cultural cleavages and ethnic sentiments can be wholly derived from purely economic and spatial characteristics' (1983: XVI), A. W. Orridge is less negative, accepting that 'uneven development has played an important role in the genesis of many forms of nationalism' (1981: 189), though in other instances it was 'at most a subsidiary factor' (ibid.).

The contributions of Tom Nairn to a general theory of nationalism are contained in chapter nine of his *The Break Up of Britain*. Stemming from a Marxist tradition, but acknowledging that 'the theory of nationalism represents Marxism's great historical failure' (1977: 329), Nairn insisted that only by focusing on the ravages and contradictory effects of uneven development, could we hope to understand nationalism. Capitalism may have unified mankind, but at the price of great desequilibria and tremendous antagonisms which have triggered off a process of socio-political fragmentation, affecting even the Old Continent. Nationalism was the result of certain aspects of the world political economy in the modern era; it was a way that peripheral countries found to defend themselves against the core. This was done by interclass mobilization on the basis of a different identity from that of the alien dominating state (1977: 340). Nationalism had of necessity to express itself through the cultural peculiarities of each area. In conclusion, for Nairn nationalism was the socio-historical cost of the accelerated implantation of capitalism at a world level. It is arguable how reductionist Nairn's theory is, though in Anthony D. Smith's survey it is classified as 'an economistic model of nationalism' (1983: XVI). Nairn maintains that nationalist phenomena cannot be reduced to economic trends, rather that the former are given real force by the latter.

Finally, I would like to make a brief reference to Benedict Anderson's *Imagined Communities*, which emphasizes a somewhat neglected area in the relations between capitalism and nationalism in the early modern period. Anderson's definition of the nation as an 'imagined political community – and imagined as both limited and sovereign' (1983: 15) has had an extraordinary appeal, as if people had been waiting for such an expression to be coined. His argument about the origins of nationalism lead him to focus on the tremendous impact of print capitalism. The book was, after all, the first commodity produced in a massive way. This was one area in which early capitalists, using the new technology of production available, were able to make great profits. Having exhausted the market in Latin, capitalists turned to the vernaculars. The effect of print-language was felt on national consciousness by means of creation of a unified language which allowed a sizeable part of the population to read the same texts and identify with each other. Furthermore, by giving a fixity to language it was possible to develop the idea of the antiquity of one's nation. Anderson concluded that 'what made the new communities imaginable was a half-conscious, but explosive interaction between a system of production and productive relations (capitalism), a technology of communications and the type of fatality of human linguistic diversity' (1983: 46). At a later stage in history state consolidation both at home and in the colonies created groups of people who felt politically and culturally excluded and by imagining themselves as communities were able to shake off alien rule.

In this chapter I have tried to assess a point of view which has insidiously penetrated a good number of arguments on the origins and growth of nationalism. It is simply the assumption that (industrial) capitalism is the *deus ex machina* of modernity, and that nationalism, as part of this modernity, is its necessary outcome. I have said that I have no quarrel with this idea if capitalism is conceptualized as a self-generating and comprehensive reality encompassing everything that is modern; in any case, expressed like that, this proposition can only be true at a tautological level, and as such has limited scientific scope. At the other extreme, there are those authors who believe that it is possible to establish a causal connection between the development of the capitalist mode of production *strictu senso* and nationalism; in other words, that the latter can be accounted for in terms of economic factors. In this conception the focus is on the creation of a national market by the bourgeoisie and on nationalism as an ideology generated by the latter to hide class exploitation. My argument is not that the bourgeoisie has not used nationalist ideologies to further its economic objectives and political domination. The issue here, which seems to escape vulgar materialists, both of

Marxist and non-Marxist persuasions, is that the complexity of nationalism precludes such simplistic assumptions.

One of the encouraging developments of the past few years has been a move against the economistic approaches of the past. A common denominator of recent theories has been the centrality of the state, conceived as a more or less autonomous entity, in the generation of nationalism. In this sense, the capitalist mode of production has ceased to be the single factor accounting for nationalism. However, a negative development has been the emphasis on industrial capitalism, precisely because it appears in the Western European horizon *post festum*, when national identities are already there. Industrialism may accelerate the nationalist process, but it does not create it. I believe that this overemphasis on industrialism is the result either of ignoring the medieval national legacy or, what comes to be the same, of adopting a modernist definition of the nation. There is still much to be explored about the early development of capitalism and nationalism. Anderson's print capitalism is an excellent example of how to relate one to the other. As to the spread and consolidation of nationalism under industrial capitalism, we had a number of original contributions, such as Giddens' idea of the connection between the capitalist commodification of time and space and nationalism. However, before reaching any final conclusion we should look at the impact of the formation of the Western European states on nationalism.

Bibliography

Anderson, B., (1983) *Imagined Communities*, London: New Left Books.

Braudel, F., (1986) *L'identité de la France*, Paris: Flammarion, 3 vols.

Gellner, E., (1964) *Thought and Change*, London: Weidenfeld and Nicholson.

— —, (1964) *Nations and Nationalism*, Oxford: Blackwell.

Giddens, A., (1981) *A Contemporary Critique of Historical Materialism*, London: Macmillan.

— —, (1985) *The Nation-State and Violence*, Cambridge: Polity Press.

Hechter, M., (1975) *Internal Colonialism*, London: Routledge and Kegan Paul.

Hechter, M. & Brustein, W., (1980) 'Regional Modes of Production and Patterns of State Formation in Europe', *American Journal of Sociology*, 85, pp. 1061–94.

Hechter, M. & Levy, M., (1979) 'The Comparative Analysis of Ethno-Regional Movements', *Ethnic and Racial Studies*, 2, pp. 260–74.

Hobsbawm, E. & Ranger, T. (eds), (1983) *The Invention of Tradition*, Cambridge University Press.

Llobera. J.R., (1987) 'Nationalism: Some Methodological Issues', *JASO*, XVIII: pp. 13–25.

MacFarlane, A., (1987) *The Culture of Capitalism*, Oxford: Blackwell.

Mann, M., (1986) *The Sources of Social Power I*, Cambridge University Press.

— —, (1992) 'The Emergence of Modern European Nationalism' in J. Hall & I. C. Jarvie (eds) (1992) *Transition to Modernity*, Cambridge: Cambridge University Press, pp. 137–65.

Marx, K., (1973) *The Communist Manifesto*, New York: International Publishers.

Nairn, T., (1977) *The Break-Up of Britain*, London: New Left Books.

Orridge, A. W., (1981) 'Uneven Development and Nationalism, I and II', *Political Studies*, XXIX, 1–15, pp. 181–90.

Smith, A. D., (1981) *Ethnic Revival*, Cambridge University Press.

— —, (1983) *Theories of Nationalism*, London: Duckworth.

Stokes, G., (1986) 'How is Capitalism Related to Nationalism?' *Comparative Studies in Society and History*, 28, pp. 591–8.

Wallerstein, I., (1974) *The Modern World-System I*, New York: Academic Press.

— —, (1979) *The Capitalist World-Economy*, Cambridge University Press.

— —, (1980) *The Capitalist World-System II*, New York: Academic Press.

— —, (1987) 'The Construction of Peoplehood: Racism, Nationalism, Ethnicity', *Sociological Forum*, 2, pp. 373–88.

-4-

State and Nationalism

That there is a close relationship between state and nation is well illus-trated in the everyday vulgar parlance, but also in the politically literate one, which confuses one with the other, or rather by assuming the total hegemony of the nation-state refers to each state as a nation. Contemporary states inexorably call themselves nations independently of whether within their territories other nations different from the domi-nant one may exist. What is obviously crucial here is the fact that in modern times the nationality principle is so pervasive as a way of legiti-mation that no state can survive without it. According to William McNeill (1986) this is in sharp contrast to earlier periods of history in which polyethnic structures were the norm. 'The idea that a government rightfully should rule only over citizens of a single ethnos started to develop in Western Europe towards the end of the Middle Ages' (1986: 7); it took off by the end of the eighteenth century and had its zenith after World World I.

In theory, of course, the state can and often does use force to achieve obedience from its subjects. But forced loyalty is at odds with the mod-ern ideology of both the liberal-democratic and totalitarian conceptions of the state (though in the latter, in fact, it is just a façade), as well as being difficult to obtain except when physical and moral violence needs to be exerted on only a relatively small, dissident minority. It is an important feature of the modern state that it transmogrifies itself into a nation ('an imagined political community' in B. Anderson's appropriate expression), which is an object of love, attachment, devotion and even passion; and for which one is prepared to undergo the most harrowing sacrifices (including giving one's life) and commit the most horrendous of crimes (against other nationals or against 'traitors'). In many modern states the processes of state-building and nation-building have gone hand in hand, often being the distinguishable but inseparable parts of the same phenomenon. Expressed in a different way, the structures of the modern state can neither be left empty nor can they function with any other content than the one provided by the national idea. What the expression may evoke in different historical circumstances and in different countries will obviously vary, and no doubt the reference to the community will take an array of different, often tortuous paths.

The idea of the modern state, an expression which occurs with predictable monotony and practically a total consensus in the specialized literature, refers to the centralized, territorial polity which began to take shape by the thirteenth century and was completed, in its essentials, by the seventeenth century. As we have seen in Part I, the modern state emerged, through a slow and uneven process of construction, from the raw materials of a situation – the early medieval world – in which sovereignty was fragmented and multidimensional, the idea of territorial unity was practically non-existent and the administrative apparatus was personalized and reduced to a minimum. The medieval state was in the words of Heinrich Mitteis 'an association between persons' (1975: 5), usually between unequal partners (lord and vassal); the process by means of which this *Personenverbandsstaat* was transformed by the monarchy into a territorial and institutionalized state is graphically referred to by Mitteis as *Verstaatung* (statification). That the modern state is different from the medieval or feudal state (assuming that the latter deserved the name of state at all) is all too obvious. How *sui generis* the modern state is as compared with the ancient state is another matter. In fact, Dolf Sternberger (1984) has convincingly shown, the ancient state contained at least some of the essential characteristics – securing citizen's freedom, for example – of the modern state.

The Western European experience of medieval state-building is commonly seen to follow two basic patterns, which for the sake of the argument can be referred to as the French model and the English model (Strayer, J.R. 1970). In the French model, state-building is said to have taken place in the context of the monarch having to bring together a variety of territorial principalities with idiosyncratic linguistic, cultural and institutional characteristics. In this case, the process of state-building was of necessity slow and subject to ups and downs, and the homogenizing task was far from being completed by the end of the medieval period. If at the administrative level what kept the state together was, as we have seen, a number of key institutions which were enforced by the presence of the king's representatives in each of the principalities and provinces, at the ideological level it was the invention of the nation, 'France' in this case, that cemented the kingdom. In the English model, the process of state-building is said to have followed a much smoother path because the kingdom was already unified and homogeneous by the time the modern state emerged. This would partly explain why the ideological need for seeing the kingdom, England in this case, as a nation was a less urgent and easier task. On the other hand, the idea of England is problematic as a model because it abstracts from the historical reality of a state incorporating the Celtic lands.

By 1470 Sir John Fortescue, an English jurist, had already articulated, in an idiosyncratic anglophile way, the main features of the two types of state. Using the Aquinian classification of governments into *dominium regale* (absolute rule), *dominium politicum* (popular rule) and *dominium regale et politicum* (popular sovereignty delegated to the monarch), Fortescue characterized the French model as that leading to an absolute monarchy – 'what pleases the prince has force of law' – while the English one led to a constitutional monarchy in which the king governed with the consent of Parliament – 'the king exists for the sake of the kingdom, not the kingdom for the sake of the king' (Stubbs, W. 1897, III: 247). Although Fortescue favoured the *dominium regale et politicum*, he was well aware that 'different countries might require different laws' (Plucknett, T. 1931, 6: 388), and hence, long before Montesquieu, '[he] sought for the spirits of the laws of England and France' (ibid.).

The assumption, however, that these two models can account for the experience of medieval state-building in the whole of Europe is, in my opinion, unwarranted because both models lead to the national state if not the nation-state. It implies that alternative models (city-states, small states, federations, empires) not only soon disappeared but contributed little or nothing to the shape of the modern state, while in fact the very opposite is true. Patriotism, for example, was originally associated with the city-state (particularly in Italia), while it was in the small states or principalities were modern political institutions like parliaments, or rather *Stände*, first emerged. Federations regretfully were not the preferred model of the early modern and modern periods, but they have a strong appeal today, while empires, always on the wane according to the heralds of the nation-state, have survived well into the twentieth century (at least in Central and Eastern Europe); furthermore, many a nation-state turns out to be a multinational state on close inspection. Charles Tilly (1975: 26) is right in saying that from the perspective of the fourteenth century there is no way of predicting which type of state is likely to emerge in a later period, but he is wrong in insisting that by 1500 the national state had established its hegemony. My point here is that the medium-sized so-called national state is not the only form that the modern state takes, and for two reasons. First, this is because other forms obviously persisted practically into our days; and second, because what is labelled a national state is often, even today, a multinational state, and in any case it only became a unitary state rather late and imperfectly (for example the eighteenth century for the Spanish state).

Is it possible to identify the necessary steps for the medieval development of the modern state? Joseph R. Strayer (1970: 5–10) has suggested the existence of the following signs:

(1) There must be a political unit with a defined territory and a time dimension. One of the preconditions of state-building is the continued presence of people who live and work in the same area for generations. An additional but crucial element is the presence of a core area which acts as a centre and motor for the whole process of the making of the state. The end of the era of invasions made possible a more stable society and allowed for spatio-temporal continuities.

(2) There must be long-lasting institutions served by a permanent, impersonal and specialized efficient bureaucracy. The Church was undoubtedly a speculum into which states could gaze for institutional models.

(3) The polity must be able to generate feelings of, if not absolute, at least of paramount loyalty from all its subjects, making sure that other loyalties (family, religion, province) are subordinated to the loyalty owed to the state.

(4) The appearance of the idea of sovereignty. This was related to the idea that the ruler – the monarch – was the final legal authority and the guarantor of justice. No doubt the impact of Roman law accelerated the process.

In an earlier contribution, Strayer (1963) had examined more specifically the connection between state formation and nation-building. His main proposition was that where a medium-sized *regnum* (that is, originally a barbarian kingdom) was turned into a single state, national identity developed without major frictions and without the need to use highly pitched emotional calls; linguistic and cultural variations progressively disappeared or were disarmed of their centrifugal potential. No doubt unitary states like England had an advantage over mosaic states like France and managed to develop national unity at an earlier stage. However, when different states were created as a result of breaking up a *regnum*, the development of nationhood was very problematic, argues Strayer, because 'there was no correspondence between the political framework and the ancient traditions of the people. The historical, cultural, and linguistic group to which people felt they belonged was always larger than the state to which they were supposed to give their allegiance' (1963: 24). The existence of the state bureaucracies was also an impediment to the creation of a nation-state out of a multiplicity of small states in the nineteenth century. Germany and Italy are well known cases in point. Even more complicated was the condition of the Habsburg and Ottoman empires, which were 'mosaic states largely made up of splinters of several *regna*' (1963: 25). How could a sense of nationhood develop there? Things are, however, more complicated than they appear in Strayer's model. In my view he gives too much importance to the *regna* as *deus ex machina* of the European nations. Furthermore, he contradicts himself by, on the one hand, asserting the original ethnic diversity of the *regna* only later to assume that a splintered *regnum* breaks up a unity. In general, he is also prisoner of the idea that the nation-state must of necessity have a medium-sized territorial dimension. He rightly emphasizes, though, the role of the medieval state in shaping nationhood.

At a more abstract level, Norbert Elias (1982) has discovered some key mechanisms of the period under consideration (late medieval and early modern). The first he refers to as the monopoly mechanism, and it is the tendency to formation of territorial and political monopolies from a starting point in which a plethora of territorial principalities compete within a given area. Elias' point is that in the long run the stronger states tend to absorb the weaker ones. The ideal model for this type of development is France (Gallia in our terminology), but the mechanism obviously has wider geographical application. The second mechanism is the institutionalization of power. With the increased penetration of royal power into the different layers of society and with sustained economic development the tendency of the state is to specialize its functions and to develop impersonal bureaucracies. This is also a mechanism which applies generally, but in the early period it is typical of England. Finally, there is the royal mechanism. It refers to the ability of the state to centralize functions and maximize power by playing the different *Stände* and provinces against each other within a given country. The French and Castillian monarchies were both succesful at this game.

Elias has explored this process of long term state formation by focusing on certain behavioural patterns (etiquette, ritual) developed by the aristocracy during the late Middle Ages and culminating in the early modern period. The so-called 'civilizing process' turned warriors into courtiers through the imposition of strict rulers of behaviour at a number of levels. It is Elias' contention that these changes closely correlated with the progressive monopolization of military and fiscal power of the state. Elias' *magnum opus* in two volumes was originally published in German in the fatal year of 1939 and had little sociological impact until the late 1960s when it was reprinted and later translated into different languages. It is difficult to know the real, underground influence of

Über den Prozess der Zivilisation during its wilderness years. What is obvious is that Elias anticipated many theoretical developments in the area of state formation that are now taken for granted. Another matter is what to make of some of the claims made by the participants in Elias' honour. Koenigsberger (1977: 300), for example, assures us that Elias' theory is more powerful than the classical class-struggle centred Marxist theory, for two reasons: when dealing with the late medieval and early modern period it avoids the anachronistic concept of class, and it is void of teleology. Despite the praising, Koenigsberger is well aware of the limitations of Elias' theory. For all their abstractness, Elias' mechanisms derive too closely from the experience of only two countries (England and France). More importantly, Elias provides us only with a probabilistic theory of state formation, with no reference to either where the centre or the boundaries of the state would be. Furthermore, the model is also too vague concerning the time-scale of its development.

How does Elias conceive of the relationship between state-formation and nation-building? Renan's celebrated dictum that nations are not eternal but rather new phenomena is Elias' starting point. Both, of course, define nations in political terms; it was the transition from people being subjects to people being citizens that inaugurated the nation-states in the second half of the eighteenth century. In other words, for Elias, the long transition from a dynastic to a national state has to do with 'changes in the distribution of power within a state society. It was on the one hand a change in the distribution of power between social strata as well as in the nature of social stratification. It was on the other hand a change in the distribution of power between governments and governed' (Elias, N. 1972: 279–80).

Now, according to Elias, the emergence of the nation is the long term result of two types of processes: territorial or regional integration and strata integration. The overall process was extremely slow; in fact, Elias insists that the privileged groups controlling the state (mostly landowners), kept their positions of power until 1914. So, for Elias, a fully-fledged national state only occurs when the working classes achieve a degree of political power within modern society. It is in this sense that the expression 'industrialization and nation-building are two facets of the same transformation of societies' (1972: 282) must be understood; that is, what matters are the long term changes towards a more representative type of government that heralded the emergence of the modern nation. In looking at the past the focus should be on the role played by the parliaments and the *Stände*, and particularly the transformation of the Third Estate during the French Revolution; in the nineteenth and twentieth centuries the rallying points have been the political parties.

Nation-building, as defined by Elias, is far from having been accomplished even in the most industrialized countries, in so far as the integration of the population within the state in terms of distribution of economic and political power is still imperfect. The recrudescence of economic and political hierarchization on a regional or a class basis in recent times, has recreated in a different, maybe less extreme form, the 'two-nations situation' described by Disraeli in the nineteenth century.

At this stage it is again important to remind ourselves that the modern state did not appear in a political vacuum, but rather in the context of a number of other emerging, sovereign states; in other words, what characterized Western Europe from the late medieval period onwards was the existence of a system of states within the same civilizational *ecumene*. Neither *imperium* nor *ecclesia* succeeded in imposing their domination: the consequence was a constellation of autonomous states. This was indeed a rare development in a world in which despotic-theocratic empires were the rule. We will return to this topic later.

Otto Hintze (1975) was not only one of the first theoreticians of the state to distinguish clearly and analyze the internal structure of the state and its external existence; more importantly, he established the way in which the development of the state, in connection with its neighbours, affected its internal organization. Conflicts and wars between states in a given arena are within the normal horizon of a state, that is, 'the external configuration, the size of a state, its contiguity (whether strict or loose) and even its ethnic composition' (1975: 160). Internal political developments can only be studied in the changing context of the external existence of the state, because it is the latter which, in each historical period, gives us the appropriate framework. A typology of state 'shapes' and its corresponding constitutional forms was schematized by Hintze: empires are correlated with despotism, city-states with direct democracy, territorial states with estate systems and national states with representative systems.

If we want to understand how the European countries slowly developed their sense of nationality, we can only find the answer in the different ways in which states were created and grew. Hintze was critical of the attempts to explain the different types of state by exclusive reference to the then – Hintze was writing at the turn of the twentieth century – popular idea of *Volksgeist*. In the end, there is of course a reciprocal relationship between the internal and the external aspects of the state; Hintze's conception is here organismic rather than mechanical, and he envisaged the inner and outer worlds of the state as living, interacting forces. In his own words: 'The process by which a state is shaped produces aims, habits, needs and views, and these create among leaders and masses a distinct intellectual disposition that favours a particular type of constitutional structure' (1975: 162).

Hintze rightly emphasized the anomalous character of the modern European state system; the historical rule was rather world-empires (the city-states of Ancient Greece and Italy were after all developments within narrow geographical spaces). Europe was, in the final resort, a failed empire: the end product, by default, of the struggles between the Papacy and the Holy Roman Empire. The appeal of the idea of a European (universal Christian) empire was there all the time, but by the end of the Middle Ages a number of sovereign states, that is, independent from Pope and Emperor, had appeared. Within the limits of custom and force, European states recognized each other's right to exist, and from that emerged a framework of inter-state law on which to operate. It was in the context of such an interaction that many internal state developments took place. Hintze explained the appearance of the *Stände* as a result of the conflict between spiritual and temporal power and the existence of a coordinated but competitive system of states.

One of the crucial problems for Otto Hintze was how to account for the transition from the territorial states with *Stände* to the modern, unitary, national states. Here is where absolutist rule played a key part. However, what triggered off the absolutist process is not that clear, though Hintze placed great weight on the French development of military might as a result of France's confrontation with the Habsburg Empire in the early modern period. With the emergence of a strong French state the other European powers had no option but to follow suit if they wanted to preserve their sovereignty, and the only way of doing that was by developing a number of features (centralization, monopoly of force, homogenization, bureaucratization, etc.) which are typical of the modern state. We shall return to this issue when considering the work of Charles Tilly.

Not all European states, however, developed absolute monarchy in the early modern period; some small states, the Netherlands and Switzerland for example, avoided it altogether, while the Spanish monarchy, excepting the Castilian domain, did not become absolutist in Hintze's terms until the eighteenth century with the abolition of the parliaments of the different principalities of the old Kingdom of Aragon. England's geographical situation, its homogeneity and early development as a unified state, made absolutism unnecessary. Hans Kohn (1940) saw in sixteenth-century England the first European nation, but even such statements have to be qualified. There was a small number of people, an elite of about five per cent of the population, who derived a certain amount of solidarity from considering England as a community, as a nation. However, their loyalty was only in part patriotic; it was based, more importantly on bonds of common interest and in the adherence to the monarchic legality. In the history of the English idea of nation the cultural element was often subordinated to the process of extending political rights to ever-expanding layers of population.

It is true that the success of the different European states in creating a unified political structure varied from state to state, but none of them totally accomplished the task they set themselves to achieve. The reasons for this failure are only too obvious: the resistance, not only regional, that they encountered inside their borders. Nonetheless, some countries, like France, were remarkably successful in breaking down the internal barriers and intermediate forces which existed between the state and the individual. This process of atomization is what characterizes the modern state; and it is in this context that the idea of citizen and citizen's rights appeared. It was precisely the process of political uniformization – every man as a taxpayer – that made it possible. Hintze concludes that this type of state allowed for the development of an incipient common interest, stemming from the fact of belonging, as objects of rule, to the same polity. Under the appropriate circumstances, for example, the French Revolution, a sentiment of political nationhood may spread like fire to engulf the whole territory. *La nation c'est le peuple, parce que le peuple c'est la nation.*

H.G. Koenigsberger (1977), who has tried to combine Hintze's typological correlations with Elias' long term historical dynamics, still ends up with a number of unsolved problems. To start with, a number of European monarchies did not operate within enclosed political systems, that is, they were composite systems in which they had multiple parliaments which could take momentous decisions affecting the monarchy. Catalonia within Spain, and Scotland within Britain are cases in point (at least until the beginning of the eighteenth century). Second, the process of state building could be stopped by foreign intervention, an event difficult to predict. Third, the conflict between king and parliament occurred at a time of religious confrontation, with a danger of religious splits and alien interventions. Finally, a number of other elements could affect the outcome (specific parliamentary rules, the role of a great statesman, the presence or absence of male heirs to the monarchy, etc.).

In recent years the most influential text on the origins, structure and dynamics of the national state has been a book edited by Charles Tilly under the title of *The Formation of National States in Western Europe.* Once again it should be made clear that what is meant by the label 'national state' is not necessarily a strictly defined nation-state, but rather a modern state which is neither a city-state nor an empire, and which exhibits the following features: '(1) it controlled a well-defined, continuous territory; (2) it was relatively centralized; (3) it was differentiated from other organizations; (4) and it reinforced its claims through a tendency to acquire a monopoly over the concentrated means of physical coercion within its territory' (Tilly, C. 1975: 27). In the early modern period, the ethno-national element was not central for the emergent state; in fact, as I have already said, during the absolutist era the ethno-national element receded into the background, because the power politics of territorial expansion was paramount and such a policy was not particularly congenial to ethno-national considerations. None of the three major ideologists of the emerging modern state – Machiavelli, Hobbes and Bodin – had much place for the ethno-national element in their characterization of the state (Passerin d'Entreves, A. 1967: 170–1), though in Machiavelli there was a nationalist angle of sorts.

It is well known that Machiavelli was the first modern political thinker who really understood the origins, structure, meaning and consequences of the modern state. His radical break with medieval thinking is best exemplified in his attitude towards the theocratic principle. He not only paid no attention to it, but on the whole he assumed that the state was associated with power of the secular type. For Machiavelli religion was to have a subordinate role as an instrument of power, and that is why he favoured earthly religions rather than otherworldly ones. With Machiavelli the state comes up of age, and its sovereign finds its justification in itself rather than in God. Although his political experience was that of the small Italian principalities, his perspective was that of a man who scanned the Western European horizon (Cassirer, E. 1946). It is true that nationalist considerations did not enter into Machiavelli's legitimation of the state, which in Gramsci's words was either by force or consent. Now the last chapter of *The Prince* contains a vibrant exhortation to liberate Italy from the Barbarians. Many commentators, including Cassirer, have considered this chapter an anomaly, a rhetorical and emotional call in the midst of cool political theory, and have gone as far as to suggest that it might have been added to the original text. One has to admit that Machiavelli's extemporaneous appeal to *italianità* may sound out of place and out of character, but in fact it was in line with a prior humanistic concern for the fate of Italy which was there before (in Dante, Petrarca and others), as well as a serious commitment in Machiavelli's part (Gilbert, F. 1954).

Returning to the issue of the national monarchies, J.A. Maravall (1961), who had an axe to grind in relation to the Spanish monarchy of the early modern period, insisted not only that there were clear 'proto-nationalist characterisitcs' in the states of the period (particularly France, England and Spain), but also even that 'the policies of the great monarchs of the late fifteenth and sixteenth centuries were based on a pre-national type of community consciousness' (1961: 795). He was aware, however, that the policies of the kings were not limited by national considerations. What cannnot be denied, of course, is the existence of voices which might have put forward patriotic or even nationalist ideas to reinforce the state. The case of the so-called Spanish monarchy is, however, dubious as an example because until the eighteenth century there is no clear idea of the boundaries of Spain. Furthermore, and as H. Koenigsberger has remarked, 'the Spanish monarchy ... was singularly ineffective in promoting either institutional or emotional unity among its Spanish kingdoms' (1975: 171).

Tilly's remark that by 1500 there were about five hundred more or less politically autonomous units in Western Europe, while by 1900 there were only about twenty-five independent states, is a poignant reminder of the ferocious state struggles that characterized the period. The kind of question that needs answering is, what sort of features are required in a given polity for it to '(1) survive into the following period as a distinct unit; (2) undergo territorial consolidation, centralization, and differentiation of the instruments of government from other sort of organization and monopolization of the means of coercion; (3) become the nucleus of a national state?' (Tilly, C. 1975: 40).

In the end Tilly and his colleagues come out with the ten commandments or general conditions which account for the survival of the political units:

1) Thou shalt have extractible resources.

2) Thou shalt live spatially and temporally in a protected position.

3) Thou shalt produce a continuous crop of statesmen.

4) Thou shalt be successful in war.

5) Thou shalt create a homogeneous population.

6) Thou shalt ally with the landed aristocracy.

7) Thou shalt be aware of how expensive state building is.

8) Thou shalt realize that there is a close connection between war, military organization, the fiscal system and decentralization.

9) Thou shalt know that the different types of government are largely the result of the changing coalitions between the central power and the major social classes.

10) Thou shalt be familiar with the fact that in the long run homogenization is a key variable in order to explain the 'structure and effectiveness of government' (Tilly, C. 1975: 632–3).

There is no way of quantifying the relative weight of each factor, but no doubt their presences and absences tended to balance each other. Repeated military defeats were determinant in erasing or keeping political units under control. Catalonia is a case in point of a political unit which failed to appear as an indepedent state (though it preserved a strong sense of identity) in modern times because of continuous defeats in war; Holland and Portugal successfully disengaged themselves from the Habsburg monarchy in the seventeenth century. The eighth commandment is of the greatest importance, in spite of its apparent circularity. Homogenization is a factor which duly becomes important only in modern times.

There are three main areas in which a parallelism can be established between Tilly's approach and that of Wallerstein's world system perspective. First, national states become dominant organizations as the capitalist system expands and as particular parts of the world become integrated into that system. Second, the chief forms taken by the national states depend on the identities of their dominant classes. Third, the economic strength of those dominant classes (modified by the extent and character of their dependency on the dominant classes of other states) determines the strength, durability, effectiveness and responsiveness of the state.

What is obviously missing from the list of conditions or commandments laid down by Tilly is a more explicit reference to the fact that Western Europe can only make sense if it is taken as an inter-state system. Tilly is well aware of this issue (1975: 45) but does not develop it at any length. How this system was created in the late medieval and early modern period cannot be explained in terms of Wallerstein's materialist world-system theory, which contemplates political structures as epiphenomena of economic structures or as the result of systemic needs, and cultural systems as determined both by economic and political structures. What should be suggested instead is an approach which conceives of the period in terms of three autonomous but interrelated structures. Concerning the political sphere, A. Zollberg (1986), following ideas put forward by O. Hintze and B.F. Porshnev, took as the central premise of his work the assumption that, in considering early modern and modern Europe, states should not be taken in isolation from each other, but as part of an inter-state system generated by the action of the individual states to expand into other states and the reaction of the latter. In other words, what can be observed is the appearance of an inter-state system as the unintended result of state forces generated to avoid the emergence of an empire.

Both Tilly (1975) and Wallerstein (1974), when considering the period of state formation in early modern Western Europe avoided or diffused the issue of the connections between state and nationalism. Tilly was candid enough to admit that his original plan was to 'analyze state-making and the formation of nations interdependently' (1975: 16). One of the reasons why the project failed was the contentious character of the term 'nation'; but, more importantly, it was his belief that in early modern Western Europe nationalism, mass political identity and cultural homogeneity were very scarce commodities. Wallerstein insisted also that the rise of the nation and of nationalism took place at a much later stage; absolutism was the typical ideology of the long sixteenth century and later, and as such it was the ideology of the rise of the state as a social force. However, Wallerstein admitted that the proponents of absolutism would, in the long run, cultivate national sentiments as a way of reinforcing their position. If a collective sentiment existed to a certain extent at this time it was not directed to the collectivity as a whole but to the ruler. As to the connection between state and nation in general, Wallerstein seems to consider the former as a necessary but insufficient condition for the emergence of the latter.

One author who has tried to look into the systemic properties of Europe as a whole is Stein Rokkan. He developed a territorial model of politics based on the ideas of centrality and peripherality. What defines a periphery is distance, difference and dependence; the latter is not exclusively economic, but also political and cultural. In a pioneering paper (Rokkan, S. 1975), Rokkan tried to account for the differences in state-building and nation-building which occurred in Western Europe by means of a complex model and daring generalizations. Rokkan's model considered a number of phases in the political development of Europe. The process of initial state-building encompassed the period between the high Middle Ages and the French Revolution. After this stage, we see a progressive presence of the masses in the system (schools, armies, etc.) and an active participation of them in the political system (elections, etc.); finally, the state administration becomes more present in the life of the individual (welfare state) (1974: 571–72). These four phases he referred to, respectively, as penetration, standardization, participation and redistribution.

There are six constants in the formation of centre and periphery in Western Europe:

> First, the heritage of the Roman Empire, the supremacy of the Emperor, the systematization of legal rules, the idea of citizenship; second, the supraterritorial, cross-ethnic organization of the Catholic Church and its

central role in the channelling of elite communications during the millennium after the fall of the Western Empire; third, the Germanic Kingdoms and the traditions of legislative-juridical assemblies of free heads of families; fourth, the extraordinary revival of trade between the Orient, the Mediterranean, and the North Sea after the defeat of the Moslems and the consequent growth of a network of independent cities across Western Europe from Italy to Flanders and the Baltic; fifth, the development and consolidation of feudal and manorial agrarian structures and the consequent concentrations of landholdings in important areas of the West; and sixth and finally the emergence of literatures in vernacular languages and the gradual decline of the dominant medium of cross-ethnic communication, Latin, quite particularly after the invention of printing (Rokkan, S. 1975: 575).

According to Rokkan these 'givens' shaped in important ways the long initial period of state formation in Western Europe. A number of dimensions became essential to explain the way in which the different states managed to consolidate their positions. To start with there was the geopolitical position in relation to Rome; second, the geopolitical distance to the urban and industrial centres; third, the nature of the peasantry (concentration of landholdings); finally, the question of cultural, linguistic and religious variation within each state (ibid.: 575–76). Ultimately, what Rokkan was saying was that 'in combination these four variables yield a plausible account of the geographic pattern of state-making' (Tilly, C. 1975: 67). Although Rokkan's generalizations are not without major problems because of the constant introduction of ad hoc explanations and perhaps also because his model is more descriptive than causal, his contribution offers valuable insights into the nature of state-building as well as nation-building.

The literature on nationalism has long been plagued with a false dilemma: either the state maketh the nation or the nation maketh the state. That there are good historical arguments on both sides is undeniable, particularly when the focus is on the modern period. This apparent contradiction dissolves, however, if we take the perspective of the *longue durée*. As we have seen in Part I, in the medieval period state and nation often went together and they fed on each other. There are, though, two major caveats to this statement. First, state competition and struggle meant, in the long run, that some states consolidated and grew in size, while others were absorbed or disappeared. Second, ethno-national identities developed as a result of outside pressures even when a proper state did not exist to facilitate the task. Now, I would agree that the bond of nationality developed slowly, though there is little doubt that the love of country (*patria*) existed in the medieval period, particularly in the city-states. The question that is often asked is, how was the transition operated from a very localized love of *patria* to the love of this imagined community that is the nation?

What I have shown in Part I is precisely that the idea of nation as an imagined community is far from being modern and that it was in the Middle Ages that many of the Western European nations were created by a sheer jump of the imagination in the circles of the literati, most commonly, but not always, around the monarchs. What is modern about the nation, then, is fundamentally its potential as a mass belief; not its existence as an imaginative vision. What is true is that from the medieval period to the eighteenth century the principle of nationality was one among other bonds of state legitimation; it was only after the French Revolution that it became the strongest pillar of the state (Passerin d'Entreves, 1967: 178). This is best exemplified by the notion that the nation-state is the hegemonic political form of modernity. I have already criticized this conception, although it is valid at the ideological level; so I would rephrase it to say that the ideology of the nation-state is hegemonic in the modern period, whatever the multinational realities that we may find behind each state.

In the argument about whether in relation to the state the nation is a dependent or independent variable, most authors tend to give primacy to the political structures over the ideological forms. It is alleged that even if it does not have the legitimizing authority, the state certainly has the legal power and the brute force to impose itself on its subjects. It would appear that the process of national homogenization should have been an easy objective for the state, particularly after the French Revolution. Furthermore, when a state has had centuries to impose a certain idea of nation it should have been successful easily. But history seems to negate this assumption; even the 'oldest' Western European state – France – has not managed this feat. What we know for sure is that ethno-national identities forged in the medieval period die hard. And in addition, there has been the problem of the changing of state borders, even up to very recent times. In these cases the nationality principle is bound to be an embarrassment, unless properly manipulated (like the claims by the French state that Roussillon was geographically French, Savoy was linguistically French and Alsace was historically French). In modern and contemporary times the creation of new states has always been the result of the inter-state system and of the balance of power within it, so there is a limit to the idea that nations make states.

In conclusion the only thing that we can say with certainty is that the nationality principle that seized the Western European imagination in the late eighteenth century revolutionized the world in which we live; but the outcome was not a landscape of nation-states, but rather a confused puzzle. What we have seen in the past two centuries are political structures (states) being subverted by an extremely effective ideological power (nationalism). I have said repeatedly that the *mot d'ordre* of modernity – no nation without a state and each state must be a nation – is pure humbug, or rather a make-believe ideology. State and nation make strange bedfellows, basically because they are organized on very different principles. Furthermore, there are two additional problems: the inertia of the state in relinquishing territorial sovereignty and the unpredictability of nationalist ideology in defining its circle of application.

Bibliography

Abrams, P., (1982) *Historical Sociology*, London: Open Books.

Cassirer, E., (1946) *The Myth of the State*, New Haven: Yale University Press.

Elias, N., (1972) 'Processes of State Formation and Nation-Building', *Transactions of the World Congress of Sociology*, Sofia: ISA, VIII, pp. 274–8.

— —, (1982) *The Civilising Process*, Oxford: Blackwell, 2 vols.

Ergang, R., (1971) *The Emergence of the National State*, New York: Van Nostrand.

Finer, S., (1974) 'State-Building, State-Boundaries and Border Control', *Social Sciences Information*, 13, pp. 79–126.

Giddens, A., (1985) *The Nation-State and Violence*, Cambridge: Polity Press.

Gilbert, F., (1954) 'The Concept of Nationalism in Machiavelli's Prince', *Studies in the Renaissance*, I, pp. 38–48.

Gramsci, A., (1971) *Selections from the Prison Notebooks*, London: Lawrence and Wishart.

Hall, J., (ed.), (1986) *States in History*, Oxford: Blackwell.

Hintze, O., (1975) *The Historical Essays of O. Hintze*, Oxford University Press.

Kiernan, V. G., (1965) 'State and Nation in Europe', *Past and Present*, 31, pp. 20–38.

Koenigsberger, H. G., (1975) 'Spain and Portugal' in O. Ranum (ed.), *National Consciousness, History and Political Culture in Early Europe*, Baltimore: The Johns Hopkins University Press.

— —, (1977) *'Dominium Regale or Dominium Politicum et Regale?* Monarchies and Parliaments in Early Modern Europe', in P. R. Gleichman et al (eds), *Human Figurations*, Amsterdam: Sociologisch Tijdschrift.

— —, (1978) 'Monarchies and Societies, *Theory and Society,* V.

Kohn, H., (1940) 'The Origins of English Nationalism', *Journal of the History of Ideas*, 1, pp. 69–94.

Lubasz, Heinz (ed.) (1964) *The Development of the Modern State*, New York: Macmillan.

Mann, M., (1986) *The Sources of Social Power I*, Cambridge University Press.

Maravall, J.A., (1961) 'The Origins of the Modern State', *Cahiers d'Histoire*, 6, pp. 789–808.

McNeill, W., (1986) *Polyethnicity and National Unity in World History*, Toronto University Press.

Mitteis, H., (1975) *The State in the Middle Ages*, Amsterdam: North Holland.

Passerin D'Entreves, A., (1967) *The Notion of the State*, Oxford University Press.

Plucknet, T., (1931) 'Fortescue, Sir John', *Encyclopaedia of the Social Sciences*, 6, New York: Macmillan, p. 388.

Poggi, G., (1978) *The Development of the Modern State*, London: Hutchinson.

Rokkan, S., (1975) 'Dimensions of State Formation and Nation-Building' in C. Tilly *The Formation of National States in Western Europe*, Princeton University Press.

Sternberger, D., (1984) 'Ancient Features of the Modern State', *History of European Ideas*, 5, pp. 225–35.

Strayer, J., (1963) 'The Historical Experience of Nation-Building', in K. W. Deutsch & W. Foltz (eds) *Nation-Building*, New York: Atherton.

— —, (1970) *On the Medieval Origins of Modern State*, Princeton University Press.

Stubbs, W., (1897) *The Constitutional History of England*, Oxford: Clarendon Press, 3 vols.

Tilly, C., (ed.) (1975) *The Formation of National States in Western Europe*, Princeton University Press.

Wallerstein, I., (1974) *The Modern World-System I*, New York: Academic Press.

Yates, F., (1975) *Astraea*, London: Routledge and Kegan Paul.

Zollberg, A., (1986) 'Strategic Interactions and the Formation of Modern States' in A. Kazancigil (ed.), *The State in Global Perspective*, London: Gower.

–5–

Class, Civil Society and Nationalism

In the previous two chapters 'capitalism' and 'state' were treated, on the whole, as abstractions with only passing references to the groups operating within these structures. I shall start this chapter by considering the limits of class analysis, in particular the thesis that the nation is the creation of the bourgeoisie. Later I will introduce the concept of civil society which, although it has a long and often contradictory pedigree, I believe is a richer and more supple tool than the concept of class, particularly when the latter is understood in strict economic terms. I take it, with John Keane, that civil society can enlighten us about the 'origins, patterns of development and transformations' of the nation (1988: 14).

The idea that nationalism is the ideology of an ascendant industrial bourgeoisie which tries to secure a market for its commodities is typical of traditional Marxism. In this conception nationalism is basically understood as economic nationalism, i.e. as the idea that nascent industries need protection from foreign competition if the objective is to achieve the economic development of the country. Traditional Marxists would insist that the idea of the nation as a cultural artifact is nothing but a complex ideological excrescence developed by the bourgeoisie to masquerade its economic interests. The coincidence that arises between national and class (bourgeois) interests is typical of a specific stage in the development of the capitalist forces of production. If the industrial bourgeoisie of a country wants to succeed at all it must first of all gain the monopoly of the 'national' market through protectionist measures. At the state level it is crucial that the interests of the industrial bourgeoisie should predominate in one way or another. But why the industrial bourgeoisie should require nationalist clothing to cover its own naked economic interests may need some clarification. The emerging industrial bourgeoisie of a country could argue its case strictly in economic terms, trying to show, for example, that protectionism is, in the long run, in the interest of the country as a whole. Historically, it did this, more or less convincingly, by insisting that its class interests coincided with the interests of the society as a whole. But by grafting the national element into its protectionist discourse, the nascent industrial bourgeoisie was able to enhance its argument by presenting the economic policies as a part of a wider conception which encouraged what was nationally produced (whether culture, language or commodities).

I accept that at a certain level the traditional Marxist account of nationalism as an ideology of the nascent industrial bourgeoisie is historically correct in that this class did actually use nationalism for the purposes stated above. A classical example of the appropriation of a nationalist ideology to defend economic interests was the German industrial bourgeoisie of the nineteenth century. In this case, it could be argued that the construction of a large and modern state was the precondition for the realization of economic interests (the vast economic market prepared by the *Zollverein*) and/or the satisfaction of wider nationalist aspirations. This example, however, should be taken with a pinch of salt, as we shall see when we consider the German case in more detail. There is a danger, of course, of ontologizing what is merely a specific occurrence within certain structural-temporal parameters. What does not follow is either that the bourgeoisie is the only class that can appropriate nationalism or that nationalism can be explained by reference to class interests. The former was, of course, already accepted by Lenin when he stated: 'The nation is a necessary product, and inevitable form, in the bourgeois epoch of social development. The working class cannot grow strong, cannot mature, cannot consolidate its forces itself, except by "constituting itself the nation", without being "national" (though not in the bourgeois sense of the word)' (Lenin, V.I. 1930: 31).

It is true that Lenin, like Marx before him, believed that the development of capitalism would lead to demise of the boundaries of the nation-state, and in that sense this national stage of the proletariat was a passing one. Most modern Marxists have come to accept, rather reluctantly it must be said, that the nation is here to stay. The periodization of the nationalist movement in Catalonia into three stages according to the hegemonic class that led it – a bourgeois, a petty-bourgeois and a working class one – was first advanced by Communist Party ideologists.

It is unfortunate that economic explanations of nationalism – in terms of the strict class interests of the bourgeoisie – are still rife in Marxist and Marxisant circles, as I have indicated on a number of occasions. The problem with these interpretations is the refusal to see the specificity of the nation, that is, the fact that although this entity has been, and still is, appropriated by different social groups, this in no way indicates that it can be reduced to the interests of any class. A national ideology may occupy, for economic reasons, a prominent place in the discourse of a class or of a political party, but this hardly exhausts the nationalist domain. The Scottish Nationalist Party, for example, may want to appeal through an economic argument – the exploitation of Scotland by England – to rally opinion for an independent Scottish nation. This point, the truthfulness of which is not at stake here, only touches upon one dimension of national identity and in no way can it be metamorphosed, as often happens in the English media, as the main or only rationale for a separate Scottish state.

In the Marxist tradition, Nicos Poulantzas exemplifies a courageous attempt to deal with the theoretical, and practical, deadlock facing the national question. Although not willing to say with Tom Nairn that the greatest historical failure of Marxism is its theory of nationalism, Poulantzas is prepared to accept that 'there is no Marxist theory of the nation' (1978: 93). He starts by stating that the 'nation is not identical with the modern nation or with the national state, such as they appeared with the rise of capitalism in the West ...; [it refers to a] specific unit of the overall production of social relations that existed long before capitalism ... [and] it coincided with the passage from classless (lineage) to class society' (ibid.). Poulantzas admits that even in the framework of capitalism the state cannot 'entirely encapsulate the nation' (1978: 94), while nations which have not managed to create their own states are 'no less of a nation for that' (ibid.). It is true that under capitalism there is a tendency towards the creation of national states, but this does not mean that the nation loses its specificity.

Poulantzas is critical of the idea of the internal market theory of the nation, on the strength that the internationalization of the market and of capital in no way affects the basis of the nation. Generally speaking, he accepts the thesis that the state creates and shapes the modern nation, at least where state and nation coincide. After all it is through the state apparatuses that the nation 'acquires flesh and blood ... and it becomes the anchorage of state power in society and maps out its contours' (1978: 99). The two words that reflect the relation between the state and the nation in modern times are Jacobinism and separatism; the reason is simple: in modernity the nation either fuses with the state or constitutes a new state. Nations without states are in great danger of having their culture, language and historical memory obliterated by the state under which they exist. The situation arises precisely because 'the state establishes the modern nation by eliminating other national pasts into variations of its own history' (1978: 113). Here is where one can apply Engels' reference that nations without state become peoples without history.

Poulantzas is careful not to see the modern nation as a creation of the bourgeoisie but rather the 'outcome of a relationship of forces between the "modern" social classes – one in which the nation is a stake for the various classes' (1978: 115). Each of the major classes (bourgeoisie and proletariat), as well as the other classes (petty bourgeoisie, peasantries) and the fractions within each class, have a relationship with the modern nation and shape it in their own way. To be sure, in so far as the bourgeoisie is the hegemonic class the nation bears its stamp prominently. Poulantzas was well aware that he had left many questions unanswered, but at least he had the courage to acknowledge that the nation had a tremendous 'endurance and resistance' (1978: 120), which the classics of Marxism had not foreseen. His clear distinction between nation and modern nation allowed him to avoid the pitfalls of many of those, both Marxists and non-Marxists, who postulate a clear cause-effect connection between capitalism and nationalism. Finally, he was careful enough not to see the nation as an ideological subproduct of the economic interests of the bourgeoisie. Poulantzas' definition of class takes him beyond economistic and homogenous conceptions of social classes, and in that sense his concept of an overall, complex social structure constitutes a link with the idea of civil society that I shall consider next.

I have said at the beginning of this chapter that the idea of civil society has a long and confused history. The concept originated in Locke and was developed by the thinkers of the Scottish Enlightenment (Hume, Smith and Ferguson) in an attempt to characterize the modern civilized societies of the West in opposition not only to the state of nature but also to the barbarian and despotic regimes of the Orient. For Hegel, civil society was the self-regulatory realm of the social relations generated by individual needs (including material interests), and it was differentiated from the state which was the sphere of morality. Marx inherited the Hegelian conception, though for him the political (state) was subordinated to the economic (civil society). For the Marx of *The German Ideology* civil society was the cause, the real theatre of history, while the state was just visual and sound effects. In Gramsci, civil society experimented a further twist in that it became the private, non-political part of the superstructure. In this sense, the civil society exercised an indirect, hegemonic effect through a variety of ideological means, while the state domination was based on the monopoly of force.

What are we to make of these disparate definitions of civil society? In an attempt to integrate these approaches, S. Giner (1985) has proposed the following definition of civil society: 'an historically evolved sphere of individual rights and of voluntary associations in which the peaceful political competition of individuals and groups in defence of their varied concerns, intentions and interests is guaranteed by the state' (1985: 73). Five major dimensions characterize civil society according to Giner: individualism (the individual is the only and ultimate reality of social life; social groups are only aggregates of individual wills), privacy (as opposed to participation in politics or public life), market (competitiveness in all spheres of social life), pluralism (power is diffused all over society and is fragmented on the basis of the different ideological divisions) and class (the unintentional result of the competition for commodities and power).

In a recent book, Anthony Black (1984) has examined the appearance in Western Europe, between the twelfth and the seventeenth centuries, of a distinctive combination of politico-economic values; on the one hand, civil society in the sense of personal freedom, legal equality and property, and, on the other, communal values, mutual aid and craft honour. Civil society, in the widest sense of the term as it occurs in Hegel, emerges with the progressive dissolution of the 'natural bonds' of the feudal order; a new social structure appeared, mostly in towns, where craftsmen, small businessmen and merchants developed new forms of social organization, while developing new economic activities. It is important to emphasize here that this civil society was both a *Gesellschaft* and a *Gemeinschaft*, to use Tönnies terminology. It is from these medieval origins that the bourgeoisie started to develop (Gouldner, A. 1980: 358–60). The history of Western Europe is the history of its civil society; but the combination of the different values varied from time to time and from place to place.

This detour on the concept of civil society has of yet produced only a few insights on the national question. In fact, the issue has not arisen much in the literature, perhaps because there has been little theoretical use of the concept of civil society by contemporary social scientists. So in which way do I think, as I promised at the onset of this chapter, that the concept of civil society can help us to understand the development of nationalism? Before anything else I believe that it is important to introduce, once again, the concept of the state. A common feature to all the authors hitherto considered, except perhaps for some of the early liberals, is that they oppose, for different reasons, civil society to the state. The point emphasized here is that civil society and state may have different social referata. While civil society is the sum of social relations and institutions that develop spontaneously out of a situation in which people interact in a variety of spheres, the state may be, and often is, imposed from the outside.

In the medieval period, civil society had to fight against the state on two different fronts, first, to have its autonomy recognized against feudal regulations, and second, to avoid impingement or domination from neighbouring states. In the city-states of this period, whether in Italia, Germania or elsewhere, civil society and state tended to a great extent to overlap. We have already come across, considering the city-states of northern Italia, the patriotic feeling that developed in their midst. This happened in city-states like Florence, Venice, Genova etc. where the *vita civile* was thriving. Even admitting to the changing meaning of words, the term nation (*natio*) was associated with merchants, students, etc. from a city-state when established temporarily outside, particularly outside the Italian peninsula. Admittedly in latter circumstances, sentiments of cultural *italianità* also emerged on account of recognized linguistic similarities and Roman ancestry. Even the urban centres of small states, like the case of Barcelona within Catalonia, could become relatively autonomous if they had a strong civil society. However, this is not to say that the concept of nation was limited to city-states or small states; along with this concept more abstract concepts of nation appeared in the medieval period, such as the creation of 'France' as an imaginative vision of the literati around the Capetian and Valois monarchs clearly shows.

Peter Burke has emphasized the fact that both the Dutch and Swiss states emerged as federations of city-states aimed at defending their autonomy; in the case of the United Provinces the existence of a thriving and patriotic civil society was a key factor in assuring their success against the centralizing aims of the Habsburg monarchy (Burke, P. 1987: 145).

It may be argued that the medieval and early modern periods are too controversial in terms of the national question; that opinions are too divided as to whether nationalism existed at all; that although a connection existed between the love of the city-state as *patria* and modern nationalism, the link is not always straightforward. As K.R. Minogue put it: 'the difference between nationalism and patriotism is to be found, then, both in the unit to which allegiance is given, and also in the very manner of that allegiance' (1976: 57). A similar argument has been raging on the modernity of civil society. How developed can civil society be said to be in the medieval and early modern periods, even in the city-states that I have mentioned before?

I believe that the link between civil society and nationalism stands or falls on the strength or weakness, respectively, of the case that can be made for it in the modern and contemporary periods. And that the best laboratory to judge that statement is not an examination of those countries where state and civil society have common if not identical national interests, that is, where in Gramscian terms they constitute a historical bloc, but in connection with situations in which civil society finds itself under the domination of a state that is felt to be alien in national terms. The demonstration should be applicable both in the case of new state building (for example, Italy in the nineteenth century) and in the case of ethno-nationalisms against the state (that is, oppressed nationalities within a state).

Let me start with the case of Germany where, although a case of new state building, the problem was not so much foreign rule but fragmentation of sovereignty in the area I called Germania and where there was 'awakening' to German cultural nationalism at the turn of the nineteenth century. In Part IV I intend to deal with the German case in detail, but at this stage suffice it to say that, in the final resort, the formation of the German state in 1871, was basically, as an end product, engineered, led and executed by Prussia. However, in the long and tortuous process that started with the Napoleonic invasion of Germania, the role of civil society is crucial to understand the cultural, political and economic German nationalism of this period. More interestingly, it was not so much the *Besitzbürgertum* (industrial and commercial capitalists), but the *Bildungsburgertum* (intellectual bourgeoisie, that is, civil servants, university professors, liberal professions, intellectuals, artists, journalists, clergy, etc.) which played the key role, through their private associations, in the social, cultural, political and constitutional changes of the period. As to the nationalist movement, from 1789 onwards it was up to clerics, university professors, artists, journalists, professionals, etc., that is, up to the intelligentsia to create the appropriate conditions for the birth and development of German nationalism (Kocka, J. 1986).

As Dieter Düding has shown, between 1811 and 1866 there were four well differentiated phases in which different types of associations (recreational, artistic, political, etc.) 'played a major role in the development of the German people into a modern nation' (Düding, D. 1987: 21). These groups were committed to the creation of a German nation-state. And it was precisely through these organizations and their activities that the nationalist movement became consolidated. This is not, of course, to ignore the importance of economic nationalism from the List-inspired *Zollverein* to the impact of industrialization. In the end, the Bismarckian solution of creating, against the will (weak by the 1860s) of the private associations, the new Reich from above and by force, left many cultural Germans (particularly in Austria) outside the German nation-state. Needless to say, it was in this state-imposed solution to the German national problem (Bismarck's *Kleindeutschland*) that the root lay of the instability of the German state from 1871 until 1945.

The creation of the Italian nation-state in the nineteenth century offers strong parallelisms with that of the German case that I have briefly analyzed. There are, however, some important differences. By 1815, some of the key, economically developed territories within the Italian peninsula, to use Metternich's dictum that 'Italy' was only a geographical expression, were occupied by a foreign power (Austria). The spread of industrial capitalism was taking place at a much slower rate than in Germania, and it was concentrated practically in the north (Lombardy and Piedmont); and last, but not least, the intelligentsia was proportionally much smaller. In its origins, in the late eighteenth century, the process known as *Risorgimento*, was a cultural and ethical movement aimed at restoring Italia to a leading place in European civilization after three centuries of decadence; at the start, it was an affirmation of the linguistic and cultural unity of Italia. The Napoleonic invasion contributed to the collapse of the structures of the ancient regime. Napoleon created an Italian state in the north of the country, bringing with him not only the ideas of the French Revolution, but also an efficient bureaucracy, and encouraged economic development. If the Restoration after 1815 meant a return to the old scheme of things, the ideological hurricane brought by Bonaparte was there to stay.

The explosion of *italianità* that gathered momentum after 1815, manifested itself in a literary and musical renaissance, which helped to fix a national language (on the basis of Tuscan) and to awaken national sentiments. Furthermore, the obsession of the Austrians with keeping the most advanced part of Italia, created a discontent in the dispossessed Lombardian intelligentsia that no doubt contributed more than anything else to the emergence of political nationalism. It was not uniting Italia, but freeing it from alien rule that became the motto of the Italian patriots. The mercantile and industrial classes of Lombardy, Piedmont and Tuscany soon appreciated the importance of having an all embracing Italian market, without the barriers and tariffs imposed by the existing states; but it was only when other methods of achieving this unified market failed, that they joined the nationalist movement (Mack Smith, D. 1969).

The fact that conditions in Italia were different, meant also that the nationalist movement followed an idiosyncratic path. It was not only the question of spreading *italianità* by a minority group of intellectuals, artists, novelists, poets, musicians, journalists etc., but also challenging the reactionary and oppressive regimes of the different Italian states, and, more importantly, foreign rule. To that end secret societies were formed (Carbonari, Young Italy, etc.), insurrectional movements were fostered and terrorist acts performed. It is important to see that all these processes, be they cultural, economic, political or revolutionary, were the work of a small group of dedicated people, with different class backgrounds, led by an intelligentsia and operating outside and against the policies of the existing Italian states, and obviously against the foreign, Austrian rulers. Here is another case, then, of a civil society taking the lead and sponsoring the creation of the Italian nation-state. It is true that, as in the German case, the actual formation of the Italian state in 1861 was the result of force as well: the lead taken by Cavour's Piedmont to unify Italy by military means, and the acquiescence of France in such a move. That the might of the state and international conjuncture (in terms of the balance of forces at a given moment in time) should be the final determinants as to whether a new state emerges or not should not be surprising. This does not disqualify the thesis that the Risorgimento was a movement brought about by small, active intelligentsia within a civil society which, except in the north of the country, was weak and divided. Here we have, though, an unanswered question: why should civil society be fostering nationalism ?

Nationalisms against the state present an even better case for exploring the link between civil society and nationalism. In such a context, nationalism has not only to be 'created' or 'awakened', but in its diffusion it has to compete against the existing state nationalism. The comparative study of Western European cases seems to suggest that even where there is a strong ethno-national identity, the presence or absence of a thriving civil society is a determinant factor in the appearance and consolidation of nationalism, both ideologically and politically. Let us take, for example, Occitania, Scotland and Catalonia in the second half of the nineteenth century. From a cursory examination of three cases, we might conclude that the failure of the Occitan idea, the fact that it had no impact beyond a very reduced circle of people, can be attributed first of all to a weak ethno-national potential, but also to the absence of an active civil society. Scotland and Catalonia both had strong ethno-national potential, and yet only Catalonia managed to articulate, at that stage, a nationalist movement. Here it could be argued that Scotland had a wider 'national' autonomy within the UK than Catalonia had within Spain. However, it is also true that the Scottish civil society looked more towards London than towards Edinburgh, while in Catalonia the civil society had been promoting from 1835 to 1885 Catalan language and literature, music, the arts, etc. In short, it had been developing, through private associations, a sense of national identity at the cultural level, which towards the end of the century became a fully-fledged nationalist ideology, later to constitute the ideological basis for a political movement of self-determination.

What seems to be the common denominator of the different cases that I have briefly looked into, is that successful nationalisms seems to be going hand in hand with a well-developed, dynamic civil society. One could go even further and suggest that for a civil society to flourish there is a need for a thriving modern economy to exist and a bourgeois class to act as the motor for such capitalist development. We have now come full circle. The chapter began with a rejection of the vulgar Marxist thesis that nationalism was the ideology of the bourgeoisie in its attempt to have exclusive access to a market – the 'national' market. I agree that the bourgeoisie may have thought in such terms, and in that sense it may have used the nationalist ideology to attain its objectives. However, as I have repeatedly said, this specific use of the nationalist ideology by a given class – the bourgeoisie in this occurrence – does not exhaust nationalist ideology, nor does it account for its origins and development. By focusing on civil society in the widest sense of the term, we have seen how powerful the idea of nation had become in the aftermath of the French Revolution. Nationalism was not created but 'manipulated' by the bourgeoisie to achieve its economic ends. In fact, what is wrong in vulgar Marxism is the idea of the bourgeois as exclusively an *Homo economicus*. It is because of this reductionist vision of class that the introduction of the idea of civil society is theoretically useful. In historical practice, many bourgeois were also cultural and political nationalists, even if at times this might have collided with their strict economic interests. In any case, nationalism cut across classes and, as we shall see, it had strong popular support, even if initially it was the intelligentsia, and not the bourgeoisie, that spread it.

What we have come across again and again is the harsh reality that nationalism is not easily reducible to other, more structural realities, even if, of course, capitalism, the state, classes and civil society, have shaped it in different ways. It would appear as if nationalism has an ideological core which is to a certain extent autonomous and independent of the structures of modernity; that, in modern times, the idea of national identity is a given, and not an epiphenomenon of any other sphere. In other words, that it is a long historical precipitate and not a byproduct of modernity, even if the latter might have given it a larger than life image. Behind many of the reductionist conceptions of nationalism there is the conviction that ideas cannot be material forces that move society. That's why our next task should be to consider the nationalist ideology itself, before we can see its force in changing the modern world. But before we examine the birth of the modern nationalist ideology, we must look into religion, first institutionally, as a structure, with the objective of trying to ascertain the role of the 'national' churches in the development of nationalism; and secondly, and more importantly, to examine the transformation of the idea of religious community into national community in the context of the process of secularization characteristic of Western Europe since the Enlightenment.

Bibliography

Black, A., (1984) *Guilds and Civil Society in European Political Thought from the 12th Century to the Present*, London: Methuen.

Burke, P., (1987) 'City-States' in J. Hall (ed.), *States in History*, Oxford: Blackwell.

Düding, D., (1987) 'The Nineteenth Century German Nationalist Movement as a Movement of Societies', in H. Schulze (ed.), *Nation-Building in Central Europe*, London: Berg.

Giner, S., (1985) *Comunió, domini, innovació*, Barcelona: Laia.

Gouldner, A., (1980) *The Two Marxisms*, London: Macmillan.

Keane, J., (ed.), (1988) *Civil Society and the State*, London: Verso.

Kocka, J., (1986) 'La bourgeoisie dans l'histoire moderne et contemporaine de l'Allemagne', *Le Mouvement Social*, 136, pp. 5–27.

Lenin, V. I., (1930) *The Teachings of Karl Marx*, New York: International Publishers.

Mack Smith, D., (1969) Italy. *A Modern History*, Ann Arbor: The University of Michigan.

Minogue, K. R., (1976) 'Nationalism and the Patriotism of the City-States', in A. D. Smith *Nationalist Movements*, London: Macmillan.

Poulantzas, N., (1978) *State, Power, Socialism*, London: New Left Books.

–6–

Church, Civil Religion and Nationalism

The history of relations between papacy and state in medieval Europe is often obscured by the assumption that the ecclesiastical power prevailed over the civil one. The pope had no doubt a range of religious sanctions, which he could often back up by indirect military force, to impose his prescriptions. However, one should also be aware that the pope was at the mercy of the manipulations and pressures emanating from the different Christian kingdoms. At the local level the Church hierarchies, the religious orders and the rank and file clerics were, up to a point, attached to and dependent on the state. During the long medieval period there developed a close, organic connection between church and state which has given rise to the term 'national' Church (even if it was first a state church and later national). The proto-reformers Wyclif and Huss were basically heralding a call for a curtailment of Roman intervention and correspondingly for an assertion, to a certain extent, of 'national' values (including the use of the vernacular for religious purposes). In any case, the Western European monarchies approached the end of the Middle Ages with two clear principles in mind: that the king was the spiritual, not the temporal subject of the pope and that the local church was spiritually subordinate to Rome but temporally subject to the monarch. However, the motto *cuius rex, eius religio* did not make full sense until the sixteenth century with the generalized movement of religious reform and independence from Rome.

Although I agree with J. Armstrong that the 'nationalization' of the church on both sides of the Reformation and Counter-Reformation divide had a powerful influence on ethnicity, with the 'heightening of awareness of its linguistic component' (Armstrong, J. 1982: 232), I would insist that the effects tended to be more important in Protestant countries than in Catholic ones. Religious homogenization – one country, one religion, one church – was seen as a pre-condition for the consolidation of the state; religious dissidents, whether Jews, Muslims or Protestants in the Iberian peninsula, or Catholics in England, the United Provinces or Geneva, were seen as potentially subversive, and dealt with ruthlessly and expeditiously. Furthermore, religious radicals who wanted to bypass the alliance between church and state and who believed that Christ was the sole head of the church also represented a threat to 'national' churches and were also persecuted everywhere (Mullet, M. 1980).

The role of religious ideology emanating from these 'national' churches, no doubt helped to cement the legitimacy of the early modern European states, and contained as well a number of national themes. It could be said roughly that Christianity took as many forms as the number of states that existed, and that each prince required support for his particular brand of religious synthesis. The doctrine of princely sovereignty, which was crystallizing in the early modern period, required the existence of what Hobbes called 'one society'; no other organization, particularly an alien one depending on Rome, was likely to be allowed to operate in its midst. Consequently, as Passerin d'Entreves remarked: 'once the unity of Christendom was broken, the oneness of society could only mean that the national church completely coincided with the national state' (1967: 135). It should be added, however, that the transition to the Renaissance type of monarchy was also legitimized by the monarchies taking over certain symbolic aspects of the imperial tradition. This was not only the case of Charles V, as head of the Holy Roman Empire, but also Elizabeth I in England and Charles IX in France (Yates, F. 1975).

England offers a classical example of the Erastian principle of subordination of ecclesiastical to secular power. We need not enter into the reasons why Henry VIII, whether stirred up by conscience, worried about succession or moved by lust, sought a divorce that led him into a collision course with Rome. The fact is that in 1529, as H. Cam put it, the parliament met and decided 'to cut the financial and judicial ties between the English Church and Rome; to reject the pope's ecclesiastical authority; and to declare the king Supreme Head on earth of the Church of England recognizing disciplinary powers in matters of faith and morals, and to exemplify this by dissolving the monasteries ... and transferring their property to the king' (1963: 174). It is worth noting that whatever the underlying realities of absolute rule, Henry VIII insisted in presenting the break with Rome as the decision of a sovereign parliament. This momentous decision was to enhance, in the centuries to come, the rule of law and parliament in England.

After the short interregnum of Mary Tudor, during the reign of Elizabeth I the English Church was shaped so as to produce an acquiescent clergy at all levels; this was not always easy because Puritans and non-conformists had to be kept at bay. The identification of church and nation took the form of an ideological attempt to show that from its very inception the English Church owed nothing to Rome. The 'Englishness' of the church was presented in an organized way in *De Antiquitate Britannicae Ecclesiae*, by Parker, the Archbishop of Canterbury.

Besides the Bible, the most popular and influential book in Elizabethan times, which continued to play a major role in the seventeenth century, was John Foxe's *The Acts and Monuments of these Latter and Perilous Days*. Foxe's *Book of Martyrs*, as it was popularly known, presented the stories of the Protestant martyrs of the sixteenth century, particularly the Marian ones, 'in an account of ecclesiastical history which purported to show that this faith was the same for which the martyrs of the primitive Church had died, the same which had been brought uncorrupted to Britain in the beginning directly from the apostles. This account of the Church history the book also linked to a history of the long succession of native rulers down to Elizabeth, shown as owing their authority to divine appointment' (Haller, W. 1963: 225).

The body of fact and fable which constituted England's national past was given a boost, even if some authors doubted certain aspects of it. There was Brutus and Arthur, and also Joseph of Arimathea who introduced the Gospel into Britain long before the Roman missionaries and King Lucius who established the British Church. On the other hand there were the agents of Rome from St. Augustine to the Normans and many others. However, John Wyclif and those who came after him exemplified the native spirit and kept the true Christian Gospel alive. The importance of Foxe's book for the English monarchy resided essentially in the fact that it gave the ruler a clear role in the history of the country. On the other hand, the church was firmly established within the state, as the events of the seventeenth century clearly showed.

In the religious sphere there was a crucial aspect of the Elizabethan period, which only came to full bloom in the mid-seventeenth century, but which should be mentioned here. I am referring to the idea that England had a special religious destiny to fulfill. The reading and studying of the Bible blended with the development of a history of England, produced the idea of an elect nation; the English identified with the Hebrews, and the country was seen as the people of God, as a new Israel. Haller's insistence that Foxe's *Book of Martyrs* made English people conscious of having a common destiny and of being God's elect people, have been criticized lately. It has been suggested that, in fact, Foxe conceived of the 'true church as international and mystical' (Fletcher, A. 1982: 309). This would tally with Elizabeth's theme of imperialism that I mentioned before and should be seen as an ideological justification for the control that she exerted on both state and church. However, as F. Yates put it 'the religious role of the imperial legend was easily turned in a nationalist direction as England's power and greatness expanded under Elizabeth's rule' (1975: 47).

Religious nationalism is what characterized England during the Puritan Revolution in the seventeenth century; it was a translation of Old Testament Israelite nationalism to Tudor and Stuart England. As I have mentioned, this came as a result of the pre-eminence of the Bible in the thoughts and actions of ordinary English people. Hans Kohn has remarked that Hebraism coloured totally the ideas of the period and that 'the three main ideas of Hebrew nationalism dominated the consciousness of the period: the idea of the chosen people, the covenant, the messianic expectancy' (Kohn, H. 1940: 82). It is debatable, though, Kohn's statement that 'national consciousness embraced the whole people of England' (ibid.: 91). A strong sense of English identity, however, arose among the gentry in this period.

When by the 1640s the policies of Charles I (with a popish wife and his Arminianism) were seen as seriously endangering, among other things, the Protestant-established Church, and hence English identity as well as the sovereign role of Parliament, and even the very foundations of the English state, the provincial gentry and other groups were ready for an open confrontation with the monarchy. In the civil war that followed 'the struggle to defend Protestant orthodoxy made possible the threefold identification of parliament, true religion and national interest' (Fletcher A. 1982: 316). The Church of England was able to maintain a stable and firm position in the century of revolutions by staying where Elizabeth I had placed her: at 'the centre of national life' (Haller, W. 1963: 245).

If England is the classical case of a close connection, not to speak of an identity, between state and church, there are plenty of other examples in which Protestant 'national' churches played a key role in the establishment and consolidation, or at least defence, of nations and states. From Martin Luther's apology of the German nation, and attack against the pope and Italian cultural domination (Dickens, A.G. 1974), to the powerful patriotic feelings generated by Calvinism in Geneva, Scotland and the United Provinces (Mullet, M.A. 1980: 3–4), we have a range of cases in which state and church legitimized each other in the context of the Reformation.

The allegiance to Rome of the Latin churches at the time of the Reformation should not obscure the fact that, as we have seen in Part I, by the end of the Middle Ages there was a close alliance between church and state at least in France and the Iberian kingdoms. The expression 'national' churches is often used in the literature to refer to a situation in which the church was temporally subordinated to the state, while spiritually it preserved its autonomy, but there were, of course, a lot of grey areas which account for the constant clashes that took place over a wide range of matters; in the final result it was always a question of the jurisdiction of religious and political institutions impinging on each other's domains.

The case of France in the early modern period exemplifies a situation in which religious disunity threatened the state. Religious divisions, particularly during the latter part of the sixteenth century, tore the country apart to the point of endangering even 'national' unity and territorial integrity. What was happening is that the struggle between Catholics and Protestants was sapping the legitimacy that Christianity had provided to the French state for centuries. The French monarchy, it is true, basically supported the Catholic Church and engaged in a bloody repression of Huguenots, though at times it tolerated the Protestants with a view to not alienating foreign Protestant states, but it also (particularly after the Edict of Nantes of 1598) had to fight against ultramontane Catholics. The Huguenots were a small, geographically localized, active minority (about five per cent of the French population at their peak). For about forty years, between 1558 and 1598, there was a civil war between the Catholic League led by the Guise famile and the Protestant party. Both doctrinally and practically the Huguenots challenged the traditional legitimacy of the monarchy (espousing the right to rebellion) and under Calvinist influence they insisted that the government should be by consent. François Hotman, the leading Protestant political theorist, insisted that the monarchy was originally elected by the 'people' (or rather its representatives). This theme was taken up in *Vindiciae Contra Tyrannus* (1579), a book attributed to Du Plessis Mornay, who added that there was another agreement which gave legitimacy to the monarchy: the established balance between the king and his subjects, on one side, and God on the other. The religious war had some particularly vicious events like the infamous St. Bartholomew's Night in which 20,000 Protestants were massacred in 1672.

What is interesting about the French case is that the major religious confrontations that I have just referred to led to a weakening of the traditional gallicanism that had characterized the relations between the state and church towards the end of the medieval period. It was not until after the murder of Henry IV in 1610 that we can observe a slow return to the old values. The idea that the monarchy was a divine right was one of the principles which were reemphasised in the Estates General of 1614: 'There was no temporal or spiritual power which could deprive them [the French kings] of their sovereignty nor absolve their subjects from the fidelity and obedience they owed ... Gallican sentiment became a crucial element in absolutist ideology and could be utilized by government as needed' (Parker, D. 1983: 50). In the end, though, gallicanism was not the only factor that contributed to the development of absolutism in France; unwittingly, the ultramontanes also gave a lift to royal authority. The Counter-Reformation not only helped to stop the development of Calvinism in France but also 'recharged the ideological batteries of the divine right monarchy' (ibid.: 51). By being forced to return to the old religious status quo, the crown was able to instill a 'degree of conformity and reverence for authority ... into a restless community' (ibid.).

The French Revolution created another major chasm between state and church. This was the attempt of the revolutionaries to create a state religion and a state church that conflicted with the interests of the Catholic Church. Even after the Napoleonic Concordat, the relationships between the French state and the Catholic church were far from peaceful. The fact of the matter is that the modern state encroached progressively on the traditional domains of the Catholic church from education to the social services. At the ideological level there was a clash between the secular and republican ideology and Catholic doctrine. In the end, the only solution, not perfect by any means, was the separation of state and church. What is the case, as Bellah has pointed out, is that not all societies solve the problem of creating a non-problematic civil religion. And France is a case in point because the civil religion which came out of the French Revolution was anti-Christian; during the nineteenth and twentieth centuries there has been a major chasm between Catholic symbols and the symbolism of 1879 (Bellah, N. 1970: 181). It is not surprising, then, that nation-building in modern France has relied more on republican than Catholic values and symbols.

As the next case study in the connection between state and church I would like to consider the Habsburg monarchy in the sixteenth century, with special reference to Hispania. In Part I, I have challenged the preposterous thesis of Spain as a Visigothic nation. Many authors assume the existence of a Spanish 'national' church in the Middle Ages out of a combination of laziness, ignorance and modern nationalist distortion (Linehan, P. 1982). The fact is that in the different Hispanic kingdoms the Christian church developed specific characteristics. The religious component of national identity in the face of the crusade against Islam was much stronger in Castile than in Portugal and Catalonia. The reason is simple: both Portugal and Catalonia had completed their Reconquest approximately two and a half hundred years before Castile. Furthermore, Portugal's identity was forged in a constant struggle against Castile (Ricard, R. 1956: 14). In the Catalan case the problem is more complicated because of its dynastic union with Aragon, but initially Catalan identity was forged against the Capetian monarchy, later against the Muslims, and finally against the pressures, successful in the long run, to impose a Castilian dynasty on the Catalano-Aragonese federation.

In 1469 the marriage of Ferdinand of Aragon and Isabella of Castile paved the way for the dynastic union of the two kingdoms. Each kingdom was to preserve its institutions, so there is no way in which we can speak of the birth of a nation, and not even of the emergence of a new state. However, it is true that there were ideologists who thought in terms of Hispania as a nation. Because the fifteenth century had been a disastrous century for Catalonia as a result of the peasant war, and because Castile was stronger numerically and materially, the union of crowns, which was meant to be a union among equal partners, respecting the political autonomy of each of the constituent parts, was in the long run slanted towards Castile. The first manifestation of this unevenness was in the religious sphere: the introduction of the Castilian Inquisition in the territories of the crown of Aragon and the nomination of Castilian (and Castilian-speaking) bishops to Catalan sees, and the flooding of Catalan monasteries with Castilian monks. It is interesting to note that in the Middle Ages the ecclesiastical boundaries did not always coincide with the boundaries of the kingdoms, but the Catalano-Aragonese monarchs, like those of Portugal, tried successfully to create jurisdictions which were independent from Toledo.

In addition to having exacted from Pope Sixtus IV the right to appoint inquisitors to prosecute dubious Jewish converts (*conversos*), the Catholic Kings Ferdinand and Isabella obtained the privilege of the royal presentation of bishops, abbots and other religious dignitaries (*Patronato Real*) and substantial economic advantages from the church. With them begins what has been known as 'Spanish regalism'. What we have here is the emergence of a missionary monarchy, which presented itself as an institution at the service of the church, but in fact carefully controlled it. Charles V and Philip II maintained and reinforced this regalism, to the point of even having the right to censor the publications of the church, including those of the pope. The *Regium Exequatur* meant that many papal criticisms of the Habsburg monarchy never saw the light in Hispania. The defence of the Catholic faith was the ideology of the Habsburg monarchy, but in practice the religious ideals often masqueraded political ambitions. This is not to deny the heartfelt religiosity of the monarchs. Some authors have seen the regalism of the Habsburgs as both absorbent and protective. It was also an attempt to avoid Roman centralism and protect the traditions of the Hispanic churches, especially the Castilian one. The Habsburg presence in Italia meant, however, that clashes with the pope would be inevitable.

Charles V had many problems with the papacy, and not only because the imperial troops sacked Rome in 1527 and made the pope virtually a prisoner. Philip II also had serious clashes because Pope Paul IV wanted the Habsburgs out of Naples and out of other areas of Italia as well, so that he could expand the papal states. As a result of this, the policy of Philip II was to make sure that newly elected popes would be favourable to his policies. Pius V was a good case in point. With the defeat of France and the Council of Trent, Catholicism became a Habsburg preserve and Philip II could present himself as the defender of Catholicism *par excellence*. It is reported that his ambassador in Rome *de facto* dictated policy to the pope. In conclusion, the sixteenth-century Habsburg monarchy may appear at first sight as the paladin of Roman Catholicism, but on close inspection we have seen that the Habsburgs dominated the papacy, and in a sense they determined what Roman Catholicism was.

Of all the institutions of the Hispanic Church under the Habsburgs, the Holy Office of the Inquisition was undoubtedly the one that the monarchs relished most as an organ of social control. I have already mentioned that the Inquisition was granted by the pope to the Catholic Kings on an *ad hoc* basis to deal with a specific situation: the recanting of Andalusian Jews. In the long term, however, the Inquisition developed into an impressive bureaucracy which tackled religious dissent of all sorts by repressive methods, including torture and death by burning. The Inquisitor General had jurisidiction over all the territories of the crowns of Castile and Aragon. All the officers of the Inquisition owed their allegiance to the monarchs, and were basically their servants. The pope had in fact little to say on the matters of the Holy Office. The attempt to create a religiously homogeneous society based on the newly revived Catholicism of the Council of Trent is what the Inquisition succeeded in enforcing. In that sense, the Habsburgs tried to develop a Hispanic identity based on a 'Catholicism' which was their own creation. One of the many effects of the persecution of the Jews (*conversos*) in the Catalan-speaking areas of the crown of Aragon, was that the major source of patronage of Catalan literature came to a halt (Lovett, A.W. 1986: 295).

What we have seen in all the cases that we have fathomed, in Protestant and Catholic countries alike, is that in early modern Europe the church was basically subordinated to, and an instrument of, the state. One could say that in the period under consideration, feelings of national identity tended to be expressed essentially, though not exclusively, in religious terms, and the church contributed in different ways to consolidate such sentiments. In the long run, however, religion was not sufficient to define national identity, particularly in religiously homogeneous areas, where there was more than one nation competing for hegemony. In such cases, the local church, and particularly the rank and file clerics – who were closer to the people – might have helped to vehiculate a nationalist ideology which went against state nationalism. Also, in these cases, as Van Gennep remarked, 'what relates the individuals and makes a coherent group out of them on the basis of common sentiments and concepts is not religion in itself, but the acceptance of a certain given dogma, the practice of certain rites, the acknowledgement of a certain clergy, in a word, the fact of belonging to a particular religion' (1922: 27).

The case of Catalonia is a good example of that type of 'national' church. It came into existence in the medieval period in the framework of the formation and consolidation of Catalan political, cultural and linguistic autonomy. In the early modern period, after the union of crowns, it suffered the same decline as Catalan society in general, but preserved a strong attachment to Catalan identity. Many clerics were at the forefront of the fight against Castilian encroachment, and in the eighteenth century many priests were persecuted for having remained faithful to Catalan institutions and language. In spite of the appointment of non-Catalan bishops, the ordinary parish priests continued to preach in Catalan, and catechisms in the vernacular were always available in spite of numerous prohibitions to the contrary. The Catalan Church was also in the vanguard of the *Renaixença*, with grammarians, poets and intellectuals. By the end of the nineteenth century Bishop Josep Torres i Bages had produced an ideological blueprint in which Catholicism was an indispensable component, or precondition, of Catalan national identity; hereafter the Catalan Church embraced the dictum: 'Catalonia will be Christian, or she will not be at all'. In the more recent period – the Francoist era – the Catholic Church in Catalonia exhibited, on the whole, a commitment to defend Catalan language and culture against the penetration and impositions of the Spanish state. In this sense, and because of its relative autonomy from the Spanish state, it was the only collective entity which at times was in a position to articulate and propagate Catalan identity to the vast masses of the population. In Gramsci's terms we could say that it was a civil society within civil society; in fact it was the only civil society which was allowed to function more or less freely. With a homogeneous ideology, a well-organized clergy and the appropriate channels of diffusion, the Catalan Church managed to reach the different layers of the population.

A similar demonstration could be established on the basis of the Basque Church, with the proviso perhaps that originally, and for most part of its history, modern Basque national Catholicism was predicated in opposition to the Spanish state which was seen as secular (Garcia de Cortazar, F. 1988). In opposition to that, the Irish case presents a novelty in so far as for approximately four centuries, Ireland not only kept its

Catholicism in a Protestant political space, but it had Protestants settling in its own territory, particularly in Ulster. While anti-Catholic repression, particularly under Cromwell, was brutal, Irish national and religious identity survived. In fact, the church was the only Irish institution left, and provided spiritual and temporal leadership to the people both in rural and in urban environments. In addition to the Catholic Church there were two more 'churches' in Ireland: the official English Church of the administrators and landed aristocracy and the Presbyterian Church which was that of the Scottish immigrants in Ulster. After the French Revolution, the lower Catholic clergy became more and more identified with Irish national ideals, even going as far as espousing the Irish revolutionary cause; they were also active in the literary renaissance as well as politically. The attitude of the hierarchy was much more ambiguous, often supporting the status quo. In spite of that, there is little doubt that Irish identity was maintained by the church, and this identity, although pervaded by Catholicism, meant also the Gaelic language and an ethnic cluster of values and customs (Carey, M. 1983).

There is no way that in the previous short perusal we could account for the complexity of the state-mediated relations between church and nationalism. My intention was only to draw the conclusion that such a relationship was worth considering and that in modern times it is particularly relevant, in order to explain nationalisms against the state.

Max Müller said somewhere that in their origins all religions are 'nationalities', a formula that E. Durkheim would have approved of if for 'nationality' we just read 'society'. It is not my intention to argue in favour or against Müller's dictum, though one would have a difficult case to prove with universalist religions. More importantly, by confusing nationality with state cult (or the cult of society) Muller committed the well-known sin of projecting modern categories into the past. Modernity seems to have reversed Müller's motto in the sense that nationalism has become the functional equivalent of religion; or, expressed in a more pungent way, nationalism has become a religion – a secular religion where god is the nation. What is meant by that is not only that modern nationalism has all the trappings and rituals of a religion, but also that, like religion, it has tapped into the emotional reservoir of human beings. Religion, it has been said, operates at the same level as nationalism: the level of deep elementary emotions (Johannet, R. 1918). Hayes has expressed that in a forceful manner:

> Nationalism, like any religion, calls into play not simply the will, but the intellect, the imagination and the emotions. The intellect constructs a speculative theology or mythology of nationalism. The imagination builds an unseen world around the eternal past and the everlasting future

of one's nationality. The emotions arouse a joy and an ecstasy in the contemplation of the national god who is all-good and all-protecting, a longing for his favours, a thankfulness for his benefits, a fear of offending him, and feelings of awe and reverence at the immensity of his power and wisdom; they express themselves naturally in worship, both private and public. For nationalism, again like any other religion, is social, and its chief rites are public rites performed in the name and for the salvation of a whole community (Hayes, C., 1960: 164–65).

Nationalism, as the main form in which the religious sense of human beings has manifested itself in modern times, is seen by Hayes as a large-scale tribalism, as a doctrine which, although inspired by the Christian religion, owes more to the ideals of the tribe than to the universalistic message of world-wide religions. The idea of nationalism as a tribal religion is echoed by Ninian Smart who, paraphrasing Renan, calls the nation a 'daily sacrament', in so far as it is 'the communication of substance throughout the very language itself and through the innumerable assumptions and celebrations of identity' (1983: 21). In this vision of the nation as a phenomenological construction the emphasis is on the performative acts or celebrations in which participants communicate and share values (land, history, ancestors, myths, etc.). Modern national identity appeared in Western Europe at a time when all the intermediary bonds of society were collapsing, and religion itself was losing its grip on the masses. Religion was a ready-made model for nationalism and in many cases, as we have seen, it was also a powerful ally, reinforcing emerging nationalism. As compared with religion, though, Smart finds nationalism weak in terms of doctrine, but strong in myth, ethics and social form; the ritual of nationalism tends to be intermittent, while it is moderately strong in terms of experience (ibid.: 27).

It remains to consider the idea of civil religion. J. J. Rousseau introduced this concept in the last chapter of his *Du contrat social* (1763) to refer to a kind of religion which elicits love of country in its citizens and which compels them to perform their duties. This civil religion should not be incompatible with transcendental beliefs. A civil religion finds its expression not in dogma, but in some basic 'sentiments of sociability without which it is impossible to be a good citizen and a loyal subject' (Rousseau, J.J. 1964, III: 468). The crime against civil religion is not impiety but unsociability. Rousseau thought that the dogmas of civil religion should be few in number and expressed in precise and clear terms; he singled out the belief in a divinity, the belief in another world, the belief in the punishment of evil and the reward of good, and the belief in the sanctity of the social contract.

As we have seen, in modern France, religion (Catholicism) and nationalism followed diverging paths. The French state was not only non-confessional, but explicitly secular and even anti-clerical. After the French Revolution abstract concepts such as Fatherland (*Patrie*), Reason (*Raison*), Liberty (*Liberté*), etc. became deified and were worshipped as gods (or rather godesses). All the paraphernalia of a new religion appeared: dogmas, festivities, rituals, mythology, saints, shrines, etc. To what extent can we refer to that as a civil religion, when the transcendental element seems to have faded away? Are we not witnessing the emergence of the nation-god (or the state-god)? Norbert Bellah, who has written extensively on the idea of civil religion, would agree with such a conclusion, but the lines are often blurred. To Bellah, civil religion is 'that religious dimension found in the life of every people, through which it interprets its historical experience in the light of transcendental reality' (1975: 3). A civil religion is supported by myths which try to idealize reality and in so doing bring ' moral and spiritual meaning to individuals or societies' (ibid.: 2). Bellah chose the American civil religion as a case study. In opposition to France, in the USA, the civil religion was not only not anti-clerical, but was rather built upon the basic themes of the Old and the New Testaments. In fact, state and church have worked historically in unison to develop 'powerful symbols of national solidarity and mobilize deep levels of personal motivation for the attainment of national goals' (Bellah, N. 1970: 181). It is interesting to observe that most part of his critics have read in his work an endorsement of 'an idolatrous worship of the American nation' (ibid.: 168). In reply to these critics Bellah insisted once again that in a civil religion the nation has to be subordinated to moral principles that transcend it and that the nation should be judged according to whether it stands up to these principles. So Bellah sees in civil religion the embodiment of certain critical principles which 'undercut the everpresent danger of national self-idolization' (ibid.: 168).

It would appear as if the self-regulating mechanism of civil religion that is supposed to protect us against nation-worship is at best faulty. As we shall see, the tendency of modernity has been to consider the nation-state as a god: fascism, as the culmination of state nationalism, pitched this idolatry at the highest level hitherto known. E. Durkheim, who was aware of the dangers of nation-worship, felt however that the nationalist tide was unstoppable in the forseeable future. He did not think that religion could provide any longer the kind of humanist values that he felt were necessary for world peace. Instead, he felt that respect for the person should be enshrined in all societies; and that each state should try to realize human ideals within national bounds rather than to pursue expansionist policies against neighbouring states. For Durkheim 'what gives the nation its moral value is that it most closely approximates to the society of mankind, at present unrealized in fact and perhaps unrealizable, yet representing the limiting case, or the ideal limit toward which we always strive' (1975: 81). Durkheim has been castigated for his French chauvinism, much explicit in his wartime writings, and for trying to 'attain human ideals within the nation itself' (Mitchell, M. 1931: 106). In so doing, says Mitchell, he defied the nation and was a precursor of an extreme nationalism which conceives of the 'nation as supreme reality, and humanity as the highest ideal ... [and] in which the nation fulfils the requirement of both' (ibid.: 106). Recent critics of Durkheim are not as harsh as Mitchell, although they acknowledge that Durkheim's problem – how to reconcile cosmopolitanism with nationalism – is a very real one. (Llobera, J. R. 1994)

I would like to conclude this chapter by emphasizing the centrality of religion in the development of nationalism. It is not only that institutionalized religion (the church) often played an important role in the legitimation of the state and in fostering nationalist values, but more importantly that nationalism tapped into the same reservoir of ideas, symbols and emotions as religion; in other words, that religion was metamorphosed into nationalism.

Bibliography

Armstrong, J., (1982) *Nations before Nationalism*, Chapel Hill: The University of North Carolina Press.

Bellah, N., (1970) *Beyond Belief*, New York: Seabury Press.

— —, (1975) *The Broken Covenant*, New York: Seabury Press.

Cam, H., (1963) *England Before Elizabeth*, London: Hutchinson.

Carey, M., (1983) 'Catholicism and Irish National Identity' in P. Merkl & N. Smart (eds), *Religion and Politics in the Modern World*, New York University Press.

Dickens, A. G., (1974) *The German Nation and Martin Luther*, London: Edward Arnold.

Durkheim, E., (1975) *Moral Education*, New York: Free Press.

Fletcher, A., (1982) 'The First Century of English Protestantism and the Growth of National Identity', in S. Mews (ed.), *Religion and National Identity*, Oxford: Blackwell.

Garcia de Cortazar, F., (1988) 'Iglesia, vasca, religión y nacionalismo en el siglo XX', in F. Garcia de Cortazar & J. P. Fusi, *Política, nacionalidad e iglesia en el País Vasco*, San Sebastián: Editorial Txertoa.

Haller, W., (1963) *Foxe's Book of Martyrs and the Elect Nation*, London: J. Cape.

Hayes, C. J. H., (1980) *Nationalism: A Religion*, New York: Macmillan.

Johannet, R., (1918) *Le principe des nationalités*, Paris: Alcan.

Kohn, H., (1940) 'The Genesis and Character of English Nationalism', *Journal of the History of Ideas*, 1, pp. 69–94

Linehan, P., (1982) 'Religion, Nationalism and National Identity in Medieval Spain and Portugal', in MEWS, S., (ed.) *Religion and National Identity*, Oxford: Blackwell.

Llobera, J. R., (1994) 'Durkheim and the National Question', in W. Pickering and H. Martins, (eds.), *Debating Durkheim*, London: Routledge.

Lovett, R. W., (1986) *Early Habsburg Spain*, Oxford University Press.

Mitchell, M. 'Emile Durkheim and the Philosophy of Nationalism', *Political Science Quarterly*, XLVI, pp. 87–106.

Mullet, M., (1980) *Radical Religious Movements in Early Modern Europe*, London: Methuen.

Parker, D., (1983) *The Making of French Absolutism*, London: Edward Arnold.

Passerin D'Entreves, A., (1967) *The Notion of the State*, Oxford University Press.

Ricard, R., (1956) 'La dualité de la civilisation hispanique et l'historie religieuse du Portugal', *Revue Historique*, 216, pp. 1–17.

Rousseau, J. J., (1975) *Du contrat social et autres oeuvres politiques*, Paris: Garnier.

Smart, N., (1983) 'Religion, Myth and Nationalism', in P. Merkl & N. Smart *Religion and Politics in the Modern World*, New York University Press.

Van Gennep, A., (1922) 'Religion et nationalité', *Journal de Psychologie Normale et Pathologique*, 19, pp. 24–46.

Yates, F., (1975) *Astraea*, London: Routledge and Kegan Paul.

Part III

The Development of Nationalism: Ideological Factors

–7–

Political and Cultural Nationalism

Introduction: Some Terminological Problems

Paraphrasing Marx, one could say that nationalist ideology becomes a social force when it seizes the masses of a country. The question is, of course, under which conditions or circumstances does this take place? Ideologies surely do not fall from heaven nor are they the result of deranged or isolated imaginations; they arise from, and are part of society, and they evolve with society. However, once they have appeared they have a life of their own, independent of the conditions that have created them, and they also have effects which need to be carefully scrutinised.

It is not my intention to enter here into a consideration of the filiation of the idea of nationalism, whether in the Graeco-Roman idea of patriotism, in medieval Christian religion, in the Biblical themes of early modern Europe or in the democratic traditions. All these things have been mentioned, although some only in passing. The main objective of Parts I and II, however, was to provide a comprehensive framework within which to account plausibly for the appearance and development of modern nationalist ideology. But nationalism as an *ideé-force* has changed the existing social reality and has shaped the modern Western European world in its image, at least to the extent that it has managed to neutralize or overcome opposed forces. Certain historical events, like the French Revolution, gave nationalism a tremendous boost; then it followed its own course, inflating or deflating according to the international conjuncture and the resistance encountered.

My initial goal, in fact, is to establish with the figures of Rousseau and Herder, the modern beginnings for the ideas of political and cultural nationalism, respectively, although, as we shall see, both authors were well aware of the two dimensions of the nation. With Rousseau and Herder there is a qualitative change in the idea of nation which explains its success. How was that achieved? Firstly, by defining the nation politically as a way of incorporating the individual (the citizen) into the wider political unity; it contained the idea of freedom of the individual who together with other individuals formed the polity by consent. Secondly, by defining the nation as a community (cultural, linguistic) which was a projection of the individual in traditional society. The nation was a family (tribe) writ large. Thirdly, by bestowing upon the nation the quality of sacredness borrowed from religion.

Before I consider Rousseau's political nationalism, I should like to clarify some of the terminological confusions that bewitch anybody approaching the eighteenth century with a mind of the late twentieth century. The problem is not so much that the word *nationalisme* did not exist in the French language but that words like *patrie*, *nation* and *peuple* had different meanings which need to be ascertained before we can proceed. It is no coincidence, though, that it was after 1750 that these words and their derivatives started to acquire the meanings that we associate with them today (Palmer, R. 1940; Godechot, J. 1971; Suratteau, J. 1983).

Let us start with the word *patrie*, which translates poorly into English; while fatherland would be the literal equivalent, country or home are more appropriate and of more common usage. (However, the derivatives, *patriote* and *patriotisme* have been popularized.)

By the mid-eighteenth century the term *patrie*, which was not used as often as *nation*, had a variety of meanings. Most commonly, it referred to the place of birth, which could be a village, a province, a region or a *pays*. In schools it appeared in the classical Graeco-Roman texts with its traditional meaning. An interesting development had taken place at least from as early as the late seventeenth century: the idea that *patrie* and freedom were closely connected. Both La Bruyere and Montesquieu had stated that there was no *patrie* under despotism. A number of texts contributed to the idea that *la patrie* was the land where people were free and happy. Particularly important in this sense was the publication of Bolingbroke's *The King Patriot* (1730) and *On the Spirits of Patriotism*, which appeared in French in 1750. Bolingbroke popularized the words *patriote* and *patriotisme* in France. Patriotism in Bolingbroke was a feeling that legitimated opposition to a corrupt government; this idea came from a variety of sources: the classical belief in balancing monarchy, aristocracy and democracy, the need to reform the system and the idea that freedom was born in England (Cunningham, H. 1981: 9–10). Also published in the same year was a *Histoire de la patrie*, which was the history of a free country – the United Provinces. In *De l'esprit des lois* (1748), Montesquieu had also recorded this meaning of *patrie,* and he clearly differentiated it from the state, as when he said that in a monarchic government 'the state survives independently of the love of country' because the law takes the place of this virtue (Montesquieu 1987, I: 147).

Prior to 1750 the term *nation* was mostly used in a neutral sense to designate, as the *Dictionnaire de l'Académie* (1694) suggested, a group of people who lived under the same laws and used the same language; the territory could be the state, but also the *pays*. There is no doubt that the word *nation* also referred to France, and that a sense of national pride, honour and superiority had existed for a long time, but still the term was not emotionally charged as it would become afterwards. In eighteenth-century Italia, for example, the term *nazione* was also used in a variety of ways: to refer to an 'urban or regional political community, to Italy as a community of literary language, and to Europe as a community of culture' (Alberini, M. 1969: 5).

The controversy over the term *patrie* started in 1754 with the publication of *Dissertation sur le vieux mot de Patrie* by the Abbé Coyer. In his pamphlet, which was basically a response to Voltaire's cosmopolitan idea that *patria est ubicumque bene* (and not the country of birth or where one lives), the author claimed the ancient use of the *patria* needed to be reinstated. Coyer spoke the language of patriotism, advising soldiers to die for their country, priests and judges to dedicate themselves to their fatherland, women to bear children for the glory of their country etc. He wanted to see instituted rituals and awards and monuments to celebrate the *patrie* (Palmer, R. 1940: 99). This test by Coyer, along with his *Dissertation sur la nature du peuple*, was so influential that Jaucourt, who wrote the article '*Patrie*' in the *Encyclopédie*, copied long chunks from Coyer's works. Jaucourt also referred to the opinions of Montesquieu, Voltaire and Rousseau. His starting point was that while *patrie* originally indicated the birthplace, it also expressed our attachment to the society where we belong, and which is based on the rule of law and which assures our happiness. Along with Montesquieu and many others he embraced the idea that there is no *patrie* without freedom and the belief that love of country is conducive to good mores and vice versa.

If Voltaire was the representative par excellence of cosmopolitanism, Rousseau came forth energetically in defence of giving the term *patrie*, and its derivatives, the classical Graeco-Roman sense. While Voltaire in his *Dictionnaire philosophique* (1764) used sarcasm to undermine those who defined the *patrie* as the place of birth or of living, and insisted that to be a good patriot often meant to be the enemy of mankind, Rousseau stood at the opposite end, defending the classical meaning of the term and attacking the idea that the *patrie* is only the place where reason and enlightenment reign: the *patrie* is one's native land, irrespective of its political regime. In his *Contrat Social* (1763) he wrote 'what can we think of those who pretend to be cosmopolitan and, while justifying their love of country by their love of humanity, feign to love everybody so that they have the right to love no one' (Rousseau 1964: 406). And, in a letter to Usteri he conjured up the sense of modern nationalism when he said ' the patriotic spirit is an exclusive spirit which encourages us to see as enemies those who are not our compatriots (*concitoyens*); this was the spirit of Sparta and Rome'. But Rousseau's definition of *patrie* went further. In his *Emile* (1762) he accepted the possibility that in modern times the *patrie* had faded away. For Rousseau, the love of country makes people virtuous and happy; but if the *patrie* has institutions which impair the happiness and freedom of people then they have to be changed; with Rousseau the 'word *patrie* increases its revolutionary charge' (Godechot, J. 1971: 488). Rousseau had a democratic or rather popular conception of patriotism. In addition, there is also a romantic conception of the *patrie* in Rousseau which manifested itself in his attachment for his native Geneva in Switzerland (Suratteau, J. 1983: 368).

Voltaire frequently used the word *nation* but in a vague way; it was for him more often than not a geographical expression. At times, however, the expression *nation* also took its medieval meaning. In any case, Voltaire was certain that the idea of *nation,* as well as that of *patrie* would be erased from the repertoire of the 'men of reason', or those who believed in cosmopolitanism. Against what he believed was a process of uniformization, which was obliterating the distinctive national characters of the different European people, Rousseau was a fervent partisan of maintaining what is typical of each *nation*: its passions, its mores and its tastes (predelictions). It is interesting to observe how the terminology changed from the *Contrat Social* to *Considérations sur le Government de Pologne* (1771); while in the former the language used tended to be rather abstract – 'sovereign', 'general will' and 'virtue' – in the latter, these terms become more concrete – 'nation', 'will of the nation' and 'patriotism' respectively (Palmer, R. 1940: 106).

To Rousseau can be attributed the fact that the term nation received a much more precise meaning, but with a strong sentimental change. It is in this way that *nation* and *patria* converged: if not completely overlapped, they tend to be envisaged as covering a lot of common ground; nation became also the equivalent of the state, provided that the latter was understood in a concrete, even physical way (Suratteau, J.R. 1983: 369).

It would be difficult to find an influence more decisive than that of Rousseau in the shaping of the modern meaning of words like *patrie* and *nation*, and the same could be said about *peuple*. Works based on those topics did not only have an impact in France but all over Europe. It is true that the *Encyclopédie* contributed much to the spread of the new meanings, but as I have already indicated Jaucourt's entries were more ambiguous than Rousseau's uncompromising statements. In the German language, G.V. Zimmerman published a study entitled *Vom Nationalstolz* (1758) [On National Pride]; more important will be the impact of Friedrich Karl Von Moser's *Von dem deutschen Nationalgeist* (1765), which will have direct impact on Herder. But in fact, at that time at least, the most common words in German will be *Patriotismus* and *Patriotisch*; only much later, by the beginning of the nineteenth century, would Germanic words like *Volk*, *Vaterland*, and *Heimat* become popular.

The Origins of the Idea of National Character in Montesquieu and Hume

Both Rousseau and Voltaire used freely the expression *esprit de la nation* which originated in Montesquieu, though David Hume had also written an essay on the 'national character' more or less at the same time. Is it a question of different philosophical traditions that where the French refer to *esprit* the British talk about 'character' and the Germans prefer *Volksgeist*?

The concept of general spirit of the nation (*esprit général de la nation*) is no doubt one of the central tenets of Montesquieu's *De l'esprit des lois* (1748), even if the treatment that Montesquieu gave it may appear to be somewhat cursory. In Book XIX, chapter five, we are told that the spirit of the nation is formed by a variety of factors: climate, religion, laws, maxims of government, precedents, morals (*moeurs*) and customs (*manières*); and that the relative importance of each factor will vary with the prominence of the others. Among primitive peoples, nature and climate seem to rule alone, while morals, characterize the Spartans and law tyrannizes the Japanese.

The idea of spirit of the nation took a long time to mature in the work of Montesquieu. He basically followed a Newtonian model of science and tried to discover, through observation and comparison, the relationships between natural and social phenomena. He conceived of society as a sort of nature, no matter how complex and variable, but open to study and explanation (Vlachos, G. 1974: 29). As we shall see, for Montesquieu it was the interaction of physical and moral (social) causes which produces the spirit of the nation. Montesqueieu has been repeatedly charged with the crime of climatic determinism, and it is true that he discussed climatic conditions extensively, but only a superficial acquaintance with the title of the book, *De l'esprit des lois*, can lead one to ignore the sophistication of Montesquieu's arguments and to conclude that he did not consider other bad environmental causes in the shaping of the spirit of the nation.

Montesquieu's concern for the idea of spirit of the nation can be traced back to the period after the publication of *Lettres persanes* (1721). It is in a fragment entitled *De la politique* (1725) that we find Montesquieu's first reference to his notion. There he stated his belief in the existence of a soul or character of society which he conceived of as the result of an infinite chain of causes, and which, once formed, tended to dominate society. Later on, in his *Pensées* (1731–3) he elaborated on the causes, and came out with the five following factors forming the spirit of the nation: religion, maxims of government, laws, morals and customs. He insisted on the existence of a close connection between them, to the extent that if one of the factors changed, the others would be affected as well. A few years later in the *Considération sur les Romans* (1734), he insisted that the spirit of the nation could only be tampered with at the risk of losing the original qualities of the nation, but it was not until his *Essaie sur les causes* (1736–43) that Montesquieu made a clear distinction between physical and moral causes, incorporating for the first time the climate as a determinant element. It is important to emphasize here (because of repeated misinterpretations of his work) that Montesquieu believed that the spirit of the nation was the result of a combination of *all* the different factors. Furthermore, he felt that it was crucial to keep a proper balance between the different causes. He believed that moral and physical causes, except in very primitive societies where the latter dominate, need each other to produce the desired effects. In *Essaie sur les causes* he went as far as to assert that in the formation of the spirit of the nation, moral causes are more important than physical ones. With the development of civilisation, climatic influences are tempered by the emergence of religion, morals, law etc. In addition, Montesquieu saw it as the task of the legislator to impinge upon the domination of the climate, trying to weaken its grip, provided of course that the general spirit of the nation was not interfered with. In any case, in developed societies the legislator had to operate mainly through moral causes because, as said earlier, the role of the climate becomes less forceful (Shackelton, R. 1961: 318).

In his short essay *Of National Characters* (1748), David Hume (1964, III) assumed that each nation had a peculiar set of manners and that these can often be explained by reference to physical (climate) and moral (government, wealth etc.) causes. Hume was a firm believer in the action of moral causes on the national character, although he admitted that climatic extremes could affect it, even if he preferred to offer non-physical but rather biological causes to account for the inferiority of the peoples living in the temperate climates. Hume provided a long list of examples across time and space to show the effects of moral causes:

1) Governments which have existed for a long time in a vast territory cause the spread of the national character over the whole area, e.g. China.

2) Small nations living contiguously have different characters even if the climates are the same, e.g. Athens and Thebes.

3) National characters follow political not geographical boundaries, e.g. Spain and France.

4) The people of a nation scattered in a diaspora, provided that they keep their original national character by maintaining close contact and keeping their habits, will be different from the other peoples among whom they live, e.g. the Jews.

5) If two nations living in the same territory do not mix because of linguistic, religious or any other differences, they will keep for centuries different national characters, e.g. Turks and Greeks.

6) The national character will follow a nation in its world expansion, e.g. the Spanish, English, and French colonies in America.

7) National characters may change quite substantially from one historical period to another due to a variety of reasons (changes of government, ethnic mixtures etc.), e.g. Ancient and Modern Greeks.

8) Adjacent nations which are in close political, commercial or any other form of contact with one another, will develop certain common national characteristics.

9) Some nations exhibit a perfect combination of manners and characters with the result they do not have a pronouced national character, e.g. England, but not Scotland despite its similar climate.

Rousseau and Political Nationalism

For purposes of exposition and to maintain a traditionally accepted distinction, I shall present Rousseau as the founder of political nationalism because he 'is said to have equated nationhood entirely with the expression of a people's will' (Barnard, F.M. 1983: 231). According to this viewpoint what mattered for Rousseau was the making, maintenance and reawakening of the nation as a political community of a state. And yet Rousseau could not conceive of the state without the nation; in fact

he saw the nation in the cultural sense of the term, as the logical and historical precondition for the state.

In trying to ascertain Rousseau's concept of the nation, it may not be
an idle pursuit to look first into his anthropological theory. As Lévi-
Strauss has rightly insisted, one of Rousseau's major concerns early in
his career as a writer was the question of the transition from nature to
culture, from animality to humanity. In the *Discourse on the Origins of
Inequality Among Men* (1755), he saw this issue in terms of a sort of
evolutionary process from a posited and speculative first stage which he
referred to as the state of nature, that is, a pre-cultural situation, to a final
stage in which civil government is instituted. There is not much difference between men in the natural state and animals, except that the former are better organized and had more 'choice', something which was
absent from animals due to their more instinctive behaviour. This is a
stage in which there is no language or family and where individuals are
basically on their own; in other words, there is no society. Rousseau
accepts only the existence of two principles: self-interest (preservation
of oneself) and pity (towards other beings, particularly of the same
kind). In the state of nature there was no distinction between good and
evil (Crocker, L.G. 1968, I: 56–8). In general, Rousseau insists that
without using the capacity to make standards, society cannot change. It
is well known that in the *Second Discourse* Rousseau celebrated the natural state as peaceful and stable, and how the absence of passions made
natural man a happier being than civilized man.

It was an external force, the growth of populations, which brought,
along with other concomitant factors, an end to the state of nature and
gave rise to what we might call the state of savagery. The pressures created by the increase in numbers slowly forced natural man to come to
terms, reflectively, with his environment, including his equals. Hunting
and fishing were developed along with their appropriate artefacts. A
strategy had to follow to cope with his surroundings. The first act of cultural man was to create a standard by which he felt proud of himself; it
was the 'awareness that he was not an animal' (Cohler, A.M. 1970:
116). With the idea of helping each other, individuals formed loose
associations and developed rudimentary language, that Rousseau
labelled universal, and that consisted only of gestures and cries.
Families were established and the sexual division of labour followed.
Eventually, families converged into aggregates to form tribes and the
physical separation of these groups led to the development of conversa-
tional languages. To all ends and purposes these were basically egalitarian societies (Crocker, L.G. 1968, I: 261). It is in this context that what
we might call the primitive nature appears. It is towards the beginning of
Part II of the *Second Discourse* that Rousseau described this momentous

change: 'Men who until this time wandered in the forest, having adopted a more permanent settlement, slowly came together, united in different hordes and finally formed in each territory (*contrée*) a particular nation unified by its customs and character, not by regulations and laws, but by the same way of life and eating habits and by the common influence of climate' (Rousseau, 1964, III: 169).

But we have to look into *The Essay on the Origins of Language* if we want to find out more about the development of (primitive) nations. It is here that Rousseau places language at the centre of what is most distinctive between one nation and another. Furthermore, because language is the originial social institution par excellence it must come from the outside, it must be the result of natural, external causes. The origin of language, he argued, cannot be due to the physical needs of the individual, but to the passions, that will eventually result in the *amour propre*, a 'sentiment produced by the capacity to see oneself and another in terms of some external standard of comparison' (Cohler, A. 1970: 110). The force of language, once created, was unstoppable, and had its own dynamics. Rousseau presented also a climatic theory of nations and languages. He distinguished between northern climates and southern climates; in the former, harsher climate, the language of the nation was geared towards reason (mutual aid); in the latter, softer climate, towards emotion (love and pity). These developments, one should insist, took place prior to the development of civil government. For Rousseau this was probably *the happiest state of man.*

With the invention of agriculture, which according to Rousseau was the result of further population pressure, the division of labour followed (particularly between agriculture and metallurgists), property rights were instituted and inequality began. In this stage, co-operation gave way to exacerbated competition and the worst passions began to affect human beings: envy, hypocrisy, selfishness etc. It was a society in which wealth was the measure of all things. In the end it became the war of all against all, a situation in which *homo hominis lupus.*

The idea of a civil government, that is the institution of laws and a judicial system, was a scheme, according to Rousseau, conceived by the wealthy to protect themselves against the poor and hence to perpetuate their position in society. It was the most ingenious ideological plot ever conceived by the human mind to dupe the poor and dispossessed. The *Second Discourse* finishes with the uncompromising statement that the progress of society was the progress of inequality. With the last stage of society, human beings finally lose their harmony with nature and act against their natural inclination. The artificial inequality created is a source of unavoidable unhappiness.

In later writings, and particularly in *Du Contrat Social*, Rousseau moderated his radicalism. The establishment of government was not only envisaged as a defence of property, but as something which could also help in the sociability of the nation as well. Rousseau still believed that inequality was the source of all social problems, but he also believed that private property adequately regulated and limited was essential to political society. Furthermore, he used the idea of natural equality, that is the conception that human beings were originally free, and not dependent on others, to assert logically that the only justification for civil government was the consent of the individuals and that inequality was the death of freedom. The law, as the expression of the general will of the people, supposed that all citizens were equal. In the end, the idea of the egalitarian state of nature, although it was a stage to which societies could not return, could serve as a yardstick, as a model by which to judge political society (Derathé, R. 1982).

Cohler concludes her analyses of the origin of nations in Rousseau with the idea that Rousseau put forward three values, three standards for human beings: 'language, wealth and the laws. The third, the laws, is different in that it is an ordering of the first two common standards' (Cohler, A. 1970: 128), but it can also become autonomous like the others, and can lead to further inequalities. Rousseau believed that language bound people together, though at a rather non-reflective, non-conscious level; the absence of a government to protect it was also another negative factor. In addition, language was unable to protect society from further inequality. Only in government, as we have just seen, was there the possibility of putting a halt to the degeneration of human society.

If the *Second Discourse* deals with the origins of nations, the *Social Contract* is concerned with how a nation united by 'bonds of origin, interest or convention but which has not yet known the true yoke of the law' (Rousseau, 1964, III: 169) becomes conscious of itself and how it acquires a civil government, a state. What is needed if we want to ascertain the true foundation of society and how it becomes a political nation, says Rousseau, is to examine how a people becomes a people (Rousseau, 1964, III: 390). To use Hegel's terminology, what Rousseau tries to account for is the transformation of nations *an sich* – 'unreflective collectivities' as F.M. Barnard (1983: 237) calls them – into *für sich*. It is in this context that Rousseau's concept of the general will seems to be relevant. Among other things, this idea is Rousseau's response to cosmopolitanism, because 'it can come to men only when they acquire that *moi commun* which arises out of close association with their fellow citizens' (Shklar, J. 1969). Does the general will assume, then, the existence of a national character? This would appear to be the case, because what are all those things that are common to the members of society if not the national character? Shklar, however, seems to believe that for Rousseau the national character is artificially imposed on the people from the outside by the legislator. As we have seen the idea of a national character was very much part of the heritage that Rousseau received from Montesquieu, Hume and Voltaire. It certainly would be incorrect to make of Rousseau a Herder *avant la lettre*, but nonetheless he seems to believe that the national character, if it is not perhaps the characteristic of every people, it ought to be. In his unfinished *Project of Constitution for Corsica*, he bluntly stated that for such an endeavour, 'the first rule to follow is the national character. Every people has or should have one, and if the national character is lacking one must begin by giving it to the people' (Rousseau, 1964, III: 913). In the latter case, as we shall see, it is up to the legislator to give a people its distinctive national character. In fact, for Rousseau 'the particular character which it is assumed that each people should have is dictated partly by what is appropriate in the actual circumstances of the state and partly by the ideal which the legislator sets before himself' (Cobban, A. 1964: 109).

We have seen how Montesquieu listed a number of causes which contribute to the formation of the *esprit général d'une nation* – climate, religion, laws, maxims of government, customs etc. Montesquieu is not the climatic determinist that many believe him to be; climate seems only to take precedence over other factors in very primitive types of societies. What is certain is that he held that it was dangerous to tamper with the national character, and that laws should not be in opposition to it. Rousseau also considered a variety of factors that moulded the national character. These certainly included the geographic surroundings of a country: Rousseau speculated on the impact of the mountains for Switzerland or of insularity for Corsica. Again he believed that people in the countryside tend to preserve the national character, while the burgers tend to be cosmopolitan, not patriots. Language, as we have seen, is also an important element in shaping the spirit or character of a nation, though Rousseau does not envisage the identity of language and nation which is typical of Herder; in fact, he at first contemplates also the possibility that it is the national character which moulds language.

The examples that Rousseau proposes of unsullied national characters tend to be from antiquity. The problems with the European peoples of the eighteenth century was that they were not patriotic at all: different nations were converging into the same type of education, the same literary taste, the same habits, the same type of governments, the same entertainments; Rousseau even found that love-making was at fault for not being national enough in character (Palmer, R. 1940: 107). Critics have seen a rhetorical aggrandizement in this kind of statement; after all

Rousseau was obviously referring to a very small minority of European cosmopolitans; and yet what is important to emphasize here is that Rousseau castigated a tendency towards European uniformity, which he profoundly abhorred, deplored and fought (successfully) against.

That the national character is not just the outcome of the unconscious history of a people, I have already pointed out. Sometimes the national character has to be created and imposed on a nation. And here is where the legislator plays a key role. A distinction should be made, however, between primitive and modern nations which neither Rousseau nor most of his commentators seem to make. It is one thing to say that Moses created a Jewish nation, and a very different one to say that Peter the Great failed to give the Russians an appropriate national character (Shklar, J. 1969: 161). I have indicated before that comparison between the *Social Contract* (1762) and the *Considerations on the Government of Poland* (1771) shows a much more 'nationalistic' – patriotic would probably be a more accurate word – language in the latter than in the former. In the *Social Contract* the legislator, who is described as a god-like figure, is normally an outsider; he must be endowed with great political qualities and a great sense of appeal, because he can neither impose the laws by force nor has he any position in the civil government. The charismatic figure of the law-giver appears as if he is speaking in the name of God, and that is why Rousseau says that in the origins of nations, politics and religion go hand in hand, one being an instrument of the other (Rousseau, J.J. 1964, III: 283–4). It is interesting that although using one of the same classical examples – that of Lycurgus – Rousseau's reference to the legislator in *Considérations* is dramatically different in emphasis. In modern nations there are no legislators, only law-makers. What a difference from say Moses, who gave the Jewish people a political character, customs and freedom which have lasted five thousand years, including the diaspora. Lycurgus taught the Spartans love of the *patrie* by a constant emphasis on their laws, their games and their festivities and their amorous practices. In a word, all the ancient legislators tried to build up links which would bond their citizens to their *patrie* and among themselves.

It is essential that the legislator, in imposing laws from the outside, should have drawn them up not in abstract, as the best possible ones, but as the most appropriate ones for the country of reference. The institutions that are given to a country by the law-givers should be in tune with the existing national relations, and only destined to combat, to destroy, the vice and degeneration that the nation had suffered. J. Shklar (1969: 161) seems to have exaggerated the arbitrariness of the national character to be imposed upon a people; in fact as F.M. Barnard has remarked, 'there was not the slightest chance, according to Rousseau, that a political nation could be created independently of its nature, culture, history. Nation-building, in other words, is not simply a matter of national purpose and political will. To be a nation requires continuity as well as identity, a tradition of culture as well as the creation of a political structure ' (1983: 239). Institutions then, had to be introduced at the right time; he felt that Corsica was ripe for a legislator, but the attempt by Peter the Great to create a Russian nation came too early, as well as being unoriginal and inadequate. Because he had the classical models in mind and he was concerned about the intensity of national feelings, Rousseau believed that small states were in a better position to succeed in developing the patriotic feelings of their citizens than large ones. Corsica was about the right size, while Poland was definitely too large.

We come now to the final element, but certainly not the least important, of Rousseau's conception of how the nation and its character are moulded. For him, more was required to create a national consciousness and an *esprit de corps* than the work of the languages. The will of all did not necessarily coincide with the general will. To that end, Rousseau put great weight on what we could call national or public education. The model chosen by Rousseau for education is the Spartan one, in which what matters most is not so much knowledge but the forging of patriotic citizens; it is an education under the rigid control of the state which aims at creating a strong national character. In such a system education is a means to an end: giving individuals a strong sense of national identity. Unlike *Emile* (1762), which is a scheme for a private, idealistic education of human beings, *Considérations* (1771) continues some of the ideas on public education, following the state dictat, which Rousseau had first presented in his article *Economie Politique* (1755). As Shklar has rightly remarked: 'A cohesive community cannot be built by those who cherish the *moi humain*. That is why civic education and the education of the individual have nothing in common' (1969: 160). Rousseau was well aware of the dilemma, that one had to choose between private and public education, and it would appear that in his later writings he opted for patriotic education.

It is interesting to note the different role played by the teaching of history in the two different schemes of education. While in *Emile,* Rousseau considers history as a dangerous discipline because it encourages a partial and passionate vision of events, in the *Considérations* he advises that by age sixteen, the Polish youth should have imbibed the whole history of their country. In general, national education was intended, in the words of Rousseau, 'to give to minds the national form, and to direct their opinions and tastes so that they become patriots by inclination, by passion and by necessity' (1964, III: 966). Schoolchildren were to be required to play games which might encourage their patriotic feelings as well as to be taught the traditional customs of their country. Public festivals of all types which encouraged civic participation were another way conceived by Rousseau to rekindle the patriotic flame. Finally, the existence of a citizens' militia would complete the task. The idea was that a citizen would constantly be participating in celebrations of one type or another which would make the love of country (patriotism) their strongest, indeed their only passion. Religion, as I have said above, was seen by Rousseau as a cohesive force, and hence something to be used by the state to enhance the national spirit. The idea that religion could sanctify the nation, and in this way make it more the object of worship, did not escape Rousseau who often referred to the example of the Jewish nation (Cobban, A. 1964: 114).

In spite of his reliance on the patriotism of the classical city-states as a model for his political nationalism, Rousseau imagined a nation indivisible made by the communion of members or citizens; what was essential for Rousseau were the laws, the customs, the government and the constitution; in a word, the relations between the state and its members. He believed that nations were unique and by existing and realizing themselves they contributed to give variety to the world. There was, however, a tension between statehood and nationhood: the former was based on reason and the latter on sentiment. In the final resort, when Rousseau had to decide which 'theory of public willing' was more justifiable, he chose patriotism (Barnard, F.M. 1984: 260–1). This is because love of one's country was for Rousseau one hundred times more ardent and delightful than that of a mistress.

Herder and Cultural Nationalism

As in Rousseau's case, I shall start with the received wisdom that Herder was the founder of cultural nationalism, that is, of a doctrine which defines a nation in terms of its ethnic features, but I hope to show that Herder was also concerned with the political society and its legitimation (Barnard, F.M. 1983: 232). It is interesting to remark that the political emphasis of Rousseau and the cultural emphasis of Herder were also reflected in their own presentations of the self: Rousseau as a 'citizen of Geneva' and Herder as a 'cultural German'.

F. Meinecke has said that Johann Gottfried Herder's conception of nationality was the result of his experiences as a young man in his twenties in the city of Riga. In this Latvian city he experienced the 'pressure upon a small subjugated people by a large ruling nation' and wondered 'how long this popular culture, with its original language, songs and customs, could possibly last in face of the corrosive or destructive influence of modern ways' (Meinecke, F. 1972: 305).

That Herder should have felt such a concern for the value and uniqueness of each culture, to the extent of saying that each nation had its own centre of happiness and should be left to its own means, was certainly a novel and revolutionary thing to say in the second half of the eighteenth century in a Germania with little sense of patriotism, at least the patriotism stemming from the existence of a German people. Herder castigated and ridiculed his compatriots for their despite of things German and their love of French language, culture and habits. Many of the writers and politicians had cosmopolitan leanings, and words like *Nation* and *Vaterland* were rarely if ever used to refer to the German people as a whole. Outstanding as an exception of German patriotic feelings before Herder was Friedrich Karl von Moser, who in 1765 published *Von dem Deutschen Nationalgeist* and the *Patriotische Briefe* the year after. Moser was the first to use the expression *Nationalgeist* in the German language – a term which in the form of *Volksgeist* will be central to German thought from Herder to Savigny, as we shall see below. Moser firmly believed in the existence of a single German people characterized by its common language and common institutions. However, it was Herder who often coined, and in many cases popularised the key terms of the nationalist vocabulary in the German language. I am referring to expressions such as national language (*Nationalsprache*), national history (*Nationalgeschichte*), national education (*Nationalerziehung*), national traditions (*Nationaltraditionen*) and many others. Interestingly enough he never used the expression *Volkgeist*, but rather *Geist des Volkes* and *Geist der Nation*, and of course *Nationalcharacter*.

Herder and Rousseau have been presented as arch-enemies of the Enlightenment, and no doubt they were both critics of the rationalist excesses of some *philosophes;* however, they were passive heirs of the Enlightenment even if they tried to temper the extremes of the cult of reason with the passion of emotions. In stating that Herder was the founder of cultural nationalism one should not assume that he favoured a kind of exclusivist and xenophobic nationalism. The very opposite is true: 'to Herder', as Cassirer has appropriately reminded us, 'every nation was only a voice in a universal, all-embracing harmony' (Cassirer 1979: 185). Particularlism, then, was not incompatible with universalism; in fact it was its presupposition. Herder shared with the Romantics the celebration of *all* forms of national life; the goal of historical knowledge and the familiarity with world literature were means to the end of feeling and enjoying the existing national *differences*. Herder was explicit in condemning the exaltation of one's nation at the expense of others, and he can rightly be seen as the father of German cultural nationalism; he justified his love of things German as a reaction against those in his country who had adopted foreign –

French – affectations and had forgotten their true national selves. In this sense Dumont's assertion that Herder's ethnic theory of the nation was a 'vindication of German culture against the cosmopolitanism of the Enlightenment' (Dumont, L. 1986: 593), is incomplete and misleading because the problem is not so much cosmopolitanism but the domination of French culture in Germania. Furthermore, Herder cannot be blamed for the fact that his 'successors', Dumont dixit, 'have more often hierarchized the cultures or nations with their own at the top of the value scale, than they have valued them equally' (Dumont, L. 1983: 21). The problem with Dumont's characterization of German ideology in general, and of Herder in particular, in that it purports to have found a continuity of thought between Herder and Hitler, is not only that it is hardly new, but also that it is profoundly ahistorical and Gallocentric. Is it another case of *La France au dessus de tout*?

Herder's starting point is man in society: a man with a culture and with a language and living in a polity. There is no hypothetical isolated natural man, closer to animality, who progressively evolves into a human being by step by step acquisition of human features. 'Man', said Herder, 'is not a Hobbesian wolf, nor a lone creature of the forest, as Rousseau would have it; for he has communal language in which to communicate' (Herder 1969: 167). Ape and man are clearly distinct species and there is no continuity between one and the other. It is nature, or divine providence in religious terminology, which creates the social group, whether it is the family or the nation of people (*Volk*), which after all is nothing but a sort of enlarged family. Man cannot be conceived of in isolation from society; he depends totally on social organization in one form or another. Furthermore, Herder, unlike Rousseau, cannot conceive of man without a political organization, that is, without a system which regulates human relations. In that sense, then, political organization is as natural to man as language. The individual can only be fulfilled within the nation which is conceived of by Herder as an organism – as a plant in the garden of humanity – with all the characteristics entailed by that: plants grow, flourish and languish.

In his *Yet Another Philosophy of History* (1774), Herder states that each people plays the role that divine providence has assigned to it; a few years later, in his *Ideas for a Philosophy of Mankind* (1784–91) he is more concerned with explaining the diversity of nations, each characterized by a peculiar culture, language, religion, political institution, art, literature etc. Each nation is different because the combination of these elements makes it an original society. Big or small, each nation, as part of the divine plan, brings to humanity a certain experience and way of being, feeling or doing that no other nation can provide. And in this respect it is irreplaceable because it represents a cultural enrichment for all human beings. How can we account for this diversity? Certainly not by reference to race, which according to Herder was not a valid way of classifying human beings and had no genetic power to account for human diversity. Human beings belonged in a single human species; this is the way the Bible tells the story of the origins of mankind (descended from one stem) and it was also confirmed by research into the different branches that studied man.

If national differences are not the result of differences in origin, how did different cultures come to exist? According to Herder they developed as the result of the combined effects of certain factors. Outstanding among these was the geographical environment, that is, a God-willed natural phenomenon. The main features of each nationalist group, be it language, customs or character, were shaped, Herder maintained, by climate, mountains, rivers etc. Once the milieu had created a national character, then heredity made possible its transmission from generation to generation. Another influential factor was education; it helped to shape the nation in one or another direction. Then, of course, according to the degree of interaction with other peoples, the national character may be more or less peculiar. Herder was aware that the extreme isolation of nations might be conclusive in developing an inflexible national character, while national contact and competition may produce a more versatile one. Finally, tradition is also a factor shaping the nation. By this term, Herder meant ways of conceiving, of seeing, of feeling and of expressing things. Here, of course, is where language becomes essential, because it is the way in which traditions are passed to the next generation (Ergang, R. 1931: 89–94). It is obvious that for Herder the development of a nation was the result of natural factors; human intervention could only help to enhance this process, but in no way could it be in a position to impose change from the outside.

The centrality of language in Herder's definition of the *Volk* cannot be overemphasized. At times it would appear as if a national community is defined mainly, if not exclusively, by its language, and the genius of a nation would seem to find its expression in the language of the community. Even when he considers other factors affecting the nation, they are always reflected through language. A good case in point is Herder's *Von Geist der Ebraischen Poesie* (1782–3). The Hebrews represented for Herder a people with an authentic and remarkable national spirit which had lasted for centuries. Besides language, Herder recognized the existence of a number of elements in the history of the Jews which explained the strength of this nation. For example, Herder listed the compact between God and the Israelites and the respect of the Hebrews for their ancestors and for the territory they had inhabited. All these elements, however, were closely related; they were part of an organic totality which was made possible by the existence of the Hebrew language and its literature, as well as being externalized through it (Barnard, F.M. 1959).

In the beginning there was one single language: in that, Herder followed the Biblical story. But for him, language was neither the result of divine creation nor human invention. In fact, language is implicit in the definition of a man as a rational being. Herder would have nothing to do with attempts to explain the origins of human language by looking at the transition from animality to humanity. In spite of believing in some sort of single organic plan, Herder was no transformist, and for three reasons: the uniformity of the plan was simply Leibniz's scale of beings writ large in the light of comparative anatomy (the Creation was a single work which reflected the creator), species do not descend one from another (this specifically applies to the idea that men do not have any kinship with apes) and no new organic forms had appeared since the Creation. His concept of *Humanität* was very much inspired by Christian thinking and it was a reaction both against the idea of man as an animal and against mysticism (Rouché, M. 1962: 21–3).

From the original single language, all the languages of the world developed. The peculiarities and idiosyncracies of each language can only be explained by reference to its own natural history, including first and foremost the effects of the environment, but also the customs of the nation. As Herder put it: 'there came into being a thousand languages according to the climate and the customs of a thousand nationalities' (Herder, J.G. 1911, I: 1).

A language for Herder is not only the most distinctive expression of the spirit of a nation, but also the only way in which the latter can manifest itself. Language is the royal path to the identity of a nation; *Volk* and language cannot be conceived of independently of each other. Many things in the life of *Volk* can be lost, including its political independence, but if the language is preserved, the essence of the nation will survive. For Herder the world consists of a variety of linguistic nations, which have grown naturally over a long period of time. The language of each nation is the most valuable wealth that it possesses, because this language is the abode of the religious beliefs, the customs and the history of the nation. It is only with one's own mother tongue that the communication of emotions, thoughts and ideals is made possible. The common native language allows all different layers of the population to develop a common patriotic sentiment. Herder felt strongly that languages should be allowed to develop independently of each other, without mixtures and borrowings. This was the natural order of things and the world should remain this way.

Is it surprising that for Herder, nationhood should be the basis for statehood or that no other state could be justified unless it was congruent with the nation? In his *Ideas for a Philosophy of the History of Mankind* he clearly stated that:

> The family is a product of nature. The most natural state is, therefore, a state composed of a single people with a single national character. A people can maintain its national character for thousands of years and, if its prince, who has this heritage, has a concern for it, it can be developed through education along the lines most natural to it. For a people is a natural growth like a family, only spread more widely. Nothing seems, therefore, more clearly opposed to the aims which all governments should have in view than the expansion of states beyond their natural limits, the indiscriminate mingling of various nations and human types under one sceptre (Herder, J.G. 1911, XIII: 384).

Herder's tirade against multinational states and empires was precisely based on the idea that they were monstrous assemblages, like the Beast of Revelations lacking a national character. What comes out of Herder's perspective is that the natural type of society for human beings to live in is the nation, and not the artificial state. Furthermore, there is no order of rank in nations; they are all part of the divine providence and have the right to develop according to their national spirit.

Barnard has emphasized that Herder's political model is one that follows from Mosaic Law. First of all, it emphasizes a somewhat inflexible and legalistic republican type of constitution. Second, it conceives of the nation without a central focus of power, but rather encouraging self-government for the different sectional groups. Third, the legislative power is in the hands of the elders, who are seen as the representative body. Finally, the individual is part of the whole which is the nation (Barnard, F.M. 1965: 65–67).

Quite a large part of Herder's concern for language was in connection with the situation of German in his day and age. Because he thought that there was a German *Volk* and a German language, and that the mother tongue was an essential element of the nation, he was appalled by the low prestige of German among his compatriots and he felt that the honour of his country was at stake. He became an ardent propagandist of the German language, praising its qualities as a robust and philosophical language, comparable to Greek and Latin. He insisted that only the use of the native language could help to expose the German national character in literature. He urged his compatriots to speak the language on all occasions and to find inspiration in its history and idioms. Particularly important for Herder was that schooling should be in the mother tongue, and not a foreign language (not even in Latin, as it was often in his time). A patriotic feeling could only be instilled in pupils, when the training was in the mother tongue; no genuine German culture could emerge and develop without the use of German. Finally, Herder also wanted the use of the vernacular in the Church; as he put it: 'The language in which we make love, pray and dream, that is our most intimate language, our language of worship' (Herder, J.G. 1911, XXIV: 43). Now I have said earlier that this passionate defence of the German language was not chauvinistic, but just a crusade to give German the right place in the life of his country; otherwise, Herder encouraged the knowledge of other languages and literatures in line with his strong belief that they promoted universal harmony and understanding, because after all every nation was only an individual expression within a world in which flourished many nations. No single nation could pretend to be the 'chosen people' because 'each nation by fully realizing its distinctive essence enriched the quality of humanity at large' (Barnard, F.M. 1983: 234).

Hegel on the *Volksgeist*

There is hardly any doubt that there is close dependence between Montesquieu's general spirit of the nation and Hegel's *Volksgeist*. Hegel was the first to acknowledge his debt to Montesquieu, and credited him with having adumbrated the idea that nations had a character and an individuality. It was Hegel's holistic perspective that led him to state that it was because Montesquieu was able to understand the whole that he was able to understand the parts. In his early religious writings, however, Hegel seems to have been under the spell of Herder's concept of the *Volk*. He envisaged religion in Herderian terms, that is as a manifestation of the spirit of the people. Each nation exhibited its own peculiar *Volksgeist*, with a set of social and cultural institutions which corresponded to it (Avineri, S. 1962: 468). Later on, as a result of the French Revolution, Hegel's idea of *Volksgeist* became more political and less cultural. In fact he conceived of political phenomena as the essence of the *Volksgeist*; *Volksgeist* changes when political insitutions change and not vice versa. Being a people meant for Hegel being organized in a political framework, that is a state, though not necessarily a modern state (ibid.: 470). According to Avineri, in the *Philosophy of Right* (1821) Hegel stated that 'the *Volksgeist* does not *create* the unique character of each people, but it is the product of its concrete arrangements in the realms of religion, tradition and the like ... For Hegel the *Volksgeist* is identical with the features it is creating and does not *create* them, as the Jurists and Romantics generally held' (ibid.: 476).

It should be emphasized that Hegel gave the notion of *Volksgeist* an historical character, that is, he believed it to be an exteriorization of the *Weltgeist*. In fact, it was the world spirit which propelled the nations to realize their own peculiar national spirits. Individual nations were just playing the part assigned to them by world history. In addition, and as N. Rotenstreich has remarked: 'Hegel identifies the spirit of the people with its historical and cultural accomplishments, namely its religion, mores, constitution and its political laws. They are the work of the people, they are the people' (1973, IV: 492). In his *Philosophy of History*, Hegel periodized history in four stages, each stage representing a different type of consciousness. He distinguished then four types of cultures or *Volksgeister*: the Oriental, the Greek, the Roman and the Germanic-Christian. Each historical epoch has its own hegemonic nation, but the domination is not political but cultural. However, Hegel maintained that each *Volk* had to be a state because the political conditions of the time so demanded. But this should not be misconstrued 'to imply the emergence of a unitary state, let alone a nation-state, nor is the dominance of any given *Volksgeist* reducible to its political power' (Avineri, S. 1972: 222). Hegel never ascribed political domination to what he termed world historical nations. The qualities he praised in his *Philosophy of Right* were literary creation, poetry, philosophy, science and the plastic arts.

Romanticism and Nationalism

It has repeatedly been said that among the many things which were vehiculated by romantic literature were national consciousness and national pride; that in fact the prodigious development of modern nationalism in nineteenth-century Europe was the result of the combined effects of the French Revolution and of Romanticism. It is no coincidence to find as forebearers of Romanticism the names of Rousseau and Herder. Romanticism was, however, a complex phenomenon which affected the whole of Europe from the late eighteenth century until at least 1850. Here I am mainly interested in the early period, often referred to as pre-Romanticism. A number of thematic ideas emerged during the last quarter of the eighteenth century which constituted the core of romanticism and which directly or indirectly contributed to the spread of the nationalist world vision. Without any pretence of being exhaustive, I would like to mention the following:

1) Pluralism

This is the term used by I. Berlin when trying to express 'the belief not merely in multiplicity, but in the incommensurability of the values of different cultures and societies' (Berlin, I. 1976: 153). This is a concept which was central to both Rousseau and Herder though it was the latter who gave it a more prominent place in his work. Most contemporary students of Romanticism seem to believe that this simple, yet revolutionary idea for the people of the Enlightenment was a key factor in the configuration of nationalism. Arthur O. Lovejoy called it 'diversitarianism' in his seminal paper and defined it as 'an assertion of the value of diversity in human opinions, characters, tastes, arts and cultures' (1941: 275). The diversity of nations was 'natural and necessary, and also supremely desirable and right' (ibid.: 277). It is arguable what kind of nationalism follows from this concern with *Eigentümlichkeit*, whether the humanitarian one *à la* Herder or the exclusivist and chauvinist one. Lovejoy, writing at a time of crisis believed that the idea of national superiority had roots in the romantic intimation of the pursuit and praise of *la différence*, which easily led to the development of prejudice against other nations. This reaction against the perceived uniformitarianism of the Enlightenment led to the belief that nations should preserve their characteristics at all costs. H. Schenk quotes Walter Scott saying: ' "Let us remain as nature made us – Englishmen, Irishmen, Scotchmen, with something like the impress of our several countries upon each" ' because 'the degree of national diversity between different countries is but an instance of that general variety which Nature seems to have adopted as a principle through all her works, as anxious to avoid as modern statesmen to enforce, anything like an approach to absolute uniformity' (Schenk, H.G. 1979: 15). Both Lovejoy and Schenk emphasize the fact that the distinctiveness of a people, expressed in its *Volksgeist*, was the rallying point for the romantic imagination and became one of the indispensable parts of the movement. The initial impulse for the national resurgence of many peoples owed a great deal to this Herderian notion of singularity.

2) Nostalgia for the past

The Romantics brought a new kind of history to the fore. While the Enlightenment believed in the *histoire raisonnée*, Romanticism was interested in the past for its own sake; the past was not only knowledge, in fact it embodied the loftiest and most worthy ideals. Novalis' *Die Christenheit oder Europa* (1799) is 'a representation of an ideal which is also a pattern for the future development of Europe' (Engelhand, D. von 1988: 117); in the words of Friedrich Schlegel: 'A historian is a prophet facing backwards' (ibid.). For the Romantics the future was of little interest; their obsession with the past was a way of justifying and giving legitimacy to a given institution or belief. The religious element was often crucial in the idealization of the past; that is why the Middle Ages had a great appeal among Romantics – because of their

Christian spirituality. From the perspective of nationalism, the nostalgia for the past took the form of looking back to a period in the history of a nation when it achieved literary fame, political success or had flourished culturally. Romantic historiography, whether to uncover the past of a forgotten country or to celebrate the past of a powerful nation was an unavoidable stage forming episodes through which all coutries went.

In the field of the romantic historical novel Sir Walter Scott excelled in awakening a patriotic interest for the lost causes of small, oppressed nationalities. The impact of Scott's novels in Europe, whatever his intentions might have been, was astonishing; the *genre* he had started found followers everywhere and contributed to create a growing interest in the forgotten history of many countries. Manzoni, whose novel *I promessi sposi* played a major role to the Italian *Risorgimento*, happily admitted to the influence of Sir Walter Scott.

In the area of law, the German Historical School emphasized that history was the source of law. This conception attacked all voluntaristic conceptions of the origins of law, and maintained that laws, like language, religion or customs, were a historical precipitate and could not be left to the will of individuals to change them. The best known representative of the School, F.K. Savigny, maintained that law was closely connected with the *Volksgeist*. Each nation has its own laws in consonance with the spirit of the nation. So law is then the result of unconscious forces, and not an 'offspring of free and conscious human activities' (Cassirer, E. 1979: 182). Savigny added another piece in the nationalist puzzle when he conceived of law as a sort of primeval national force; as he put it: 'In the earliest times to which authentic history extends, the law will be found to have already attained a fixed character peculiar to the people (*Volk*) like their language, manners and constitution' (1814: 8). Savigny will always insist that what binds a people into a whole is not something arbitrary and accidental, but some inner metaphysical necessity.

3) Organicism

The holistic conception of the nation was very much one of Herder's presuppositions. Lovejoy (1941) has insisted that the idea that the social whole was more than the sum of its parts – the individuals – was a new idea in a century where the individual was at the centre of attention and where society was conceived as finding its resolution in the analysis of the parts that made it. Metaphors of the nation as an organism (plant or animal) were rife with Romanticism. The idea of the birth, growth, maturity and decadence of the nation will be echoed in many writers following Herder's exhortations. In this scheme of things, each national organism is seen as making a contribution to Nature's plan, and each has a value in itself which is incommensurable and cannot be reduced to the individuals which compose it. But at the same time that the nation was conceived as an organism, so was the state. In fact, it was in the German philosophical tradition that both conceptions appeared.

4) Anti-rationalism

I envisage this romantic conception as multilayered. No doubt, as M.G. Schenk (1979) has noted, it was felt that the Enlightenment, with its detached concern for scientific objectivity, had stifled human emotions. Rousseau had already attacked reason for its lack of human achievements. For the Romantics emotions and imagination were more important than anything else. Patriotism, as an emotional affair, ranked high in the hierarchy of values of the Romantic man; love of country was natural, nearly instinctive, except that cosmopolitanism had killed those feelings and had to be reinstated so that the natural course of things would follow. For this a certain amount of voluntarism was needed.

Highly valued by Romantics was myth. While the Enlightenment had consigned myths to the inferno of superstitious ideas, they had become an object of worship and reverence for Romantics. They were regarded as the source of human culture, and from them emerged the highest achievements of Western civilization – poetry, art and history (Cassirer, E. 1979: 182–3). In Romantic historiography of nations, myths of origin and of development played an increasingly important role all over Europe.

Bibliography

Alberini, M., (1969) 'L'idée de nation' in M. Alberini et al. (eds) *L'idée de nation*, Paris: Presses Universitaires de France.

Avineri, S., (1962) 'Hegel and Nationalism', *Review of Politics*, 24.

— —, (1972) *Hegel's Theory of the Modern State*, Cambrige University Press.

Barnard, F. M., (1959) 'The Hebrews and Herder's Political Creed', *The Modern Language Review*, 54, pp. 533–46.

— —, (1965) *Social and Political Thought*, Cambridge University Press.

— —, (1983) 'National Culture and Political Legitimacy', *Journal of the History of Ideas*, 44, pp. 231–53.

— —, (1984) 'Patriotism and Citizenship in Rousseau', *The Review of Politics*, 46, pp. 244–65.

Berlin, I., (1976) *Vico and Herder*, London: Hogarth Press.

Cassirer, E., (1979) *The Myth of the State*, New Haven: Yale University Press.

Cobban, A., (1964) *Rousseau and the Modern State*, London: Allen and Unwin.

Cohler, A. M., (1970) *Rousseau and Nationalism*, New York: Basic Books.

Crocker, L. G., (1968) *J. J. Rousseau*, New York: Macmillan, 2 vols.

Cunningham, H., (1981) 'The Language of Patriotism 1750–1914', *History Workshop*, 12, pp. 8–33.

Derathé, R., (1982) 'La place et l'importance de la notion d'egalité dans la doctrine politique de Rousseau' in R. A. Leigh (ed.), *Rousseau after Two Hundred Years*, Cambridge University Press.

Dumont, L., (1983) 'Interaction between Cultures: Herder's *Volk* and Fichte's *Nation*' in J. B. Maier & C. Waxman (eds), *Ethnicity, Identity and History*, New Brunswick: Transaction.

— —, (1986) 'Are Cultures Living Beings? German Identity in Interaction', *Man*, 21, pp. 587–604.

Engelhand, D., (1988) 'Romanticism in Germany', in R. Porter & M. Teich (eds), *Romanticism in National Context*, Cambridge University Press.

Ergang, R. R., (1931) *Herder and the Foundations of German nationalism*, New York: Columbia University Press.

Godechot, J., (1971) 'Nation, patrie, nationalisme et patriotisme au XVIIIe siècle', *Annales Historiques de la Revolution Française*, 43, pp. 481–501

Herder, J. G., (1911) *Sämmtliche Werke*, (Hg. B. Sulphan), Berlin, 33 vols.

— —, (1969) 'Essay on the Original Language' in J. G. Herder *On Social and Political Culture*, Cambridge University Press

Hume, D., (1882–6) *Philosophical Essays*, London, 4 vols, (Reprint by Scientia Verlag Aale, 1964).

Lovejoy, A. O., (1941) 'The Meaning of Romanticism for the History of Ideas', *Journal of the History of Ideas*, 2, pp. 257–78.

Meinecke, F., (1972) *Historism*, London: Routledge and Kegan Paul.

Montesquieu, (1987) *Esprit des lois*, Paris: Flammarion, 2 vols.

Palmer, R., (1940) 'The National Idea in France before the Revolution', *Journal of the History of Ideas*, 1, pp. 95–111.

Rotenstreich, N., (1973) 'Volksgeist', *Dictionary of the History of Ideas*, Vol. 4.

Rouché, M., (1962) 'Introduction' in J. G. Herder *Idées pour la philosophie de l'histoire de l'humanité*, Paris: Aubier.

Rousseau, J. J., (1964) *Oeuvres Complètes*, Paris: Gallimard 4 vols.

Savigny, K., (1814) *Vom Beruf unszer Zeit für Gesetzgebung und Rechtswissenschaft*, Heidelberg: Mohr

Shackelton, R., (1961) *Montesquieu. A Critical Biography*, Oxford University Press.

Schenk, H. G., (1979) *The Mind of the European Romantics*, Oxford University Press

Shklar, J., (1969) *Man and Citizens*, Cambridge University Press.

Suratteau, J.R., (1983) 'Cosmopolitisme et patriotisme au Siècle des Lumières', *Annales Historiques de la Revolution Française*, 55, pp. 364–89.

Vlachos, G., (1974) *La Politique de Montesquieu en nature et méthode*, Paris: Montchrestien.

Part IV

The Development of Nationalism: Historical Processes

-8-

The Force of Historical Events: The French Revolution and its Aftermaths

Let me start with a typical statement raised by the title of this section: 'The French Revolution was a key event in the development of nationalism, both French nationalism and that of the other European countries'. This quote is extracted from Beatrice F. Hyslop's *Preface* to the second printing of her 1934 classic *French Nationalism in 1789* (1968: v–vi). Her book, based on a preliminary study of the general cahiers of grievances (*cahiers de doléances*) written on the eve of the French Revolution by the leaders of the three estates, but particularly by the representatives of the Third Estate, provides us with an 'expression of dominant opinion' (ibid.: vi) on the national question in 1789 and hence empirically confirms a generally held opinion.

Recently, in a little volume commemorating the two hundredth anniversary of the French Revolution, Conor Cruise O'Brien (1989) has suggested that to posit a cause-effect relationship between the French Revolution and nationalism is to ignore that both were coextensive; in other words, that what we know about the processes of the French Revolution indicates that from the very beginning there was a continuous and sustained manifestation of national identity and patriotism, which later culminated in the chauvinistic nationalism of France as the *Grande Nation*. What I am insisting here is that the French Revolution was the first modern nationalist revolution, and that later it became the model for modern nationalism in other European countries. It is only with this second meaning that it may make sense to say that the French Revolution generated nationalism in Western Europe. Furthermore, there are two dimensions which should be carefully distinguished: nationalism as an ideology vehiculated by the internal developments of the French Revolution and hence open to imitation by other countries, and nationalism as a reaction against the imperialist policies of Napoleon. We could say at this stage, perhaps somewhat simplistically, that the contradiction between the national ideals of the French Revolution and the practice of national oppression by Napoleon created a wide nationalist reaction in Europe against French domination.

Prior to 1789, the last meeting of the Estates General had been in 1614, so one could say that for 175 years the French people had had no voice. I need not enter into the reasons why King Louis XVI convocated the meeting; suffice it to say that he was hoping to neutralize the threat of the nobility by using the Third Estate as a buffer. He could not have suspected that once unleashed, the Third Estate would radically subvert the order of things, bringing an end not only to his power, but to the monarchy as well.

In 1789, says Jacques Godechot, '*le peuple français à la parole*', and this *parole* was expressed in thousands of cahiers which reflected the *mentalité* of the different estates (Godechot, J. 1971: 492). We know as yet little about peasant attitudes due to the fact that there is no overall study of the parish cahiers (around 40,000). Hyslop's study, although, as I said before, limited in scope, allows a first approximation to the national *mentalité* in 1789. Four distinctive features can be mentioned which Hyslop labels consciousness of nationality, democracy, *étatisme* and patriotism. It is not my intention to argue here whether these were the best possible terms, though the exchanges between J. Godechot (1975) and Boyd C. Schafer (1975) seem to indicate a basic misunderstanding between French and Anglo-Saxon researchers on the use of the word 'nationalism'. While in English nationalism and patriotism are often used interchangeably, in French *nationalisme* is envisaged as *patriotisme* taken to an extreme (ibid.: 331).

What defines, then, the French nation? To start with, one should say that both *nation* and *patrie* are terms used quite often in the general cahiers, while it would appear that the latter is practically absent from the parish cahiers. Does that mean, as Godechot has indicated, that *nation* was a term used only by the educated people? (Godechot, J. 1971: 495). Be that as it may, the fact is that the word *nation* hardly had a univocal meaning; at times it referred to the people and to its common traditions (including Catholicism), but also to the territory (though the idea of national boundaries was absent). There was a belief in the existence of a French national character, but language played a very limited role in the way of defining the nation. In a nutshell, the nation was envisaged politically, not culturally: there was a desire for unity and uniformity, as well as liberty and equality; education was seen as a tool for nation-building. The idea of democracy was particularly strong in the cahiers emanating from the Third Estate. Popular sovereignty was a key word – the conviction that all power stemmed from the nation and that the Third Estate embodied the nation. While the nobility wanted to preserve the status quo, the Third Estate was pushing for a vote by head, and the clergy was divided. The fact that the nobility and the clergy represented less than ten per cent of the French population, explains why the Third Estate insisted on asserting that because they represented the bulk of the French nation they should be better represented in the forthcoming meeting of the Estates General. An additional issue in the cahiers was the question of the attenuation of class differences. Finally, a call was also made to put an end to differences between provinces and to push for an equalization and uniformity among them.

The third element mentioned by Hyslop was *étatisme*. It is clear from the general cahiers that the state was seen as the sole and absolute sovereign; gallicanism also ran strong, reflecting among other things, an advanced process of secularization. Finally, we close the circle with patriotism. What is interesting in connection with the latter is how volatile – particularly in the light of the events of January 1793, i.e. the execution of the monarch – some of its aspects were. The patriotism of the cahiers was hardly to the nation, but to the king or at best to the king and the nation. It is true that the Bourbon kings were honoured as symbols of national unity, but in fact only very few cahiers were willing to dispose of the sanctity of the monarchy. Hyslop emphasizes that the patriotism of the general cahiers was one in which the *patrie* was envisaged both as an ideal combining the concept of a place called 'France', certain traditions, the state, etc. – and the attainment of the welfare of the nation as a goal. The cahiers also expressed an obvious concern with the propagation of patriotism through education, and saw in regional identities a major obstacle to the idea of French patriotism. We shall see in more detail how in the events of 1789 to 1792 patriotism came to be more and more identified with the defence of the Revolution; after 1792 the war against internal and external enemies defined patriotism in even more clear-cut terms, though none the less they were extremely open to ideological manipulation.

In the light of what I have been saying about nationalism not being a product but a concomitant phenomenon with the French Revolution, it is somewhat puzzling from a statistical viewpoint that according to Hyslop's definition of nationalism, out of the 522 general cahiers examined by her, only 64 held radical views on nationalism and only 121 could be labelled progressive. What may explain the success of the more advanced views on nationalism are two factors: first, the fact that only the radical cahiers circulated in the big cities (Paris, Lyon), and second, the fact that only a small percentage of the cahiers which purported conservative views on nationalism (or no views at all for that matter) were actually printed. In conclusion, one should not exaggerate the 'nationalism' emerging from the cahiers. There were strong resistances to the idea of France as a unity coming from the *pays d'état*, which often thought of themselves as sovereign states with a clearly defined national identity.

In addition to the political discussions generated by the cahiers, the pre-revolutionary period was characterized by a flourishing of political tracts and pamphlets which caused great effervescence and an intellectual and popular debate on key constitutional issues. Best known among the pamphleteers was the Abbé Sieyès, who between late 1788 and 1792 published four tracts which had an arresting revolutionary impact. Particularly influential was his *Qu'est-ce que le Tiers Etat?* (which was printed four times between January and June 1789). The *leitmotiv* of the book was that the time was ripe for the people of France – the Third Estate – to become what they righteously were – the nation of France. For Sieyès the nation was essentially, as he himself put it, 'a body of associates living under common law and represented by the same legislative assembly' (Sieyès, 1970).

With the coming of the meetings of the Estates General scheduled for May 1789, Sieyès' main concern was to ensure that the nation should reassert itself. Now it was Sieyès' contention that the rights of the nation had been usurped by the nobility in the Middle Ages. He was not however a nostalgic of the past or a purist trying to re-establish some idyllic lost paradise. He actually believed that the freedoms of individuals had been taken away by the aristocracy and had to be returned to the people of France. Furthermore, he wanted to see the end of aristocratic rule, of regional privileges and divisions and of the myriad of intermediary institutions and corporates that came between the individual and the state. Sieyès presented in fact a blueprint for the nation-state which meant subversion of the old political structure in the direction of a more democratic and unitarian type of state (Forsyth, M. 1987: 69–70).

As we have seen, Sieyès proposed a political definition of the nation in which ethnic or linguistic features played no part; the same could be said of race, except for the fact that he felt it necessary to exclude the aristocracy from the French nation, as we shall see in some detail below. In doing that he had entered into a polemic on the racial origins of the French nation which had raged for about three centuries. In the eighteenth century the controversy had polarized around the figures of Boulainvilliers and Dubos. Boulainvilliers, who was a count, had maintained that the Frankish aristocracy were the only legitimate power in France, and that they had acquired this right through conquest, that is, by subjecting the existing Gallo-Roman population. In his view, the nobility had been losing ground since the medieval period by the intrusion of the clergy and the Third Estate in the sharing of power. Boulainvilliers had insisted that only the aristocracy had the right to attend the Estates General. Dubos for his part challenged most of Boulainvilliers' theses. He was adamant that the settlement of the Franks was peaceful and had in fact prolonged Roman domination. In addition, the Franks had intermarried with the Gallo-Romans and France was the result of this blending. A key contentious point was the absolution of the monarchy; while Boulainvilliers referred to usurpation of the King over the noblemen, Dubos maintained that an institution already existed among the Franks. Montesquieu was equally critical of Boulainvilliers and Dubos, though he lampooned the latter with the famous quote: 'nothing retards more the progress of knowledge than a bad work by a famous author because before instructing one must begin by undeceiving' (1949–51, II: 905).

Against Dubos, many sustained the conquest theory of the Gauls by the Franks, but rejected Boulainvilliers' idea that the Gallo-Romans were enslaved (only the Gauls were subjected). In fact, the penetration of the Franks was more in the form of raids than full-scale invasion, hence the original population was left largely undisturbed, with their political and civil rights intact (though occasionally subjected to ransom). Montesquieu envisaged the emergence of aristocratic privileges as a result of the development of feudalism in a later period. It is in the context of this polemic that Sieyès stated that the Third Estate was the nation, and was racially composed of the descendants of the Gallo-Roman population. He saw the aristocracy as a useless and expensive alien excrescence on the French nation which had to be excised (Barzun, 1932).

To assert that the nation is sovereign and that the Third Estate is the nation was no doubt a revolutionary statement in 1789, but Sieyès went much further than that. In fact he suggested that the nation was the original, pristine social principle par excellence. As F. Feher has put it: 'The nation was prior, pre-existent to all social phenomena and institutions. The latter had to be deduced from the former, and not the other way round. The nation was the source of all authority and all rights' (Feher, F. 1987: 18). This radical conception of Sieyès implied that as *volonté constituante*, the nation was 'omnipotent and not bound by any preliminary agreement, prerogative or contract' (ibid.).

We know that Sieyès considered the nobility as a 'tiny presumptuous and useless minority that could be eliminated without loss' (Palmer, 1971: 53). However, Sieyès oscillated between the idea that the nobility was basically non-productive and financially burdensome to the nation, and a conception in which they were seen as totally alien to French society. The first view is basically suggesting that the nobility, as an order, was fundamentally dysfunctional; in this sense he criticized a structure. But Sieyès also offered a more radical critique of the aristocracy going as far as to suggest the following: 'Why should it [the Third Estate] not repatriate to the Franconian forests all these families who preserve the crazy pretentions of descending from the race of the conquerors and of having inherited their rights of conquest?' (Sieyès 1970: 128). It is not my intention to suggest that Sieyès favoured the expulsion or even less the physical elimination of the aristocracy, but his influence on the Jacobins is well-attested. In all fairness, however, during the Revolutionary Terror he wisely kept aloof of politics.

According to Murray Forsyth there are three major conceptions of the nation in Sieyès:

1. The Nation as a Moral Necessity
According to this perspective the nation is the 'union of individual wills' and the product later 'by an agreement to form a single common will for public matters' (Forsyth, M: 74). It was obvious to Sieyès that France required major political changes, including a major democratization process, before the nation could become a union of equal individuals.

2. The Nation as Politico-economic Necessity
In this context the nation was envisaged as a highly complex and structured unity, which came close to the traditional definition of state. As a 'union of private works and public necessities', the nation was able to provide better welfare for human beings than any known institution.

3. The Nation as a Historical Entity
This is the conception that we have already come across and in which the nation equals the Third Estate. Sieyès showed how it grew progressively within the framework of the old regime. He believed his task was that of 'raising the Third Estate to a true understanding of its historical mission as the dissolvent of the existing political society and the embodiment of the nation' (ibid.: 81).

The influence of Sieyès on the developments leading to the revolutionary events should not be underemphasized. Along with other leaders of the Third Estate, who for the most part were lawyers, doctors, bureaucrats etc., and who were elected national deputies, he contributed to the politization of a large section of French society and fought against the nobility who were trying to preserve their power basis by enforcing the old habit of each Estate voting separately. The king had graciously allowed the Third Estate to send 600 representatives, as against 300 by the nobility and 300 by the clergy. However, the crucial thing at the meeting of the Estates General in May 1789 was the voting procedure; while the first two orders and the king favoured that each Estate should vote separately, the Third Estate was totally opposed to a system, which was basically undemocratic. In the end, the leaders of the Third Estate, forcefully stating that they represented the nation, outmanoeuvred the aristocracy by unilaterally declaring themselves to constitute the National Assembly, and inviting the representatives of the other orders to join them as individuals. Thus, on the 17 June 1789 the French modern nation was born. The development of a feeling of national unity developed as a result of the representatives of Third Estate meeting in Paris and realizing for the first time that they formed the nation. While in the past the King could have said *la nation c'est moi*, in June 1789 the Third Estate led by Sieyès, declared *la nation c'est le Tiers*.

After the Fall of the Bastille on 14 July 1789, there followed a number of measures of the National Assembly in the direction of consolidating the new or rediscovered nation. As Lynn Hunt has put it: 'French people believed that they could establish a new national community based on reason and nature without reference to the customs of the past. Such lofty ambitions required new political practices for their realization. The techniques of mass propaganda, the political mobilization of the lower classes, and the politization of everyday life were all invented in order to regenerate the nation' (Hunt, L. 1984: 213).

One of the first decisions of the National Assembly was the decree of 4 August 1789 abolishing feudal rights and privileges. This involved what Carlton Hayes called a 'nationalistic levelling' that is, the suppression of provincial rights and boundaries. It was obviously no longer possible to keep a double 'national' identity; the regions no longer had the right to see themselves as nations; France was the only possible nation. With the Declaration of the Rights of Man and of the Citizen on 27 August 1789, the idea of national unity became even more obvious. Its Art. 3 reads: 'The principle of all sovereignty resides essentially in the nation; no body nor individual may exercise any authority which does not proceed directly from the nation'. The Constitution of 1791 (voted in September that year) reasserted the idea that 'all powers emanate essentially from the nation'. The terminological changes soon accompany the prominence of the nation in the revolutionary discourse. Not only will there soon be a national language, a national education, and national army, but the traditional *lèse-majesté* (a term for treason) will become *lèse nation/ patrie/ liberté/ humanité*. As Godechot put it 'Everything which had been *royal* became *national*: the national navy, the national police, the national estates' (Godechot, J. 1988: 15). With the secularization of the Church (in November 1789) and particularly with the Civil Constitution of the Clergy (July 1790), priests and bishops were elected by the people paid by the state and the association with Rome was only nominal. Here we have have a clear attempt not only to subject the Catholic Church to the state, but to create the new religion of French nationalism as we shall see below. On the 14 July 1790 the Fall of the Bastille was celebrated in the Champs de Mars in the presence of the king, with half a million people taking the federation oath. In July 1791 the principle of self-determination was accepted, while the new Legislative Assembly voted a plan for compulsory national education (which was never implemented for lack of funds).

I have just mentioned a few key legislative developments in the first two revolutionary years. It is important to remember that these events were the result of the complex dynamics of the correlation of forces within the French Revolution. The alliance of the Third Estate with the *sans-culottes* of Paris accelerated the revolutionary process; with the collapse of the traditional order, nationalism 'provided a basis for a new authority ... a unifying bond for the integration of the social orders' (Kohn, H. 1967: 26). As I said before, the French revolutionaries invented a new nation and consolidated it by creating a mass of symbols from the tricolour flag to the female images of France, from the patriotic altars to the revolutionary rituals, from the patriotic songs like *La Marseillaise* to the cult of the saints, from the clubs to the festivals. It was the making of a new nation and it represented a radical break with the past. Although exhibiting religious language it was not strictly speaking Judeo-Christian, but fundamentally a cult of antiquity (Greece and Rome).

In his classical work, Albert Mathiez (1904) established the religious character of the cults which emerged in the aftermaths of the French Revolution. That, he did by using Durkheim's idea that what defines a religious phenomenon is not the content but the form; that what is important is not so much the presence or absence of supernatural beings but the obligatory nature of the beliefs for all the members of the group. Out of the French Revolution emerged a new faith aimed at regenerating the nation. Barnave saw the Declaration of the Rights of Man and of Citizens as a new credo, as the national catechism. By 1791, the constitution had become a 'profession of faith' of French patriotism; those who refused to accept it were excommunicated and aliens could join the 'communion of saints' by pledging loyalty to the French nation. The new religious faith was expressed in a number of exclusive symbols and was accompanied by practices and regular ceremonies (a cult). As mentioned above, many of the symbols (objects, legends, emblems) had a Greco-Roman or a Masonic origin. The tricolour, combining the red and blue of the city of Paris with the white of the Bourbon Kings, became popular in a short time, and was made official in 1792. Another rapidly spreading symbol was the patriotic altar which was erected spontaneously in many villages and communes and made obligatory in 1792; the patriotic altars were the rallying point for pilgrimages and gatherings; they became the sanctions of the new religion and exhibited the following inscription: 'the citizen is born, lives and dies for the country'. The tablets of the Declaration of Rights (in stone or metal) were carried around in procession as if they were the Blessed Sacrament of the French and then deposited in the patriotic altars for worship. As of 1790 there emerged the trees of freedom, which were also extremely popular; they were soon sacralized to the extent that their wanton destruction was severely punished. There were still other symbols like Roman fasces, Phygian caps, etc.

Along with the symbols of the *patrie*, there developed ceremonies, festivities and regular cults. People met to communicate their hopes and fears, to celebrate their victories over despotism and generally to participate in civic meetings. The federations, where French citizens gathered to share their patriotic feelings, were the first and most important of civic ceremonies; in their midst there grew an idea of *patrie* as a real and durable fraternity, the concern for public welfare, the belief that it was worth sacrificing private to public interests and a sense of unity of France. There were different types of civic festivities. Some of them were commemorative, that is, they celebrated revolutionary past events like Bastille Day (14 July) or the Oath of the Jeu de Paume (20 May) (resistance to the king); others were political, that is they celebrated current political events, particularly important constitutional changes. There were also cults of the martyrs of freedom (Soboul, A. 1983), that is, celebrations in honour of those who had contributed to the revolutionary cause, and moral festivities in which virtue was rewarded by bestowing honours or civic crowns on deserving citizens. The important patriotic role played by songs such as *La Marseillaise, La Carmagnole, Ça Ira* and others, is well known. At the time, a now forgotten revolutionary theatre also contributed to the effervescence of French patriotism. As Mathiez rightly insisted, the majority of these developments were the spontaneous result of the 'collective imagination of the patriots' (ibid.: 59). He concluded that the revolutionary cults were the expression of a true religion that was formed on the basis of eighteenth-century philosophy, and that this religion spread fast and took conscience of itself after the clashes with official Catholicism, to the point that in 1793 the priest Joseph de Chenier suggested that the Convention should install nationalism as a state religion. The revolutionaries were mainly concerned with national unity and saw religion as totally subordinated to the state, and the latter as the guardian of virtue and the instrument of happiness. I have mentioned in Chapter Six the chasm that developed between the new religion of nationalism and Catholicism. The Pope predictably condemned the secularization decrees, and the local clergy was split down the middle, but even those who remained loyal to the Revolution were viewed later with suspicion. In the end an attempt was made to introduce a comprehensive civil regulation of the traditional key events in the life of the individual (baptism, marriage, funeral etc.) and even the calendar (with ten-day weeks) was changed to upstage the Catholic Church. Even if in its extreme form the new religion was short-lived, the gulf which separated republicanism and Catholicism was never filled.

In an otherwise insightful article, D. D. Bien and R. Grew (1978) stated that at the time of the French Revolution there was a basic agreement as to French being the language spoken in the country. The realities were, however, rather different. There were numerous parts of the country where other languages were spoken including Breton, Basque, Catalan, German and Occitan. It is true that in all these areas there were minorities who exercised class domination through the knowledge of standard French. No doubt the Revolution, through its clubs, festivals, newspapers and later on the Army, was indirectly responsible for the spread of the national language. However, the gains were rather modest, particularly after the 1794 law to create a national language failed by lack of financial means to enforce it (Certeau, M. et al., 1975). When we realize that in 1864 at least forty per cent of the population of the southern third of France, and of Brittany and Alsace did not speak French (Palmer, R.R. 1985: 185), we have a clear measure of the real situation of the French language in France even seventy-five years after the French Revolution. In fact, while the revolutionaries believed that by enforcing French they were democratizing the country, Balibar and Laporte (1974) have suggested that 'linguistic disparity constituted a major obstacle to the exercise of *bourgeois* democracy, that is, to the political domination of the bourgeoisie' (ibid.: 816). From the same Marxist perspective, P. Higonnet (1980) has concluded that the bourgeois leadership of 1794, due to the unwillingness to bring property changes, 'chose to enforce equality of language as a substitute, only to deceive the people again by attaching importance to correct grammar and so reinstating class differences' (ibid.: 86).

It would be naive to expect that the French Revolution vehiculated a single conception of the nation. J.I. Guiomar (1974) suggested that at least three ideas of the nation were present. First of all, there was the Jacobin conception of the nation. Robespierre, its best known representative, followed not only eighteenth-century idealism and the doctrines of J.J. Rousseau but embraced also the idea of a nation of patriots. In this conception *patrie, patriote* and *patriotisme* are the most common terms used. *Patriotisme* is conceived as a struggle for freedom and human rapprochment; the *patrie* does not exist ideally with independence of people's behaviour. In fact one could say that it is through patriotic acts that the *patrie* is created. The second conception of the nation could be referred to as populism. It refers to the sovereignty of the *sans-culottes*. They called themselves patriots and saw the nation as an externalization of the patriotic sentiment, the essence of which was the affirmation of unity by abolishing all that separated the social body. They were critical of the use of the word nation because to them it meant basically a system of representation which excluded them from the National Assembly. That is why their motto was popular sovereignty, not national representation. Finally, there was also a centrist conception of the nation, which was typical of Danton and the Girondins. It emphasized the territorial union of the nation. On 31 January 1793, Danton stated to the Convention that the Rousseauesque voice of nature dictated that the limits of the French Republic were marked by the existence of natural boundaries: the Rhine, the Alps, the Pyrenees and the Atlantic. Of course, this statement came after France had absorbed Avignon, Belgium and the Rhineland, which were seen by the likes of Danton and Carnot, as naturally 'French' since Roman times, and hence only returning to the fold.

In this conception there was a transition from *patrie* to nation; the territory and the social body were designated by the name of the same family – *France* and *français*. The *patrie*, however, remained as a mass of sentiment affectively bonding the citizens, but now mediated by the idea of an exclusive territory. The most powerful social aspiration expressed in the ideas of nation and *patrie* was the desire to achieve unity and community, a sentiment which patriotism and nationalism had inherited from religion.

In a few years the French Revolution brought about radical changes in the conception of the French nation. From a situation in which the monarch was seen as a symbol of the nation to one in which the nation was conceived as the general will of the people, there is a great gap. Whether the nationalism that emerged saw the individual subordinated to the state, as both Kohn and Hayes have suggested is another matter.

One of the most momentous principles emerging from the French Revolution was the double idea of the unity of the nation and the centralization of the state. Because the revolutionaries identified nation with state, they solemnly declared the unity, uniformity and indivisibility of the state from the Constituent Assembly in 1791 through to the Republic of 1795. This principle was enshrined in all the constitutions of the period. These ideas did not necessarily suppress the original intimation of the nation as the general will of the people, though they progressively opened the latter to political manipulation. In fact, it is difficult to know whether, for example, when Saliceti stated in 1789 that the desire of the Corsicans was to be incorporated into the French nation, whether it was the people he was talking about or whether he was just expressing a personal preference. While at first the different provinces of France (or at least their representatives) freely and spontaneously expressed their attachment to the French nation, by 1793 the few existing federalist voices were silenced. Anarcharsis Cloots, the 'universal patriot', who in 1792 had dared to suggest that a federal state might be suited to France was immediately criticized. By then, the unity of the people was not negotiable independently of the will of the people. By 1793 those who espoused such federalist views were dubbed traitors and the federalist rebellion in different parts of France (Normandy, the Midi, etc.) was brutally repressed. The end result was an extremely centralized regime, with no parallel in the history of Western Europe.

What was the attitude of the French Revolution concerning the spread of their ideas abroad and the role of France in the world? The least that can be said is that between 1790 and 1792 the revolutionaries moved from a declaration of world peace to the invasion of their neighbours. How do we account for this radical change of attitude? It would be easy to suggest that the National Assembly was naive or that it was guided by *mauvaise foi*; in fact, what decided the fate of France was the combination of three major operating factors: the 'traditions' of the French state, the European political conjuncture and the internal dynamics of the French Revolution.

J. Godechot (1983) has insisted that the medieval idea of popular sovereignty, to which the eighteenth-century philosophers had given special emphasis and the French Revolution had enthroned as a sacred principle, was at the centre of the expansion of revolutionary France into Europe and elsewhere. The right of the peoples to decide their own future soon affected not only the German-speaking territories incorporated into the French crown a century ago (Alsace, Lorraine, etc.) as well as small neighbouring enclaves (Avignon, Comtat, etc.) expressing the will to be French, but also an array of French-speaking territories (Savoy, Switzerland, Belgium, Nice, etc.). In these territories there were patriots who expressed the desire to be annexed into revolutionary France. In addition, other areas where French ideas had penetrated deeply (Holland) were hoping to see their right to self-government helped by France. This situation created uneasiness among French revolutionaries who hesitated between helping those who wanted to free themselves and the danger of undermining the existing balance of power in Europe. In the end, after laborious discussions the first path prevailed.

Whether the war between France and some of its neighbours originated as a result of a clash between revolutionary principles and the *realpolitik* of international relations, or was rather a more mundane affair in which what counted was the real or imaginary attempts by the enemies of the Revolution to strike a deal with Louis XVI, the fact of the matter is that once the revolutionary government had conquered foreign territories by force of arms in mid-1792 (Belgium, the left bank of the Rhine, Savoy, Nice) it had to decide what to do with them. While at first the principle of the rights of peoples to self-government seemed to prevail, by the end of the same year another principle had emerged: that of the natural frontiers of France. Historical references going as far back as Caesar could be found to suggest that the natural frontiers of Gallia were the Rhine, the Alps, the Pyrenees and the sea. There followed a policy of annexation of some of the conquered territories which was carried out and legitimized by the Girondins (Danton, Cournot). To complete the framework, the idea of 'sister republic' was floated to refer to those countries in which the patriots were trying to rebel against the *ancien régime* and to apply the principles of the French Revolution; the issue was whether it was the duty of the French revolutionaries to help them get rid of their tyrannies. The best example of a sister republic was Holland, where a large number of patriots (some in exile in France) were trying to overthrow the despotic government of Stathoud, but the idea was later applied to Switzerland, Italy, etc.

One can naively ask to what extent did all these ideas originate as a result of idealistic principles? The answer is that in the final instance the historical practice indicates that it is necessary to accept that they can be accounted for in terms of ideological expediency, the purpose being the glory of the Great French Nation. No doubt there were arguments against these policies which were made vocal by certain Jacobin opponents (Robespierre), but with the victory of the Directory by 1795 the two doctrines were enthroned: 'natural frontiers for France, sister republics to protect these frontiers and to provide economic resources to the Great Nation' (Godechot, J. 1983: 85). In addition, the Republic developed another objective: expansion into the Mediterranean (particularly Egypt).

It is ironic that the man who, no matter how unwittingly, contributed most to the awakening of European nationalisms (Holtman, R.B. 1967) was himself totally inimical to this doctrine (except perhaps for his youthful Corsican patriotism), wanting in fact to revive the Holy Roman Empire and beyond. Napoleon never understood the extraordinary power of nationalism, nor did he respect the sovereignty or the boundaries of the existing European states. The only limit to his territorial ambitions was military defeat, and when the latter came, Napoleon could not even count on French patriotism. He was, however, an efficient and rational administrator, which may explain why at first the European bourgeoisie welcomed him as the solvent of the *ancien régime*. Towards the end of his life, while musing in his final exile of St. Helena, he came to appreciate the reality of nations (France and Spain, as well as Italy and Germany) as the building blocks of a European order, though his conception was still dictated by imperialist dreams and a distrust of Russia and England.

How far Napoleon was responsible for the development or consolidation of nationalism in France is a debateable issue. Napoleon believed that he represented the will of the majority of French citizens, although he had no time for any democratic expression of the will of the people, except perhaps through plebiscites; while the *Grande Armée* was victorious the French population was behind him. Hans Kohn (1967) has insisted on a rather unusual feature of Napoleon's policy: he never tried to manipulate or shape public policy, nor did he attempt to generate a state nationalism. He was only concerned with loyalty to his person and to the imperial monarchy; his appeals were not to the love of the French nation, but to the power and glory of the French state. Napoleon did not have a consistent 'national' policy towards the conquered territories. For example, while at first he appeared to foster the creation of a single Italian Republic, at a later stage he ruthlessly divided the Italian spoils to satisfy the greed of his relatives and commanders. By the end of his rule, it appeared as if the fate of Italy was to become a province of the Empire. In the next section we will have the opportunity to look in some detail at the different national reponses to the Napoleonic invasions.

Bibliography

Balibar, R. & Laporte, D., (1974) *Le Français national*, Paris: Hachette.

Barzun, J., (1932) *The French Race*, New York: Columbia University Press.

Bien, D. & Grew, R., (1978) 'France', in R. Grew (ed.), *Crises of Political Development in Europe and the United States*, Princeton University Press.

Certeau, M. et al., (1975) *Une politique de la langue: la revolution française et les patois*, Paris: Gallimard.

Feher, F., (1987) *The French Revolution. An Essay on Jacobinism.* Cambridge University Press.

Forsyth, M., (1987) *Reason and Revolution. The Political Thought of the Abbé Sieyès*, Leicester University Press.

Godechot, J., (1971) 'Nation, Patrie, nationalisme, patriotisme au XVIIIe siècle', *Annales Historiques de la Revolution Française*, 143, pp. 481–501.

— —, (1975) 'Réponse au professeur Boyd Shafer', *Annales Historiques de la Revolution Française,* 47, pp. 331–3

— —, (1983) *La Grande Nation*, Paris: Aubier.

— —, (1988) 'The New Concept of the Nation', in O. Dann & J. Dinniddy (eds), *Nationalism in the Age of the French Revolution*, London: Hambledon Press.

Guiomar, J. I., (1974) *L'idéologie nationale*, Paris: Editions Champ Libre.

Higonnet, P., (1980) 'The Politics of Linguistic Terrorism and Grammatical Hegemony during the French Revolution', *Social History*, 5, pp. 41–69.

Holtman, R. B., (1967) *The Napoleonic Revolution*, Baton Rouge: Louisiana State University Press.

Hunt, L., (1984) *Politics, Culture and Class in the French Revolution*, London: Methuen.

Hyslop, B. H., (1968) *French Nationalism in 1789*, New York: Octagon Books.

Kohn, H., (1967) *Prelude to Nation-States. The French and the German Experience*, Princeton: D. Van Nostrand.

Mathiez, A., (1904) *Les origines des cultes revolutionnaires*, Paris: George Bellais.

Markham, F., (1965) *Napoleon and the Awakening of Europe*, New York: Collier.

Montesquieu, (1949-51) *Oeuvres Complètes*, Paris: Gallimard.

O'Brien, C. C., (1989) 'Nationalism and the French Revolution', in G. Best (ed.), *The Permanent Revolution*, London: Fontana.

Palmer, R. R., (1971) *The World of the French Revolution*, London: Allen and Unwin.

— —, (1985) *The Improvement of Humanity. Education in the French Revolution*, Princeton University Press.

Shafer, B., (1975) 'A propos du nationalisme', *Annales Historiques de la Revolution Française*, 47, pp. 329–31.

Sieyès, E., (1970) *Qu'est-ce que le Tiers État?*, Geneva: Droz.

Soboul, A., (1983) 'Religious Feeling and Popular Cults during the French Revolution: 'Patriot Saints' and 'Martyrs for Liberty', in S. Wilson (ed.), *Saints and their Cults*, Cambridge University Press.

–9–

Nationalist Paths to Modernity

This chapter covers, in a few pages, ground that usually requires a book. There are, indeed, many histories of nationalism dealing with the nineteenth and twentieth centuries (Hayes, C. 1931; Weil, G. 1938; Kohn, H. 1944; Minogue, K. R. 1967; Seton-Watson, H. 1977; Smith, A. D. 1979; Breuilly, J. 1982; Alter, P. 1989; Hobsbawm, E. 1990), and there is no way in which a short text can be an adequate alternative. It is obvious, then, that the purpose of this chapter is not to present a lineal account of the historical development of nationalism in Western Europe since the French Revolution, but rather to highlight certain historical processes which I consider essential for the understanding of the period. By using the expression 'nationalist paths to modernity', I want to signify the different national patterns that have made modernity possible. This point is intended as a corrective to those authors who have assumed that there is one single national path to modernity – that of the nation-state. The point here is not to deny the importance of the nation-state as an ideology, but to challenge its existence as an established hegemonical reality across Western Europe. Another point that this chapter tries to nail down is the idea that historical precedence, whether of ideas or institutions, is not without effects. It is essential that historical sociology should incorporate within its explanatory framework, not only the continuous though changing meaning of specific, important historical events, but also the significance of 'evenemential' time.

If by the beginning of the nineteenth century the principles of cultural and political nationalism emerge victorious, it is mainly as *idées-forces* which have to embody themselves in a long and protracted process in the existing economic, cultural and political realities of the time. The fact that the political world was organized along the line of states of different types (city-states, small states, national states, multinational states, empires) is of paramount importance because, in the final instance, the state system is what will decide the scope and limits of the progress of the principles of cultural and political nationalism in the two centuries after the French Revolution. It is true that on the basis of ethnic markers (essentially, descent, culture and language) peoples or nations will be re-created or consolidated, but the principle of cultural nationalism is by definition so malleable and open to manipulation, that the coincidence between state and nation will be an exception rather than the norm. I would suggest that cultural nationhood is a value – one of the highest values of modernity in so far as it evokes the secularized religious sense of community – which different social groups, including states, will try to appropriate for themselves.

As a result of the potentially fissiparous tendency of national groups (due to the indeterminacy of ethnic markers), it is at times difficult to predict the territorial application of the national principle. For example, in the Spanish Constitution of 1812, the expression Spanish nation referred to both Spain and its American colonies, while after 1898 it referred only to Spain proper. Later on, the idea of Spanish nation would be rejected by important minorities in Catalonia and the Basque Country. There is, in principle, a possibility of cantonalism in most states, particularly in those places where historical vicissitudes have mixed population with different ethnic markers either in the same territory or in the same state. In addition, there is also the frequent case of divided nations across state lines (Catalans, Basques) or national minorities scattered in various states (ethnic Germans in Eastern Europe). Last, but perhaps least, is the economic context in which nationalism developed. Much has been made of the functional requirements of industrial capitalism in generating nationalism. I have indicated in Part III that the arguments were inconclusive and that the causal correlation only seems to make sense when the term capitalism is used in the most general sense of the term and not exclusively as an economic phenomenon. I would agree with E. Gellner (1983) that if anything the important aspect to underline would be that the uneven development of industrial capitalism was the factor most likely to affect the development of nationalism; but even more important than lopsided industrialization was the process of modernization that went along with it (urbanization, secularization, mass education, increase in communications etc.).

The French Revolution and the Napoleonic invasions heralded and to a great extent triggered-off the advent of modern nationalism in Western Europe, both in the sense of putting an end (at least temporarily) to the aristocratic conception of the nation prevailing in the *ancien régime* and modernizing the state, as well as generating sentiments of political independence and cultural autonomy among the affected countries. But the ways in which nationalism developed in Germany and Italy constituted a model for many countries, and particularly for those which had to operate within the constraining structures of a state which was felt to be alien.

In the early period of nationalist effervescence, at the height of Romanticism, the eyes of Western Europe were fixed above all on the Greeks who, after four centuries of Ottoman domination, were struggling for independence. The Philhellenic movement, steeped in the recently rediscovered models of Ancient Greek civilisation, dreamed, with Lord Byron, that 'Greece might be free', and believed that the 'struggle of the Greek people seemed to embody in the most suggestive and extraordinary way the awakening of nationalities' (Ciuffoletti, Z. 1987: 44) which was occurring at the time. As an ideal-typical construction Greece embodies not only cultural and linguistic unity but also high civic and political values. It is in this sense, as the national foundation of modernity, that Greece can become an exemplar, as it was in the classical period. Here it matters not that the realities of modern Greece often contradicted this mythological vision. The independence of Greece in 1830 was seen as the first major success of the nationalist principle. Soon afterwards, the Kingdom of the United Netherlands, which had been created in 1815, collapsed under Belgian pressure for independence from Dutch domination.

The post-Napoleonic period had started, however, in a most inauspicious way. The Congress of Vienna, which in 1815 had brought together the leading European states to decide on the future of the continent, resolutely opposed the emerging Italian and German nationalisms (as well as the Polish one) and consecrated the *status quo ante* (Strauss, A. 1949). The reasons are easy enough to understand. German nationalism only found strong support in Prussia, and perhaps more for political expediency than anything else. The major European powers (Austria, France, etc.) did not recognize the principle of nationality; as to the South German states they often considered themselves independent nations, and only felt very subsidiarily German. The British were somewhat aloof about nationalist issues, their main aim being to preserve a balance of power. In the end, the German Confederation that emerged enthroned the sovereignty of the German states; the only central institution – the Diet – was extremely weak financially and militarily. As to Italian nationalism, it faltered for a variety of reasons, but mainly because of Austria's desire to control northern Italy; the French and the British, not wanting to upset the Austrians, acquiesced. In any case, the nationalist cause in Italy was at a low ebb.

How far did the decisions taken at the Congress of Vienna manage to delay the onslaught of nationalism in nineteenth- century Western (and Eastern) Europe is difficult to assess. Equally difficult is to determine whether a different kind of nationalism would have emerged in the end had the existing states been more sympathetic to the doctrine of nationalism (but this is, of course, wishful thinking of the most hypothetical kind and totally out of step with normal state practices). In any case, very few nineteenth-century political thinkers managed to grasp the enormity of the nationalist avalanche, seeing it at most as a passing fad. This also accounts for the paucity and poverty of theoretical statements on the national question. Of the three most powerful ideologies of the nineteenth century – liberalism, socialism and nationalism – identified with the emergence of modernity and the subversion of the *ancien régime*, nationalism is the one which was the least appreciated as an *idée-force* at the time of its appearance.

Following ideas expressed a long time ago by Carlton Hayes and Hans Kohn among others, it is customary to see the development of nineteeenth-century and twentieth-century nationalism essentially in dichotomous and moralizing terms. Prior to 1870 there was a nationalism which was democratic, progressive and humanitarian; after 1870 nationalism became imperialist, authoritarian and chauvinist; the implication being, of course, that we should praise the former and loathe the latter. But as Tom Nairn (1977: 331–2) has noted, nationalism is like a double-faced Janus, and whether we like it or not we must take into account both sides of the coin (on one side of which appears a democratic, liberating nationalism, while on the other the obscenity of totalitarian nationalism). And, more importantly, perhaps, what we have to find out is under which circumstances and at the hands of which agencies nationalism becomes one thing or the other. In this context what immediately comes to mind is the paramount role of the state in generating nationalism both for internal consumption and for expansion abroad. The culmination of this state nationalism was, of course, the fascist regimes which flourished in Western Europe in the period between 1918 and 1945 (and in the cases of Spain and Portugal up to the early 1970s, even if by then their fascism had mellowed). The state appropriated the capacity of nationalism 'to provide psychic and emotional sustenance in an age marked by the decline of religion and by the dehumanisations of industrialism. Nationalism thrived because it tapped the potent emotions of history and locality to give individual lives meaning in an increasingly meaningless universe ... Nationalism can strengthen the state by endowing it with quasi-religious loyalty' (Schlesinger, A. 1981: IX).

I have already mentioned the paradigmatic character that German and Italian nationalism (and particularly the former) have had in the written history of nationalism in Western Europe. The literature on the topic has for long considered both nationalisms as 'exemplary', not only in explaining the transition from cultural to political nationalism, but also in accounting for the appearance of new, independent nation-states in the nineteenth century. Germany and Italy are both presented as quasi-perfect historical cases which exemplify the powerful effects of the nationalist principle. This conception, I will maintain, is somewhat simplistic and obscures realities which are politically much more complex. On the other hand, the 'lessons' to be extracted from these experiences varied tremendously from place to place. It would be unthinkable to expect that the French state would draw the same conclusions as the Catalan nationalist movement.

The first thing worth mentioning about the German-Italian model of nationalism (which for the sake of simplicity I shall initially take to constitute a single model) is that it appears to combine state-building with nationalism. In a nutshell, the model assumes a unity – an 'Italian' and a 'German' nation – which would have existed since the medieval period and which expressed itself in a language, a culture and a common descent. Due to a combination of internal factors (disorganization, selfishness, etc.) and external ones (foreign domination), the nation had been unable to flourish adequately in the past. The only way of doing that was for the nation to control its own affairs in the context of a modern, centralized state. This required a process of unification of the different independent or subjected political units which shared the same nationality. In essence, then, the model gives primacy to the role of nationalist ideas in the formation of the German and Italian nation-states. However, careful examination of the historical experience shows a fast changing reality even if we stick to the period between 1815 and 1870.

If it is true that in the German-Italian model cultural nationalism precedes the formation of the national state, it does not follow that the former should be seen as the most influential or decisive element in the achievement of the latter. In both cases we can observe that in the process of national state building the lead was taken by the most dynamic (either politically or economically) of the existing states in each civilizational area, that is, Prussia in Germany and Piedmont in the Italian case. But in the final instance, neither cultural, nor political or economic factors are sufficient to explain the formation of the German and the Italian national states. The international balance of power determines in each historical moment what is possible and what is not. Hence, the timing of the unification, as well as the territorial limits of the state depend on the international balance of power (including military power). The German national state was created by Bismarck's military machine, but the *Kleindeutschland* that emerged left out Austria and other culturally German territories. In the Italian case, the nationalist doctrines of Mazzini may have galvanized the Italian people, the strategic genius of Garibaldi may have brought military victories, the political cunning of Cavour may have prepared the union and no doubt the northern bourgeoisie put pressure for the creation of a large national market; but all these factors might have been insufficient had not France been interested in creating a strong, independent country which could be a counter-balance to the Austro-Hungarian empire. In addition, France obtained territorial concessions from Italy (Savoy, Nice).

The fact of the matter is that, in spite of appearances, nationalist ideas change in accordance with the different agencies that embody them or manipulate them. So it is crucial to have a detailed picture of the different contending nationalist forces in each historical period. From the onslaught of modernity, the existence of competing nationalist paradigms is the rule, rather than the exception. States, classes, civil societies, and groups of all sorts are likely to compete for the control of the nationalist space. And this prescription applies to the German-Italian model as well as to the other ones – the French model and the Irish model. It is implicit in what I have just said that national ideas have been shown not to respect boundaries or frontiers of any kind; hence the importance of looking into the demonstration effect when dealing with nationalist issues; obviously the uses of a local, given type of nationalism in other states or civilization areas requires a careful examination of the ideological transmutation which may have taken place. Needless to say, the closer the cultures are, the higher the chances that the ideological transplant will preserve its original meaning – other conditions being equal. On the other hand, which aspects of a given nationalist ideology are likely to be borrowed will not depend only on its objective qualities, but also, and perhaps more importantly, on the specific needs of the borrowing agency.

If the German-Italian model of nationalism has as its starting point the nation – understood as a cultural organism which takes consciousness of its existence and decides to take the conduct of its affairs in its own hands by constituting a state – the French model of nationalism starts at the very opposite end of the spectrum with the existence of a state, with fixed, stable boundaries and in which the nation is envisaged as a manifestation of the free will of its citizens; in Pflanze's words: 'common sovereignty provided common institutions and a common political tradition from which emerged a sense of nationhood which transcended cultural differences' (Pflanze, O. 1966: 139). Whether by historical accident or not, the French model incorporates two separate elements: popular sovereignty and historical state. And while the former acted as a catalyst in corroding autocratic monarchies, the latter had to face the onslaughts of cultural nationalisms, with varying effects and responses depending on a constellation of factors.

The French model, while generally relying on Renan's idea of the nation as a spiritual principle, characterized by a common heritage of memories and a desire and will to live together, involved also the recognition of achieving cultural and linguistic homogeneity. There was a conscious attempt to attain these objectives by state generated nationalism. Through the compulsory educational system both the medium (language, culture) and the message (civic values) were transmitted.

The Third Republic believed that one of its main objectives was to educate the people of France; education was envisaged as a school of patriots. There came the realization that although France might have been a political and administrative unit, it was far from being a spiritual one. In the aftermath of the 1870 catastrophe it was essential to recover French national consciousness and patriotism. The new educational system had to emphasize the duty of French citizens, including military service. As the work of E. Weber (1979) and T. Zeldin (1973; 1977) shows, the process of nation-building was not completed, if it was at all, until the First World War; Zeldin is unhappy with the idea of a unified France even in the twentieth century, given the diversity of regional languages and temperaments. In any case there is no doubt that this process of unification involved the subordination of all *ethnies* to the dominant French group. As Mona Ozouf (1985: 7) has remarked, the ideologists of the Third Republic in general and Jules Ferry in particular never had any doubts that the process of francization was but a blessing for the country. The sense that ethnic or linguistic peculiarities had value never occurred to them; the losers of history – the historyless nations that Marx and Engels referred to – had no other place but in the dustbins of history. At best there would be timid regionalist efforts against centralization and in defence of the local languages and cultures. But these particularisms would not threaten French unity (Vigier, P. 1977), and would be of limited importance until recent times.

State generated nationalisms with the view of creating a nation-state both politically and culturally are a phenomenon that occurs in practically all states, new and old. The German Reich will be no exception; the ethnic minorities in its midst (Poles, Danes, etc.) will suffer unsuccessful attempts at germanization (Pflanze, O. 1966: 141), while some southern states like Bavaria will cling to their differential identity for a long time. The Italian case suggests also that unification was prior to the establishment of an Italian national culture and language, which many commentators see only happening under fascism. Sergio Romano (1986) has maintained that Italian linguistic unity was only achieved in the 1970s. In the light of these observations it is appropriate to ask why there were no minority nationalist movements against the German and Italian states in the late nineteenth and in the twentieth century. I would venture to put forward two factors for the pre-1945 period: the impetus of the unification process itself, and later on a high-pitched nationalism with imperialist tendencies, followed by totalitarian nationalism. In the post-Second World War period, the federal constitution of West Germany and the Italian system of autonomous regions both helped to diffuse potential nationalisms against the state. As to the United Kingdom, with the exclusion of Ireland, a sort of British nation of nations was consolidated with the help of an empire, at least well into the twentieth century. For sure Britain must be understood both as a 'three-nation unit and a single unit, in different contexts and for different purposes' (Robbins, K. 1988: 184). This is not to say, of course, that Wales and Scotland did not resent English domination. The case of Spain exhibits similarities with that of Britain, but with the difference that Catalan and Basque nationalisms came into existence much earlier, as compared to the Welsh and Scottish ones, partly due to the collapse of the Spanish empire by the turn of the century, as well as an array of other factors.

In Western Europe the French model was favoured by the historical states, small or big, nationally homogeneous or nationally heterogeneous, independently of whether the democratic principles were properly or only theoretically applied. However only small, homogeneous countries like Holland and Portugal, or small heterogeneous federations like Switzerland were free or relatively free of cultural nationalisms against the state; the UK and Spain both experienced more or less radical nationalist challenges from some of their constituent parts. Inevitably, empires were even more prone to suffer the disintegrating effects of the nationality principle and in any case they were in no position to try to create a single national culture.

This leads us to the third model, which could perhaps be called the Irish model of nationalism. It involves a culturally defined nation, usually associated with a historical territory within a given state (or states). By choosing Ireland to represent the third model, the case with the utmost complexity in terms of the relations between an oppressed nationality and its oppressor has been selected. As Alfred Cobban has remarked: 'Differences of economic interest, religion, and descent, bitter historical enmities, the presence of an alien ascendancy, a class division largely coinciding with a national one, and both with the religious cleavage, a minority inside a minority, and an area of intermingled population, a determination on the part of the ruling power to maintain its legislative sovereignty, a revolutionary brotherhood handing down the torch of rebellion from generation to generation, vital strategic interests of the dominant power involved in the territory of the subject nation – all these were factors in the situation.' (1970: 126). The actual independence of Eire and the fact that Northern Ireland remained in the UK, was one of the possible solutions to the bitter historical dispute between the Irish and the British government:

from limited autonomy to full territorial independence for Ireland.

Although presenting some parallelism with the German-Italian model, the third model refers usually to small national units that try to break away from an existing multinational state or empire, rather than small states coming together to form a larger, nationally-based state. The objectives of the nationalisms against the state vary from cultural demands to autonomy, from federalism to outright independence. In theory all units can progress from cultural demands to demands for independence. As we have seen, the variation in objectives is a function of a number of variables, which include, among the most important, eth-nonational potential, the level of development of industrial capitalism, the dynamics of civil society, the strength of the state, the role of estab-lished religion and the international conjuncture.

The Czech historian Miroslav Hroch (1985) has shown the existence of three clearly differentiated phases in the development of minority nationalisms against the state in nineteenth-century Europe. There is a phase A, or initial phase, characterized by the presence of an active intelligentsia (journalists, writers, students, teachers, clergy, etc.) involved in the 'discovery' of the history, culture and language of a for-gotten nation. The social impact of such activities is limited to the cul-tural circles. Phase B is that of the awakening of national consciousness; it involves a wider group of people (particularly important sectors of the educated bourgeoisie, petty-bourgeoisie and others) being won to the national cause. It involves also the emergence of a small group of patri-ots engaged in political agitation. The final stage, phase C, entails the formulation of a well-articulated political project which manages to cap-ture significant layers of the population. The nationalist movement becomes a mass movement with a clear class consciousness. Now, not all movements manage to reach phase B or C, and Hroch makes it clear that patriotic agitation in itself is no guarantee of success; specific social preconditions are required. Hroch has studied in detail the social com-position of six minority nationalisms (mostly eastern European) in a comparative framework and has emphasized the role that different classes and fractions of classes play in the development of such a type of nationalism. Hroch offers these phases as ideal-types, which should be contrasted with the historical reality of each country under considera-tion. What is refreshing in Hroch as a Marxist historian is that he has not tried to impose an economistic model of explanation in which the mate-rial interests of the bourgeoisie are the paramount cause of nationalism.

That there is a contradiction between the expansionist tendencies of the state and the nationality principle is most obvious. The doctrines of political and cultural nationalism encouraged the creation of true nation-states, that is, states which contained a single nation (whichever way the latter was defined); realities were, however, rather different. Many nationalities never succeeded in creating their own state; many states were nation-states only in appearance. The state did not change its character because of the nationalist onslaught, but had to adapt to the new times and had at least to create the pretence of being a nation.

One area in which practically all Western European states coincided was in enhancing their prestige, their *grandeur,* by the possession of overseas colonies. It is somewhat ironic that at the time when the idea of self-determination was gaining ideological ground, the wildest colonial expansion overseas was taking place. This imperialist phase in European history was often justified in terms of a civilizing mission of superior races over inferior races. Imperialist countries had a 'national mission' to fulfil. The idea that the so-called inferior races could have the right to national emancipation was considered totally ludicrous by Western states.

What in fact predominated after 1870 was the naked power politics of the big states. In his *Reflections on History*, Jacob Burckhardt predicted the authoritarianism of the state; he saw a tendency towards centralized, unitarian, big states. The thing that a state abhors the most is its dismemberment. He felt that the desire of the individual is 'to participate in a great entity, and this clearly betrays power as the primary, and culture as a very secondary goal at best. More specifically, the idea is to make the general will of the nation felt abroad, in defiance of other nations' (Burckhardt, J. 1979: 139). In this context nationalism means an extreme form of patriotism, with clear jingoistic and chauvinistic characteristics within the overall framework of an imperialist policy. One could say, paraphrasing Lenin, that imperialism became the highest stage of nationalism. For the new breed of state nationalists 'the possession of an empire was an essential precondition for the free development of one's own national culture in time to come' (Mommsen, W. 1974: 126). This is not to disregard the economic reasons for imperialism: the need to export excess capital and excess human resources to other territories. In addition, the vested interests of the colonial bureaucracy helped to perpetuate the system.

The development of imperialism reinforced the determination of Western European states to contain their internal national minorities or emerging nationalisms against the state by engaging ever more actively in policies of national homogenization, as well as in outright repressive measures against the cultural and political manifestations of the awakening nationalities. By 1913 the idea that small nations could achieve independence by insurrectional or any other means was considered improbable. The model of the unitary state was pervasive. Measured in terms of national independence, for example, only Norway was a successful case of self-determination in Western Europe in the period between 1870 and 1914. However, the First World War changed things again. The collapse of empires in Central and Eastern Europe and President Wilson's commitment to see national self-determination on the agenda, produced a remarkable flurry of small independent states, even if it did not solve the national question due to the recalcitrant problem of the disadvantaged minorities in the new states.

Fascism was the culmination of state nationalism. All Western European countries developed radical nationalist movements that could be labelled, following Charles Maurras's felicitous expression, 'integral nationalisms'. They represented reactions against the new bourgeois democratic and liberal order that was emerging, and in which the working classes and the socialist parties were playing an increasingly important role. They were movements which tended to emerge as a result of a major crisis of confidence in the nation-state (international humiliation following military defeat or unsatisfied imperialist appetites). They appeared as movements of renewal, of revitalization of the perceived morbid organism. Both Nazi Germany and Fascist Italy fit the case well. Fascism focused on the supremacy of the nation conceived inseparably from the state. Benito Mussolini expressed this thought when he said that fascism considered the state as an absolute. In this conception of the state the individual was seen in a totally subordinated position. As Anthony D. Smith has rightly noted, fascism 'tends to view the nation in instrumental terms, as a "power-house", a repository and weapon for the exercise of will and force' (1975: 56). Some authors, including Carlton Hayes and Anthony D. Smith, have been reluctant to accept that there is a close connection between nationalism and fascism. Although they are right in emphasizing the specificity of fascism, by failing to see a continuity between integral nationalism and the fascist conception of the nation-state they are in danger of ignoring a major dimension of fascism.

In the inter-war period the fascist model of nationalism spread in one form or another all over Europe. Whether in power or in opposition, fascist movements were present in most countries. Where it was politically triumphant, fascism pursued extreme policies of nation-building, in an attempt at creating the national homogeneity that was required to keep the masses of the country tuned into the mythical, often mystical, ideas of the nation. Fascism emphasized indeed the myths and symbols of the national community and made sure that the distinction between the public and the private spheres was all but wiped out. Fascism, based on a combination of terror and consensus, insisted on the participation of the masses in cults which would generate a sense of belonging to the nation and which allowed the individuals to feel that they were involved in its affairs. As an extreme form of nationalism, fascism has coloured the perception that the twentieth century has had of nationalism. During the Second World War some minority nationalisms, particularly in German-ocupied territories, allowed themselves to fall under the spell or control of fascist ideologies, with predictable consequences for the post-war period.

In spite of its bad name, and against the predictions of most politi-cians and social scientists, nationalism made its reappearance in Western Europe in the form of minority nationalisms against the state in the 1960s, and has persisted unabated until the present (Smith, A. D. 1981; Tiryakian, E. and Rogowski, R. (eds) 1985). This has been a source of political destabilization affecting most countries. The radical way in which a significant percentage of the population of Nortern Ireland reject British rule may be comparable only to the militant stand adopted by ETA supporters in their struggle for an independent Basque state, but the phenomenon is more general if not always so virulent. The Welsh and the Scots in the United Kingdom, Catalans and Galicians in Spain, Friulians and other *Grenzeleute* in Italy, Walloons and Flemings in Belgium, and even the peripheral nationalities of the French state plus Corsica – all try to preserve a sense of national identity and rightly believe that this can only be achieved in the framework of a state that provides them with a substantial degree of political autonomy. In West Germany the federal system pre-empted to a great extent the possible emergence of peripheral nationalisms, but the *Nationalefrage* persisted more or less consciously in the minds of most people in so far as they did not accept the *de jure* partition of Germany into two states. The reunification of Germany proves this point.

Much has been made of the imitation effect of Third World move-ments of national liberation on Western European ethnonationalisms. That there was perhaps a rhetorical influence is undeniable, and in some cases organizational forms may have been borrowed. To what extent the anti-colonialist wave may have affected the timing of minority nation-alisms in the West is open to debate. In any case, the major cause of eth-nonational revival has to be found in the ever-growing process of the imposition of the model of an alien nation-state on the everyday life of the subjected nationalities. Melucci and Diani (1983: 147) have remarked that the two major political objectives of the ethnonationalist movements are: the right of a community (big or small) to be different and the right of a community to control its own affairs within a given territory. As predictable, ethnonationalist movements tend to occur in areas of high ethnonational potential. If anything, most part of these movements are not new, and their coalescence at a high peak in the 1970s may require, in addition to the general causes mentioned above, specific reasons for each case. Since 1989 there has been a recrudescence of ethnonationalism in the West which has been often attributed to the 'Baltic effect'. In many cases what we simply have is an opportunistic repackaging of long-standing demands.

I have already mentioned how important it is to avoid the historical fallacy of assuming that the nation-state is the only path to modernity. Appearances to the contrary, the nation-state is a rather unusual development; the common pattern is the multinational state. Furthermore, the nation-state is historically a late-comer. Even French national consciousness had to be created in the latter half of the nineteenth century. In the nineteenth century a plethora of (ethno)nationalisms developed in the womb of multinational states and empires; for a variety of reasons, mostly geopolitical but also because of the international conjuncture, self-determination was an option open to only a few of them, though others may have obtained different degrees of autonomy. The aftermaths of the First World War marked the highpoint of (ethno)nationalist successes.

It is because the nation, as I have indicated at the beginning of the preface, is the paramount value of modernity that states have tried, with varying results, to transform themselves into communities, into nations. The kind of loyalty that the modern state requires for its functioning is best achieved if the citizens participate not only in a rational-instrumental way, but also if the integrative aspects of the nation – the mythologico-ritual – are preserved and even enhanced.

The post-war period in Western Europe has been characterized by an extreme stability of political borders. Most of the states have come to the conclusion, no matter how reluctantly, that it was in their economic and military interests to create a united Europe, even if some political concessions in terms of state sovereignty had to be made. How far they are prepared to go to construct a politically unified Europe is not yet clear. And can a sense of European identity be created transcending, or maybe superceding in the Hegelian sense, the state and national divisions?

Another important development which took place in post-war Europe was the growing presence of an immigrant population often racially, culturally, religiously and linguistically different, occupying the lower echelons of society and who increasingly were perceived as a potential or actual threat to national identity by a large percentage of the autochthonous population. A number of different strategies were developed, sometimes simultaneously, sometimes succesively, to cope with the conflictual dimension of such a situation. First of all, most European states enforced stricter immigration controls than in the past. Second, an assimilationist policy was pursued, with mixed results, and for two reasons: the sheer number and the radical difference in cultural outlooks made it difficult for the immigrants to adapt easily; furthermore, Western societies have often rejected the immigrants mostly on racial grounds. Third, the idea of multiculturalism was floated as a possible alternative to the failed assimilationist policies of an earlier period. In the past few years the situation seems to have reached a stalemate, with no obvious solution in sight.

In the aftermath of the ideological thaw in Eastern Europe, the *de facto* Western European monopoly on the idea of Europe was challenged by peoples from this region and will no doubt be challenged by other nations. This brings to the fore the question: what is, then, Europe? A unique civilizational area or just a a geographic denomination? An entity of the past, of the present or of the future or maybe just a utopia? The anarchist dream of a federation of European peoples or a type of Hitlerite nightmare? A federation of European peoples large and small or a centralized, bureaucratic and uniform state? A common economic market or a unified polity? A social-democratic Europe or a free-for-all capitalist Europe? In conclusion, there are four major problems besetting the idea of a European supernation-state: the sovereignty of the states, the nationalism of the peoples, the integration of the non-European ethnic groups and the incorporation of non-Western European countries.

Ideas have their own momentum. At present the idea of the European Community is in the mind of many people both as a challenge and as an objective to achieve. It is true that it is far from clear what is at stake. There are a number of reasons, however, which account for the appeal of the idea of Europe, which I am prepared to admit is more emotional than rational. Historically, there was the conviction that Europe, which had been the main theatre of two devastating conflagrations in the twentieth century, should put an end to the state enmities that had made the wars possible. It was believed that the best course was to begin with economic integration and later slowly move towards political union. In more recent times the restricted EEC of the six provided such an attractive socio-economic and political model that other Western European countries wished to join so not to miss the opportunity. In front of a world which seemed to be constituted by giants, a united Europe (at present constituted by twelve countries) would undoubtedly be an economic force (and in the future also a political force) to be reckoned with.

It can be argued that (ethno)nations and ethnic groups have a better chance of preserving their cultural values within a politically united Europe than in their present situation. However, it is equally possible to defend the thesis that a unified Europe could become a bureaucratic and uniform superstate, which might stifle even further their demands for autonomy. Of course, we have to be aware of the consequences that each course of action is likely to produce, but in the final instance what will matter is the will of a people or of an ethnic group to survive. The living and active forces of a community must articulate projects which respond to the cultural requirements needed to preserve this community in the framework of a united Europe. The process will no doubt require a 'recreation' of ethnic/national identities in the context of the existing states and of the emerging European institutions. Paraphrasing Marx we could say that although history sets constraints on human behaviour, conscious human beings make their own history.

Bibliography

Alter, P., (1989) *Nationalism*, London: Edward Arnold.

Breuilly, J., (1982) *Nationalism and the State*, Manchester: Manchester University Press.

Burckhardt, J., (1979) *Reflections on History*, Indianapolis: Liberty Press.

Ciuffoletti, C., (1987) 'Mito e realtà della rivoluzione greca' in *Independenza e unità nazionale in Italia ed in Grecia*, Firenze: Olschki.

Cobban, A., (1970) *The Nation-State and National Self-Determination*, New York: Thomas Crowell.

Gellner, E., (1964) *Thought and Change*, London: Weidenfeld and Nicholson.

Hayes, C., (1931) *The Historical Evolution of Nationalism*, New York: Smith.

Hobsbawm, E., (1990) *Nations and Nationalism Since 1870*, Cambridge: Cambridge University Press.

Hroch, M., (1985) *Social Preconditions of National Revival in Europe*, Cambridge: Cambridge University Press.

Kohn, H., (1944) *The Idea of Nationalism*, New York: Collier.

Melucci, A. and Diani, M., (1983) *Nazioni senza stato*, Torino: Loescher

Minogue, K. R., (1967) *Nationalism*, London: Methuen.

Mommsen, W.J., (1974) 'Power, Politics, Imperialism and National Emancipation' in T. W. Moody (ed.), *Nationality and the Pursuit of National Independence*, Belfast: Appletree Press.

Nairn, T., (1977) *The Break-up of Britain*, London: New Left Books.

Ozouf, M., (1985) 'Unité nationale et unité de la pensée de Jules Ferry' in *Jules Ferry, Fondateur de la République*, Paris: EHESS.

Pflanze, O., (1966) 'Nationalism in Europe, 1848-1871', *Review of Politics*, 28, pp. 129–43.

Robbins, K., (1988) *Nineteenth Century Britain*, Oxford: Oxford University Press.

Romano, S., (1986) 'Language and Nation: The Italian Case' in J. Alpher (ed.), *Nationalism and Modernity. Mediterranean Perspectives*, New York: Praeger.

Schlesinger, A., (1981) 'Nationalism in the Modern World' in M. Palumbo and W. O. Shanahan (eds), *Nationalism: Essays in Honour of Louis L. Snyder*, Wesport, Conn.: Greenwood Press.

Seton-Watson, H., (1977) *Nations and States*, London: Methuen.

Smith, A. D., (1981) *The Ethnic Revival in the Modern World*, Cambridge: Cambridge University Press.

— —, (1979) *Nationalism in the Twentieth Century*, Oxford: Martin Robertson.

Strauss, A., (1949) *The Attitude of the Congress of Vienna Toward Nationalism in Germany, Italy and Poland*, New York: Columbia University Press.

Tiryakian, E. A. & Rogowski, R. (eds), (1985) *New Nationalisms of the Developed West*, London: Allen and Unwin.

Vigier, P., (1977) 'Régions et régionalisme en France au XVIIIe siècle' in C. Gras and G. Livet (eds), *Régions et réginalisme en France du XVIIIe siècle aux nos jours*, Paris: Presses Universitaires de France.

Weber, E., (1979) *Peasants into Frenchmen*, London: Chatto and Windus.

Weil, G., (1938) *L'Europe du XIXe siècle et l'idée de nationalité*, Paris: Albin Michel.

Zeldin, T., (1973; 1977) *France 1848–1945*, 2 vols, Oxford: Oxford University Press.

Part V
Theoretical Recapitulation

Conclusions

In the course of this book I have critically examined the key factors that I believe account for the development of modern nationalism in Western Europe. I have avoided what Max Weber would have called a 'one-sided vision of history' because I think that the complexity of nationalism precludes any explanatory framework which is strictly monocausal. If I say that nationalism can only be explained *historically* it may sound a rather banal or at least hardly novel statement, but all depends on the implicit concept of history used. What I am here referring to is not a linear, 'evenemential' history, even if such a concept does play a role in the scheme of things concerned with the development of nationalism. The concept of history that I work with is highly structured and functions like a feedback mechanism in that selective information from the past is fed firmly into the present through images, myths and symbols which allow us to interpret our times and to control and direct them in the desired way, within the limits of the existing correlation of forces.

There can never be a totally satisfactory answer to the question of why modernity values national identity so highly. At best we can map out the different elements or forces that have produced this state of things. In the context of modernity the problem is not so much to explain the salience of cultural nationalism across the board as a solid refuge for the individual at a time of accelerated secularization and of disintegration of traditional allegiances, but why the modern state did not tolerate polyethnic structures in its midst and aimed at creating, with varied success, a homogeneous space within which to project a single culture, an official language and a uniform conception of history both by persuasion and by coercion. Part of the explanation lies, perhaps tautologically, in the ideological factors explored in Part III, particularly in connection with the deification of the unitary state which was characteristic of the French Revolution. Once the idea that national cultures were worth identifying, preserving and fighting for had gathered momentum, as it did in the first half of the nineteenth century, it then followed that any ethnic unit that could make a bid for nationhood tried its luck.

Now, to make such a move, the first thing you must have is a reservoir of ethnic potential. Much has been made in the past few years of the idea that national cultures and languages are invented, i.e. that they are ideological constructs created by specific social groups (ruling elites, bourgeoisie, intelligentsia) with ulterior motives, be it the preservation of the state, economic interests or cultural frustrations. It is obvious to any detached observer that romantic historiography and cultural invention play an important role in the formative period of nationalist ideologies. This applies both to state nationalisms and to nationalisms against the state; and yet the relative success of these ideologies depends, in the final resort, on the strength of the ethnic potential they can tap. In the case of state nationalisms, the state tries to minimize the internal national diversity by diffusing, through folklorism, or by eliminating, through a combination of education and repression, the existing ethnic feelings which could generate ethnonationalist demands.

Because the 'national cultures' that most states try to impose are in fact the hegemonic cultures of the ruling cores (south-east England in the UK, Castile in Spain, the region of Paris in France, etc.) they have to be reinforced with the ideologies derived from political nationalism. But only dictatorial types of regimes can use permanent force, or the threat of it, to quieten ethnonationalist demands; the latter, however, do not disappear and sooner or later there is need for some accommodation (autonomy, federalism, independence). Because the legitimacy of the state does not depend exclusively on its ethnonational homogeneity, the issue of ethnic potential is not as essential as it is for ethnonationalist movements which recruit their clientele on a voluntary basis among those people who express an ethnic affinity at the level of consciousness. It is then true that ethnic identities can be invented, and in any case are always recreated, but in the absence of an ethnic potential locked in a more or less distant past, or of a powerful state that can foster them, they are likely to appeal to a very small minority of people and hence to have no political impact whatsoever.

I have not wanted to argue against the modernist conception of nationalism provided that it is clearly accepted that what we are referring to is *modern* nationalism, that is, an ideology which found its first manifestation at the turn of the nineteenth century. In Part I, however, I have insisted that the roots of the nation, of national identity and even of an incipient patriotic nationalism are firmly anchored in the medieval period. I do not see any contradiction in these two statements, as I think has been made clear in different parts of this book. More importantly, perhaps, I am prepared to admit that the idea of ethnic potential has to be used with great care because it is easily open to ideological manipulation. For one thing, there is no way in which medieval sentiments of national identity can be compared properly with modern ones; there will always be a credibility gap that has to be filled by fiat. But then, I have never suggested that the ideas of national identity in the Middle Ages and in the nineteenth century were the same; this is why national identities had to be 'invented', or as I prefer it, re-created. What matters is that past history should provide a plausible scenario for the re-creation of national identity; if not, it can only be maintained with the help of the state.

The effects of capitalism, and more specifically of industrial capitalism, in the development of nationalism in Western Europe are much more difficult to ascertain with precision than many theoreticians would like us to believe. There is no elective affinity between capitalism and nationalism, unless we equate the former to modern society in general, and not to a mode of production *senso strictu*. If we take the connection betwen capitalism and nationalism as a proposition concerning the development of nationalism in Western Europe, the evidence suggests that the process of industrialization made its appearance at a time when national identities were already there. Two caveats should be entered here. First, there is still a question left unanswered: in which way did the logic of industrialism and the concomitant process of modernization further contribute to the development of nationalism? Most authors would tend to agree with the idea that there is causality here, namely that industrialism accelerated the existing nationalist tendencies. I am not sure, however, whether the decisive factor is the process of industrialization or rather the modernizing elements with which it was associated in Western Europe. Second, I refrain from generalizing to other areas outside Western Europe (and particularly the Third World), though I note not only that national identities were rare elsewhere, but also that industrialization, if it existed at all, was both late and superficial. The two major processes of 'national' independence outside Europe took place in the aftermath of two specific political events which were 'nationally' charged: the American and the French Revolutions and the two World Wars. The former proclaimed that government should be based on the will of the people and that by people was meant, at least in theory, the totality of the citizens of the nation; the latter saw the beginning of the end of colonialism. What we can observe in both historical periods is that a specific form of anticolonial 'nationalism' – if this is the appropriate term – makes its appearance.

I envisage the modern system of Western European states as a historically given *datum*, a precipitate from the past; a resilient, though not permanent reality, which in the late eighteenth century would start suffering the ravages of nationalist ideology in its midst. State and nation obey different logics; the state is expansionist, that is, it aims at enlarging its territory for a variety of reasons (economic, political, military, strategic, prestige, etc.). This surge can only be checked by the presence of other states that oppose the move. War, or at least the threat of force, is the instrument historically used by the state to achieve its end. The nationality principle asserts that people with the same culture and language form a nation, and should live together, and manage their own affairs, that is, ideally they should constitute an independent state. It is not difficult to see why the appearance of the nationality principle created an additional element of conflictivity in the midst of modernity.

Of the Western European states which existed by the eve of the French Revolution, very few remained untouched by the winds of nationalism in the two centuries that followed. As we have seen, two large new states appeared in the nineteeth century – Italy and Germany – as well as a small one (Belgium). Even France saw permanent additions (Savoy, Nice) and temporary losses (Alsace and Lorraine) of territory. Ireland separated from the UK, and Basques and Catalans began pushing for ethnonationalist demands from the late nineteenth century. Only small states like Portugal, Holland and Switzerland remained largely unaffected in the long run. So much for an area with historical frontiers and stable states. It is not my contention that all these developments were the result of the activation of the nationality principle; rather that the latter played an important role in these events. Perhaps as important as that was the realization by the state that its survival was clearly tied up with an accelerated process of nation-building; in practice, this meant the erosion of all cultural and linguistic particularisms which could represent a threat to the culture and language of the dominant nation.

There is no better example of emasculation of regional identities than the France of the Third Republic. Contrary to received wisdom, we know via Eugen Weber's *Peasants to Frenchmen* that by the mid-nineteenth century France was far from being a homogeneous nation-state. The consciousness of French identity as a mass phenomenon was created by compulsory schooling, the development of communications and military conscription. With the exception of perhaps Switzerland, Western European states adopted homogenizing policies towards their subordinated nationalities and 'regions' (an often vague term, masking old, suppressed nationalities), with varying degrees of success. It is not necessary for my argument's sake that governments should have elaborated blueprints for cultural and linguistic obliteration; on the whole they were oblivious to the multinational realities, obsessed as they were with the *grandeur* of the official language and the dominant culture. There was no sensitivity for linguistic variety; languages other than the official one were seen as either *patois* or primitive, incapable of coping with the expressive and cognitive needs of modernity. Aesthetic arguments were also used to dismiss them. The same could be said about the non-official cultures of the state which at best were marginalized through folklorism.

One of the most persistent myths about nationalism is its class character. The assumption is typically Marxist, but it has had a much wider appeal. According to this conception nationalism is a product of the bourgeoisie and can be accounted for in terms of the economic interests of this class in securing the monopoly of the market – the national market. My objection to such a standpoint, as I have pointed out a number of times, is its simplistic and reductionist premises. It mistakes the uses and abuses of nationalism by the bourgeoisie – a well-known and historically verifiable fact – with its nature, which transcends class as history has repeatedly shown. This should not be read as a charter for ignoring the role of the bourgeoisie in the development of nationalism in Western Europe; however, it is not always in its economic interest to embrace it, particularly in the cases of ethnonationalisms against the state. It is because most social scientists and historians tend to operate with economistic definitions of class that I have proposed the use of the concept of civil society instead; it gives a much better sense of the dynamism of society in general and of the appearance and development of nationalism, particularly in those situations where the state and civil society do not coincide.

Gramsci avowed that the Catholic Church in Italy was a civil society within a civil society. Modernity has often seen an alliance between Church and Nation; there are cases of national-catholicism as well of national-protestantism, as the Irish and English cases exemplify, respectively. In the Catholic sphere of influence, the existence of an extra-territorial, final source of authority – the Papacy – has meant that there was always an option open to the different national churches within a state: to seek protection from the Pontifex Maximus, claiming that the state had no jurisdiction in religious matters. Now this is a controversial point given the history of state gallicanism in Western Europe, but ethnonational churches have often banked on this ambiguity to blur the difference between the religious and the political. The examples of Catalonia and the Basque Country within Spain show that the state, particularly a quasi-fascist regime like that of Franco, while purporting to be fervently Catholic can physically eliminate or ban from the country those elements of the clergy who have expressed allegiance to their ethnonation, in this case the Basque or Catalan ethnonation. As we have seen with the case of France, even in those cases where a chasm is open between church and state, the latter may be able to find a functional alternative to the church, both at the level of form and of content. The religious input in both medieval and early modern national identity, as well as in modern nationalism, was essential; it would be difficult to explain the appeal of modern nationalism without acknowledging the extent to which nationalist ideology is indebted to religion, albeit in modern times in a secularized form.

There is no better way of conceiving of nationalist ideology than as an *idée-force* (to use Fouillée's felicitous expression), i.e. as a thought that leads to action. But two questions arise immediately: why did the idea of political and cultural nationalism flourish in the second half of the eighteenth century? And why did it take off so rapidly and become an essential part of the repertoire of modernity? It has been a premise of this book that the nation can only be understood as a product of the *longue durée*; what we see in the eighteenth century is the culmination of an uneven process which had lasted for centuries (including the absolutist period in which the idea of nation was eclipsed by the might of the expanding state) and which built on the classical notion of *patria* and the medieval idea of the nation as an *imaginaire* (to use Duby's term). There is also the matter of the diffusion of ideas: print capitalism, as Benedict Anderson has shown, made it possible to enlarge the circle of readers to limits previously difficult to conceive. In one respect nationalist ideology can be pictured as a reaction against the cosmopolitanism of the Enlightenment. Mankind was perhaps too aloof a concept to serve the emotive and political needs of the people of the eighteenth century; the concept of nation was more apposite to their actual or potential realities. Organicism also played a role in this state of affairs by giving the nation a natural character.

Even if one can show that during the second half of the eighteenth century there were quantitative and qualitative changes in the concept of the nation, it is difficult to imagine what its future would have been without the French Revolution and its aftermaths. It is true that the American Revolution of 1776 was a prelude to political nationalism, but it was the combination of the French Revolution and the reactions against the Napoleonic invasions that shaped the future of nationalism. The series of events known as the French Revolution triggered off radical transformations in the political map of Western Europe and elsewhere. It was not only the internal structure of the *ancien régime* that came under fire by the emergence of the concept of popular sovereignty; with the spread of cultural nationalism the existing organization of Western European states was also profoundly undermined. But the most extraordinary thing is the speed with which the nationalist ideology spread all over Western Europe, affecting old and new states, small and not so small ethnonations.

The more we advance into the nineteenth century the more we can observe a progressive fusion between political and cultural nationalism, and an attempt by the state to consolidate itself along uniform ethnolinguistic parameters, a sense of shared history, a panoply of myths and rituals, an often exaggerated sense of national pride and a project of future *grandeur* (in which the possession of colonies was paramount). The nationalist phase of the state, if not totally opportunistic, exhibits a major contradiction, namely the incompatibility between continuous territorial expansion and cultural and linguistic homogeneity. It is not that the contradiction is totally insoluble, but it requires, in the medium term, the constant use of force and a non-humanitarian ideology involving a sense of racial and/or cultural superiority.

In chronological, as opposed to sociological history, the order of events matters dramatically. The Fichte of the *Discourses to the German Nation* can only be understood after the Napoleonic invasions; much of what Renan said in *What is a nation?* only makes sense in the context of the French defeat of 1870. However, once a statement has been made it is there to be used or abused, interpreted or misinterpreted, constructed or deconstructed, ignored or promoted, etc., by those who read it. Certain texts acquire the character of canons for a shorter or a longer historical period, and a flurry of intellectual discussions and commentaries are woven around them. For texts to find such a resonance they must have managed to grasp the essence of the *Zeitgeist*. In other cases they may be in a position to shape, to a certain extent, future public opinion (or at least certain aspects of it). In another order of things, it is worth remembering again that nationalism is no less but no more than an *idée-force*, that is, it has to operate in the real world in which it is opposed by other ideas and institutions. It is a sign of its vitality that nationalism has changed the world, but not always in the way desired by the nationalists. Italy had to shed Savoy and Nice to the French before it was able to constitute itself as a state; the Bismarckian *Reich* left out many areas which were culturally and linguistically German; many ethnonations had to accept different degrees of autonomy within their respective states because different historical conjunctures or correlations of forces did not allow them to go any further.

When confronted with the question of explaining nationalism, this book has considered the effects of four major causal frameworks: the *longue durée*, the basic structures of modernity, the force of nationalist ideology and the order and meaning of post-1789 history. An attempt has been made to ascertain the relative strengths of the different frameworks, and a number of propositions, I hasten to add restricted in principle to Western Europe, follow from the study:

1) Nations are the precipitate of a long historical period starting in the Middle Ages.

2) Nations cannot be created or invented *ex nihilo*. However, national identity may be submerged by the vagaries of history and may have to be re-created by an active intelligentsia in the modern period.

3) Nationalism *stricto sensu* is a relatively recent phenomenon, but a rudimentary and restricted national identity existed already in the medieval period.

4) The absolutist state was on the whole inimical to the development of national identity. As a result, there was a regression of national identity in the early modern period.

5) It is not possible to establish a causal correlation between capitalism and nationalism, except at the most general level.

6) It is not so much industrialization but modernization that had a positive effect on the development of nationalism.

7) The uneven development of industrial capitalism cannot be presented as the *deus ex machina* for the development of nationalism; in connection with Western Europe, such a doctrine is unable to account for the major nationalist processes.

8) From the perspective of the *longue durée* there is no doubt that wherever state and nation coincided (and this was rather rare), the state was a major factor in the shaping and promoting of national identity.

9) Because in modernity national legitimation is the most prestigious form of relating people to the state, once the nationalist principle was unfurled, states had no alternative but to pursue policies of nation-building.

10) The degree of success or failure of nation-building policies engineered by the state is in direct relationship to the high or low degree of ethnonational homogeneity which exists in the country.

11) Because nations pre-date modern classes it is absurd to see in the bourgeoisie the inventor of the nation.

12) In modern times the first mover of nationalism was the intelligentsia.

13) Because of the malleability of nationalist ideology, the bourgeoisie has often manipulated it to suit its own economic interests.

14) In trying to account for the development of nationalism, the concept of civil society is more appropriate than that of class. In those cases of nationalisms against the state, a thriving civil society seems to be a precondition for the success of nationalist movements.

15) National churches have played a significant role in the development of nationalism.

16) In modernity, the national sentiment is first of all a reaction against the cosmopolitan pretensions of the Enlightenment.

17) There is a continuity between medieval and modern conceptions of the nation, but in modernity the idea of community is usually projected to a much larger group of people than before. People are incorporated either on the basis of culture or on the basis of citizenship.

18) Cultural nationalism has tended to take precedence over political nationalism, but the creation of new states on the basis of the nationality principle has been subordinated at each historical conjuncture to the existing inter-state correlation of forces.

19) The nation corresponds to a certain stage of development of Western civilization, but it has proven more resilient than was generally expected and it is unlikely that it will disappear in the foreseeable future. However, the continuous increase in moral density is likely to make national identity less important at an individual basis and to generate increasing levels of multiple identity.

20) National identity occurs at lower levels of integration than the state, and there are good sociological reasons to believe that it cannot occur at higher ones.

21) In the final resort, the success of nationalism in modernity has to be attributed largely to the sacred character that the nation has inherited from religion. In its essence the nation is the secularized god of our times.

22) What determines the survival of a given nation is the will of its people to preserve their identity, albeit in a somewhat changed form.

Index

Index

Europe, -an, *passim*
European Community, 206–8
Extremadura, 75

fascism
  and nationalism, 197, 204–5
Fedele, P., 67
Feher, F., 183
Ferguson, A., 126
Ferry, J., 200
Fichte, J.G., 219
Fichtenau, H., 18
Finer, S.E., 42
Flanders, Flemings, 22, 46–7, 55, 119, 205
Fleckstein, J., 7–8
Fletcher, A., 136–7
Florence, 65–9, 127
Folz, R., 15, 60
Forsyth, M., 184
Fortescue, J., 108
Foscolo, U., 68
Fouillée, A., 218
Foxe, J., 136
Franco, F., Spanish dictator, 142, 217
France, French, x, xii–iii, 18–19, 21, 24,
  32, 42–58, 66–9, 74, 85, 97, 120, 128,
  130, 153, 157, 165, 179–92 *passim*,
  196, 198–200, 205–6, 214, 216–7, 219
  and religion, 137–9, 144–5
  medieval nation, 53–8, 83
  kingdom of, 48–52
  language, 55, 188
  state-building, 107–115
Franconia, 60, 183
Frankish Kingdom, *see* Franks
Franks, 5, 8, 12, 1418, 42, 56, 58, 70, 73,
  182–3
French Revolution, xii–iii, 3, 80, 11, 114,
  118,120, 130, 132, 139, 143, 151,
  170–1, 194–5, 213, 215–6, 218
  and nationalism, 179–192 *passim*
Frederick I (Barbarossa), Hohenstaufen
  emperor, 51, 62, 66
Frisians, 5, 15
Friule, Friulians, 205
Fuhrmann, H., 59
Fulbrook, M., 59

Gaguin, R., 56
Galasso, G., 68
Galicia, -ns, 70, 73–4, 76–7, 205
Gallia, 7, 11–12, 14–15, 19, 21–5, 32,
  42–58, 71, 80–1, 139
  and Christianity, 46, 51–2, 54–5
  as a mosaic state, 42–3

Capetian monarchy, 42, 45–8, 50
  myths of origin, 54
Gallicanism, 52, 138, 217
Ganshof, F.L., 18, 52
Garibaldi, G., 198
Gascony, Gascons, 18–19, 43
Gaul, *see* Gallia
Gellner, E., 85, 95, 98–9, 195
  on nationalism, 99–100
Genoa, 65–7, 127
Germania, 7, 21, 56, 58–63 *passim*, 64,
  80–2, 129
  and Christianity, 171
  and language, 60
  and national identity, 63
  and Papacy, 59–61
  lack of centralisation in, 59
Germanic peoples/tribes, 5–14, 119
  expansion, 13–16
  kingship, 9–10
  kinship, 6–7, 10, 81
  political organisation, 7–9
  religion, 10–13
Germany, Germans, 18–21, 58–63 *passim*,
  81, 110, 124, 188, 192, 205, 216, 219
  and civil society, 128–30
  and cultural nationalism, 164–70 *passim*
  and fascism, 204
  and unification, 195–201
Giddens, A.,
  on nationalism, 98–9
Gilbert, F., 115
Gilda, 28–30
Giner, S., 126
  and civil society, 126–7
Given-Wilson, C., 36
Godechot, J., 152154, 180, 185, 190–1
Goetz, W., 67
Goffart, W., 6
Goths, 5–6, 10, 12, 18
  Visigoths, 8–9, 11–15, 19, 70, 72, 139
  Ostrogoths, 10–11, 14
Gouldner, A., 127
Gramsci, A., 115, 126, 128, 217
Granada, 71–2, 76
Great Britain, *see* United Kingdom
Greece, Greeks, 6, 55, 113, 151–3, 157,
  169, 171, 186
  modern nationalism, 196
Gregory of Tours, 15
Grew, R., 168
Guenée, B., 47–8, 52, 82
Guicciardini, F., 69
Guiomar, J.I., 188
Guyenne, 47

Index

and printing, 119
in medieval France, 55, 59
in medieval England, 37–38
Leibniz, G.W., 168
Lemarignier, J.F., 47–49, 52
Lenin, V.I., 124, 203
Leon, 70, 73–4, 76
Le Roy Ladurie, E., 44
Levy, M., 102
Levy-Strauss, C., 158
Lewis, A., 44
Linehan, P., 139
List, F., 129
Lithuania, 58
Llobera, J.R., 96
Locke, J., 126
Lombardy, Lombards, 5–6, 11, 14, 17–19, 63–4, 66, 129–30
Longobards, *see* Lombards
Lopez, R., 95
Lorraine, 22, 58, 60, 190, 216
Lotharingia, 58, 60
Lovejoy, A.O., 172–3
Lovett, A.W., 141
Low Countries, *see* Holland
Luther, M., 137
Lutz, H., 63

MacFarlane, A., 95
Machiavelli, N., 68–9, 115
MacKay, A., 77
MacKitterick, R., 18
Mack Smith, A., 130
MacNeil, W., 106
Magyars, 64
Maitland, F., 35
Mann, M., 9
on nationalism, 98
Mann, N., 56, 67
Manzoni, A., 173
Maravall, J.A., 70, 115
Marca Hispanica, 19, 71, 75
Marsilius of Padua, 51
Marx, K., Marxism, xi, 111, 151, 200, 202, 208, 217
on nationalism
and capitalism, 95–6, 99, 101–2
and class, 123–6, 131–2
Mathiez, A., 186–7
Maurras, C., 204
Mauss, M., 61
Mazzei, F., 68
Mazzini, G., 68, 198
medieval nations, 80–6
Meinecke, F., 164

Melucci, A., 205
Mercia, 16
Metternich, K., 129
Milan, 65, 68
Minogue, K.R., 128, 194
Mitchell, M., 146
Mitteis, H., 33, 45, 66, 107
Momigliano, A., 7
Mommsen, W., 203
Monferrato. 66
Mongols, 13
Montesquieu, C., 108, 161, 183
on national character, 155–6
on *patrie*, 152–3
Morocco, 75
Müller, M., 143
Mullet, M., 135–7
Murray, A., 6–7
Muslims, 70–7 *passim*, 134, 139
Musset, L., 11–12, 15, 57
Mussolini, B., 204

Nairn, T., 102, 125, 197
Naples, 66, 68,
Napoleon, xiii, 62, 68, 129–30, 139, 179
and nationalism, 191–2, 195–6, 218–19
nation, nationalism, *passim*
nation,
in eighteenth century France, 154
national character,
Hegel on, 170–71
Herder on, 164–70
Hume on, 156–7
Montesquieu on, 155–6
Rousseau on, 161–2
Navarra, 70–77 *passim*
Nelli, R., 44
Netherlands, *see* Holland
Nice, 190–1, 199, 216, 219
Normandy, Normans, 23–27, 32–48
passim, 57, 65, 136, 190
Northern Ireland, *see* Ireland
Northumbria, 16, 25–29 *passim*
Norway, 203
Novalis, G., 172

O'Brien, C.C., 179
O'Callaghan, J.F., 72, 74–5
Occitania, Occitans, 44, 46, 55, 131, 188
Oriental, 171
Orridge, A.W., 101–2
Ostrogoths, *see* Goths
Ozouf, M., 200

Palmer, R., 152–4, 161, 183, 188

Index